THE IMAGE CANDIDATES

THE IMAGE
CANDIDATES

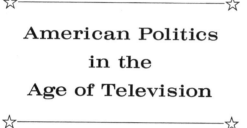

American Politics
in the
Age of Television

Gene Wyckoff

THE MACMILLAN COMPANY · NEW YORK

Library of Congress Catalog Card Number: 68-13207

First Printing

The Macmillan Company, New York
Collier-Macmillan Canada Ltd., Toronto, Ontario

Printed in the United States of America

To My Wife

CONTENTS

PART FIVE

SUMMING UP

TABLES

Whereas it appeareth that however certain forms of government are better calculated than others to protect individuals in the free exercise of their natural rights, and are at the same time themselves better guarded against degeneracy, yet experience hath shewn, that even under the best forms, those entrusted with power have, in time, and by slow operations, perverted it into tyranny; and it is believed that the most effectual means of preventing this would be, to illuminate, as far as practicable, the minds of the people at large, and more especially to give them knowledge of those facts . . . that . . . they may be enabled to know ambition under all its shapes, and prompt to exert their natural powers to defeat its purpose . . .

    —THOMAS JEFFERSON, A Bill for the More General Diffusion of Knowledge, 1779

PART ONE

Major Influences on Voting

1

PARTY LOYALTY AND CAMPAIGN ISSUES

Most adults who are aware enough to vote consistently tend to vote consistently for the candidates of one political party. The causes of this habitual voting tendency elude description, not because the causes are so rare but because there are so many factors in the life of a voter that could cause him to identify himself as a Republican, Democrat, Liberal, Conservative, or Socialist and to vote accordingly. Perhaps a Democrat who can finally afford to move his family from the city to the suburbs will want to identify himself as a Republican as self-assurance that he has indeed arrived. Perhaps a voter has gotten his political inclinations from his family or his friends, whose party loyalties in turn may stem from some political position or action their party took a generation or a century ago. Political scientists sum up habitual party loyalty as flowing from "all the inchoate pressures of socio-economic status" that cause many voters "to

3

make up their minds and act ultimately on that decision even before the campaign begins." [1]

There are recent grounds for suspicion, however, that the intensity—if not the surface identification—of American voters' loyalty to one political party is weakening. One reason for this may be the growing similarity between the ideologies of our two major parties. In his study of the 1960 "great debates," for example, Stanley Kelley found broad areas of agreement between the positions of Democratic candidate John F. Kennedy and Republican Richard M. Nixon.

STANLEY KELLEY: Nixon stated . . . that he had no quarrel with Kennedy's views on several substantive issues of importance: internal security, the need to extend economic assistance to underdeveloped countries, the defense of Berlin, and the significance that voters should attach to the religious affiliation of candidates.

Kennedy said he could find no fault with Nixon's stand on summit meetings.[2]

A second reason for the decline of party-loyalty intensity may be related to the decreasing numbers of permanent party workers due to the disappearance of patronage jobs supporting them and the delimitation of services they can uniquely render to voters between election campaigns. Civil service and municipal reforms eliminate patronage jobs. One reform of the late Mayor Fiorello H. La Guardia, for example, replaced elected sheriffs, county clerks, and numerous appointed assistants in each of New York City's five boroughs with a single sheriff and deputies chosen through competitive examination. How well they performed politically, or even whether they took an active interest in politics, did not affect their tenure in office. Government welfare programs, public housing, effective state employment services, and so forth are slowly reducing the scope of personal services that might be rendered to voters by year-around party workers. Party functions, such as rallies, are hardly the attraction they were in years before television presented candidates and political spectacles in the comfort of one's home.

Third, it is now common campaign practice for candidates to

subdue their party identity so that voters will be less prone to think in terms of the "Democratic candidate" or the "Republican." In New York City's 1961 mayoral campaigns, neither the Liberal-Democrat incumbent Mayor Robert F. Wagner nor his Republican challenger, State Attorney General Louis J. Lefkowitz, allowed mention of their party identification on much of their campaign advertising. *The New York Times* commented: "WHAT PARTY IS BACKING WHOM FOR WHAT? YOU CAN'T TELL BY THE SIGNS." [3] In 1966, partyless advertising was evident all across the country. The billboards of the Democrat running for governor in Pennsylvania simply said: "MILTON SHAPP—A MAN YOU CAN TRUST!" In Michigan, a Republican senator seeking reelection carefully avoided waving his party identification in front of voters: "YOUTH AND EXPERIENCE—U.S. SENATOR BOB GRIFFIN." In Georgia it was "GO 'BO'—CALLAWAY FOR GOVERNOR." Even the son of Ohio's late revered Republican conservative Senator Taft did not identify himself as a Republican in his billboards: "HIGH PRICES! RUBBER STAMPS! WAR CONFUSION! HAD ENOUGH?—ELECT BOB TAFT TO CONGRESS."

To further minimize the chance of voters' party loyalties working against them, candidates may practice multiple listing on the ballot. In 1961, Louis Lefkowitz appeared as mayoral candidate of the Republican, Civic Action, and Non-Partisan parties, the last two of which were little more than paper organizations with no established political positions that might repel Democratic voters (the vast majority in New York City). In 1965, New York Republican mayoral candidate John Lindsay tried to follow the same tactic with the creation of a paper Independent-Citizens-for-Lindsay party, which would allow Democrats to vote for him without forcing them to pull the possibly distasteful Republican or Liberal party levers. (Lindsay was also the Liberal candidate for mayor.) A minor mayoral candidate refused to give up his line on the ballot, however, and Lindsay had to make do with only two party listings.

Finally, in considering the influence of voters' habitual tendency to prefer candidates of one party, it should be remembered that party loyalty can be zero—a nil factor—in certain important elections, namely, primary elections in areas where voter registration in one party greatly outnumbers registration in the next largest party. When winning the majority-party primary is almost a guarantee of winning the general election that follows, the effective choice is between candidates having the same party identity.

CAMPAIGN ISSUES

The influence of issues on the outcome of elections also seems to be declining as (1) political questions become too complex for ready statement or comprehension and (2) candidates themselves avoid assuming issue positions that might be considered too extreme.

Complexity is a consequence of growth and specialization in government no less than in large business organizations. The differences between alternative ways of getting something done —since the major parties generally agree on goals—can involve such subtlety and special knowledge as to be largely unexplainable to laymen, especially in the desirable short-sentence, pithy style of campaign oratory.

In 1962, for example, Senator Prescott S. Bush (R., Conn.), long a proponent of expanded world trade, found himself talking like a diehard protectionist in campaign speeches as his opposition to President Kennedy's foreign-trade bill was reduced to catch phrases such as "thousands of jobs in our state will be wiped out by uncontrolled cheap-labor imports." That was not what the senator wanted to say at all. His opposition to the bill was based on much more subtle and expert considerations. He felt that it gave the executive branch of the federal government too much discretionary tariff-cutting power, a power that should be reserved to the Congress. But this sort of reasoning, however perceptive, did not translate into rousing oratory. He dropped from his speeches this issue and others that were similarly distorted by oversimplification until his wisdom and experience

—growing out of ten years in the Senate and a long career in private banking—was often reduced to a senatorial smile and a handshake.

The very pervasiveness of television may serve to inhibit meaningful debate on campaign issues. When a candidate is making an in-person address to a bankers' luncheon or a union convention, he can presume certain special knowledge or interests on the part of his audience and not risk boring them or talking over their heads—but not so via television, where a candidate has no way of knowing who is tuned in. His fundamental purpose—to win the election—may best be served by staying "loose" and general on the issues.

This is not to suggest that clear and genuine campaign issues will no longer arise as important, even decisive, influences on voting, but rather that they may arise less frequently and be less understood by voters. The example of the 1964 Republican presidential candidate, Barry Goldwater, will not soon be forgotten by campaign strategists. The opposition in 1964, first Rockefeller Republicans and later Johnsonian Democrats, publicly extrapolated every succinct Goldwater proposal to its worst possible consequence for the single-minded purpose of characterizing Goldwater as a harbinger of evil.

On the home screen, Goldwater's opposition to a ban on further nuclear bomb testing in the atmosphere was depicted (in Democratic commercials prepared by Doyle, Dane, Bernbach, Inc.) in images of a little girl counting the petals on a daisy while an atom bomb goes off behind her and of another little girl licking an ice-cream cone while an announcer's voice intones, "Children shouldn't have strontium 90 . . . But there's a man who wants to be president and if he's elected they might start testing all over again."

The merits, if any, of Goldwater's position on social security, foreign aid, civil rights, and the United Nations be damned. In high-level, heavily financed campaigns there is too much going on to stop for polite discussion. If the opposition says anything vulnerable, the name of the game is cutthroat.

Thus, in sure knowledge that opposition candidates and propagandists are always ready to pounce and distort any approach to public policy that might seem "different," all high-level candidates may be increasingly constrained in their campaign proposals on the pragmatic grounds that discretion is surely the better part of valor and that if they do not win on Election Day neither their announced nor their confidential issue positions will have much chance of becoming public policy.

POLITICALLY UNSOPHISTICATED VOTERS

The declining influence of political party loyalty and campaign issues on the outcome of recent elections may also reflect an increasing number of voters who tend to be relatively unconcerned with party and issue considerations.

Women, for example, have been coming to the polls in increasing numbers since the Nineteenth Amendment was ratified in 1920. They cast as many votes as men did in the 1960 national election. Currently they outnumber men by about 3 percent in the United States. Some sociologists have concluded that women tend to be less sophisticated—politically—than men because of the traditional American role belief that the woman's place is in the home: "A moralized political orientation characteristic of women, arising from maternal responsibilities, exclusion from more socially valued areas of activity and narrower orbits, tends to focus female political attention on persons and peripheral 'reform.' " [4]

This explanation of why women tend to vote more as a matter of reaction to the personal character of the candidate than as a consequence of rational consideration of the issues and party identification is probably valid as far as it goes, but does it go far enough? Does it imply that if the American woman's place was not so much in the home she would therefore be more responsive to the issues and less to the character or image of the candidates? Most candidates for our highest public offices are male. Dare we assume that the sexuality exuded by a candidate—who can be seen in close-up on television screens—affects male and female voter alike? Recent research by Dr. Eckhard H. Hess of the University of Chicago, using a pupillograph manufactured by Bausch & Lomb, measures the involuntary reaction of a person's pupil to what he sees: unpleasant images cause the pupil to contract and attractive ones cause it to expand. Dr. Hess has found that male and female viewers of a scene look at the features of that scene in different order and react (like or dislike) to different features in a manner that is distinctive to the sex. Dare we assume that these perceptual differences, by sex, have no translation into emotional differences, by sex, in response to the subject?

"DEMOCRATS SEEK NEW STAR AND SPOT PECK" announced a front-page headline of the New York *World Journal Tribune* on December 7, 1966. "Gregory Peck?" was the reaction of a housewife who normally votes Republican; "I'd elect him on the basis of *To Kill a Mockingbird* alone." Funny? President Johnson recalls the first time he escorted Peck through the White House. He found that his assistants and secretaries, who had calmly remained at their desks during visits of kings, chiefs of state, and other dignitaries, practically trampled each other to get a look at the handsome film star.[5]

Along with large numbers of women, the growing "politically unsophisticated" voter group may include men who have a low interest in the democratic process and who might normally stay home on Election Day but for the persuasion of the intensive nonpartisan get-out-the-vote drives that our mass media conduct as a public service.

HARVEY WHEELER: Voting is made to appear the proper thing to do. . . . [The drives induce] large numbers of people to vote who would not otherwise do so, and this means an increase in voting by people who have given little or no consideration to the issues. This is hardly likely to increase the rational element in electoral behavior.[6]

One group of political scientists at the University of

Michigan's Survey Research Center have concluded that today's politically unsophisticated voters show a "disproportionate amount of partisan fluidity" from election to election,[7] such as by voting for a Democratic candidate one year and a Republican the next.

"Partisan fluidity" may be an apt phrase for summarizing an increasingly apparent trend in this age of television. With respect to the elections of November 8, 1966, an Associated Press report commented: "So many voters split tickets . . . that it is impossible to categorize them strictly as Democratic or Republican. In 12 of the 22 states that elected both a Governor and a Senator last week, a Republican won one race and a Democrat the other." [8]

But politics, as nature at large, abhors vacuums and low-pressure areas. If, across the whole electorate, pressures on voters from habitual party loyalty and comprehension of campaign issues are lower than in earlier years, we should expect to find some other pressure or influence correspondingly more important in the voting decision.

This other pressure is the personal character or image of the candidates running for public office.

NOTES

1. Eugene Burdick, "Political Theory and the Voting Studies," in Eugene Burdick and Arthur Brodbeck (eds.), *American Voting Behavior* (New York: Free Press, 1959), p. 139.
2. Stanley Kelley, Jr., "Campaign Debates: Some Facts and Issues," *Public Opinion Quarterly*, 26, No. 3 (Fall, 1962), p. 359.
3. *The New York Times*, October 7, 1961, p. 10.
4. Robert E. Lane, *Political Life* (New York: Free Press, 1959), p. 216.
5. Robert E. Thompson, "Democrats Seek New Star and Spot Peck," *World Journal Tribune*, December 7, 1966, p. 1.
6. Earl Mazo, Malcolm Moos, Hallock Hoffman, and Harvey Wheeler, *The Great Debates* (Santa Barbara, Calif.: Center for Study of Democratic Institutions, 1962), p. 6.
7. Angus Cambell, Philip Converse, Warren Miller, and Donald Stokes, *The American Voter* (New York: Wiley, 1960), p. 490.
8. *The New York Times*, November 20, 1966, p. 36.

2

CANDIDATE IMAGES

The personal images of candidates for public office have long served as simple models of political reality, as political complexity and confusion abstracted into something voters believe they can judge: human character.

WALTER LIPPMANN: The real environment is altogether too big, too complex and too fleeting for direct acquaintance. We are not equipped to deal with so much subtlety, so much variety, so many permutations and combinations. And although we have to act in that environment, we have to reconstruct it on a simple model before we can manage it.[1]

Before television and radio, the most important component of a candidate's image in the United States was probably his reputation—conveyed by newspapers, pamphlets, cartoons, posters, and campaign slogans—from which voters might derive, in their mind's eye, an impression of the candidate's personal character.

Before the advent of electronic communications, a reputation as a military hero appeared to help elect several of our Presidents: George Washington, Andrew Jackson, Zachary Taylor, U. S. Grant, and Theodore Roosevelt. In 1840, Whig newspapers conveyed such a virile image of William Henry Harrison as the hero of Tippecanoe that voters chose him over incumbent President Van Buren. But in truth, the battle of Tippecanoe had taken place almost thirty years earlier and William Henry Harrison, aged sixty-eight on coming to the White House, was not really virile enough to last much beyond the exhausting round of inauguration festivities.

By allowing the electorate to hear the candidate's voice and listen to his reasoning and eloquence as clues to his character, radio probably broke the back of the newspaper industry's ability to perpetrate literary-fiction images of candidates. Franklin Delano Roosevelt, whose tenure as President spanned thirteen of radio's short twenty-five-year (1922–1947) prime, communicated an admirable character to the vast majority of voters. The printed media, largely Republican-controlled, could do nothing to stop the 1936 reelection landslide of President Roosevelt.

MARSHALL MCLUHAN: Radio affects most people intimately, person-to-person, offering a world of unspoken communication between writer-speaker and the listener. . . . A private experience. . . . power to turn the psyche and society into a single echo chamber. . . . The famous Orson Welles broadcast about the invasion from Mars was a simple demonstration of the all inclusive, completely involving scope of the auditory image of radio. It was Hitler who gave radio the Orson Welles treatment for *real*. . . .

If we sit and talk in a dark room, words suddenly acquire new meanings and different textures. . . . Given only the *sound* of a play, we have to fill in *all* of the senses, not just the sight of the action.[2]

Marshall McLuhan had not begun to develop his now-famous concept that the medium is the message by the end of World War II, when the heyday of radio was over and television began to be the most pervasive of the mass media of communication. How radio affected public comprehension of political controversy as the basis of informed voting in the Jeffersonian tradition is an academic question today. But a similar question about the long-term influence of television on American political life may be very much worth investigating. That influence is the central concern of this book.

The following survey findings convey a sense of television's growing pervasiveness in the United States.

Year	Households with TV Sets	Total U.S. Households
1950	4.2 (millions)	43.6 (millions)
1952	15.8	45.4
1954	27.6	46.8
1956	35.5	48.8
1958	42.5	50.5
1960	45.2	52.0
1962	49.0	54.2
1964	51.3	55.7
1966	53.8	57.3
1967	54.9	58.2

SOURCE: A. C. Nielsen Company.

SURVEY QUESTION: *Suppose that you could continue to have only one of the following—radio, television, newspapers, or magazines—which of the four would you most want to keep?*

Most Want to Keep	1959 (%)	1961 (%)	1963 (%)	1964 (%)	1967 (%)
Television	42	42	44	49	53
Newspapers	32	28	28	27	26
Radio	19	22	19	15	14
Magazines	4	4	5	5	3
Don't know or no answer	3	4	4	4	4

SOURCE: Roper Research Survey for Television Inf. Office.

SURVEY QUESTION: *If you got conflicting or different reports of the same news story from radio, television, the magazines, or the newspapers, which of the four versions would you be most inclined to believe—the one on radio or television or magazines or newspapers?*

Most Believable	1959 (%)	1961 (%)	1963 (%)	1964 (%)	1967 (%)
Television	29	39	36	41	41
Newspapers	32	24	24	23	24
Magazines	10	10	10	10	8
Radio	12	12	12	8	7
Don't know or no answer	17	17	18	18	20

SOURCE: Roper Research Survey for Television Inf. Office.

TELEVISION VIEWING HOURS PER DAY
BY ADULT HOUSEHOLD MEMBERS

Age	Men	Women
Under thirty-five years	3:11	4:18
Thirty-five to forty-nine	3:07	4:08
Fifty years and older	4:08	4:55

SOURCE: A. C. Nielsen National Audience Composition Report, January, 1967.

These last findings concerning the average number of hours per day spent by the average American adult in front of his television set seem most important to remember in searching out the unique influence of television on voting. Depending on what survey one subscribes to, in 1967 those hours numbered between two and four, day in, day out, year around, year after year. If the medium *is* the message, what message relative to American politics are voters getting from this incredible exposure to television?

Do candidate images conveyed to voters by television in advance of Election Day differ from images of the same candidates conveyed by the other mass media?

These questions may be immensely important in years when influences on voting other than candidate image seem to be declining. At stake is nothing less than the responsiveness of our government and its elected leaders to the opinion of the people.

NOTES

1. Walter Lippmann, *Public Opinion* (New York: Macmillan, 1922), Chapter 1.
2. Marshall McLuhan, *Understanding Media: The Extensions of Man* (New York: McGraw-Hill, 1965), Chapter 30.

PART TWO

Adventures of an
Image Specialist

CHAPTER

3

AMBASSADOR OF FRIENDSHIP

The long corridor was unnaturally quiet and unnatural, too, in that there were no knobs on any of the doors except the one at the far end labeled 800H.

In connecting suites off 800H, in the rooms behind those knobless doors, Leonard Hall, former chairman of the Republican National Committee, had set up temporary Nixon campaign headquarters. The site was hidden away in the vast recesses of Washington's Sheraton-Park Hotel because Vice-President Nixon was not yet the Republican presidential candidate. This was the beginning of May, 1960. The Nixon nomination was expected to come at the Republican Convention in July. The job of 800H was to make sure it did come.

Len Hall was a stranger to me then. My summons had come from Ted Rogers, for whom I had worked as a writer on NBC's *Home* program and *Wide Wide World*. Among writers, whose view of producers is sometimes biased, Ted had been known as the Wheeler-Dealer because he always had important phone calls to make from his hotel room when we arrived on location (while the writers wandered around aimlessly). The Rogers-Nixon relationship dated back to 1952. Nixon's campaign manager then, Murray Chotiner, had been impressed with a talk Ted gave on the political uses of television and drafted him from the Hollywood office of Dancer, Fitzgerald, and Sample to be Nixon's television adviser for that national campaign. Ted had been "producer" of the Nixon "Checkers" telecast in 1952. Eight years later, the Vice-President invited him to sign on for the big race.

TED: I've got some important calls to make. Read this and then we'll talk.

I made some notes from what I read about the candidate.

1. *Foreign policy.* Great personal travels, esp. man who stood up to Khrush.
2. *Experience counts.* Most active VP at home, took over during Ike's heart attack, Pres. of Senate, member of Ike's Security Council & Cabinet, helped settle steel strike.
3. *Ike endorsement.* This is my boy!
4. *Humble beginnings.* I believe in the American dream because I have seen it come true in my own life.
5. *More of the same.* The past eight years under Ike have been the greatest.

We talked of the organizational setup for radio, television, and film, which would be a collapsible advertising agency called Campaign Associates manned by personnel borrowed from big ad agencies and the networks. The Washington office, with Ted in charge, would take care of getting television coverage of the candidate wherever he happened to be campaigning, through a combination of purchased station time and appearances on local news and interview programs. TV advance men out of Washington would leap-frog each other to arrive at locations ahead of the candidate and make sure of station facilities, lighting, studio-audience control, and so on. The New York office of

Campaign Associates—located on Vanderbilt Avenue because Nixon did not want the Madison Avenue stigma associated with him—would be directed by Carroll Newton, a top man at BBDO, who turned out to be a little older, wiser, and quieter than most of us on the crew. My job was to write and produce television films—only some of which would require fresh material from the candidate—under Carroll's supervision.

This was the best news yet. I could commute to work in New York from home in Connecticut, where I had two children, a very pregnant wife, and a number of white goats left over from a television show about Carl Sandburg.

Whereupon Ted Rogers told me to take the first jet for Los Angeles. There was trouble in My Department.

The trouble was a Nixon campaign film that had been prepared by some surviving members of the DeMille unit at Paramount Pictures. Barney Balaban, president of Paramount and a staunch Republican, had wanted to be helpful. Now Nixon's inner circle had seen the film and were declaring it useless. Yet they badly needed a basic campaign film and they did not want to antagonize Balaban.

They screened the film for me in Washington. It was bad: weak, dull, a pious illustrated lecture. The producer had faltered at the crucial step from research to drama. He had meticulously gathered a great amount of 35mm Nixon travel footage, which was probably no easy task. But lacking a writer, and unable to rise above the material himself, he had failed to make a *moving* picture.

TECHNIQUE: DETACHMENT

The Agent from 800H sunned himself by the hotel's pool and tried to remember a college course in propaganda taken long ago and far away. "The first task is to detach...detach the audience from their own reality...from their prior train of thought . . . so that their minds are open to persuasion. . . ."

The professor had shown movies . . . *Der Triumph des Wil-*

lens . . . Triumph of the Will . . . began with clouds, banks of majestic cumulus clouds rolling toward the audience, washing over them, detaching them from all reality beyond that on the screen . . . now the gaint sound of motors, growing stronger, coming nearer . . . an airplane suddenly slashes through the clouds, the sunlight flashing on its wings, a silver chariot of the skies carrying the Nazi godhead to his admirers assembled at Nuremberg. Hitler himself had put actress Leni Riefenstahl in charge of 30 cameramen and a crew of 120 to make this film production of the 1934 Nazi party convention. With the film in mind, Hitler and Goebbels ordered grandiose architectural settings for the mass movements of a hundred thousand party faithful. Miss Riefenstahl kept her cameras moving, panning, tracking, tilting, so that audiences would not only see a feverish world on the screen, but would feel themselves caught in it. Nuremberg became a sea of waving swastika banners, the flames of bonfires and torches illuminating the nights, the streets and squares echoing with Prussian march music, the endless columns of marching men, the innumerable rows of party formations, the rows of drummers pounding away in unison, the trumpeters and the Reich eagle and Hitler—always Hitler—silhouetted against the skies conveyed an overwhelming impression that German mythology, such as in *The Ring of the Nibelungen,* had come to be real and that while the German people were still but ornaments to the will of the gods, that will was now embodied in Hitler. For students of propaganda, *Triumph of the Will* is a frightening reminder of film's potency to reduce individual viewers to mindless particles caught up in a mass hysteria that denies all traditional human values.[1]

TED ROGERS (ON PHONE): I called the studio. You were playing badminton!

GENE: Listen! I got to tell you—I got a great idea for the opening.

(*Slate:* PARAMOUNT PICTURES, #21198, REEL ONE)

FADE IN

AERIAL SHOT—

BANKS OF CUMULUS CLOUDS
ROLLING TOWARD
THE CAMERA

(*Sound:* SLOW FADE IN, AIRPLANE MOTORS)

MORE CLOUDS

NARRATOR (VOICE OVER PICTURE): This is the story
of one man
who traveled
over two hundred thousands miles
through sixty countries
of the world
to ease international problems
and foster good will
for the United States.

MAIN TITLE ZOOMS
FORWARD TO FILL THE
SCREEN, SUPERIMPOSED
OVER THE CLOUDS

(*Sound:* PLANE MOTORS STRONGER)

"AMBASSADOR
OF
FRIENDSHIP"

THE NIXON PLANE SUDDENLY
SLASHES THROUGH THE
CLOUDS, SUNLIGHT FLASHING
ON ITS WINGS

(*Music:* IN AND UNDER NARRATION)

TECHNIQUES: VISUAL LEITMOTIF AND REACTION SHOTS

In its first unusable version *Ambassador of Friendship* had two marked visual shortcomings: a lack of visual continuity and a lack of reaction shots. When these were corrected, the flow of images on the screen suddenly gave a better illusion of drama, which in turn intensified the role of the candidate in that drama.

Because campaign films often try to span high points of a political career with a hodgepodge of footage from various sources, a common failing is lack of a pictorial flow from one sequence to another that makes them all seem part of a story that is thrusting forward to a climax.

Sometimes a visual leitmotif—a symbolic scene repeated throughout the film—will help pull all the bits and pieces together. The silent feature film *Intolerance* provides a classic example of visual leitmotif. To tie together alternating sequences of four separate stories about man's inhumanity to man, D. W. Griffith repeatedly inserted a short scene of Lillian Gish rocking a baby's cradle to remind viewers of the overall theme: "Out of the cradle endlessly rocking" (Walt Whitman).

Because the theme of *Ambassador* was Nixon's international experience and because some of the footage showed him getting in or out of official-looking planes, the obvious connecting scene would be an air force transport flying over all sorts of terrain. But the Paramount stock library had no such footage listed, and there was hardly time to start looking for it in the Washington or Long Island City film libraries of the Defense Department. Someone at Paramount remembered that Jerry Lewis was using scenes of an air force transport in his *Geisha Boy* feature. The outtakes were in Cinemascope for wide-screen projection, but the center portion of each frame could be rephotographed in the optical lab without losing more than some sky to each side of the plane.

Now *Ambassador of Friendship* began to hang together and "move." Cut in as transitional scenes, footage of the air force C-54 flying over oceans, past mountain tops, and through clouds carried Vice-President Nixon from Asia to Russia to Africa and other parts of the world as identified quickly by stock close-ups of national flags (available from the United Nations) and superimposed titles.

Reaction shots are close-ups of people reacting to someone or something that affects them, underscoring the emotional impact of the happenings on the screen. Watching Frankenstein's monster stalk through the woods may be frightening, but seeing the look on his victim's face can be emotionally devastating. The big view of a welcoming parade can be colorful, but close-ups of cheering faces will suddenly translate the spectacle into human terms.

Reaction shots are so typically a technique of film and television drama that use of them in nonfiction presentations may—besides intensifying emotion—give viewers more of an illusion that they are watching drama.

A common mistake in political films is dwelling too much on the candidate, possibly through an erroneous notion that the more the candidate appears on the screen the more he is getting his money's worth. The first version of *Ambassador*, for example, had a sequence of Nixon speaking in a Russian television studio. He talked and talked. His words were good, but they were words. The picture stood still. The sense of drama dissipated.

In the remake, I opened up this sequence by cutting away from Nixon as soon as he started to talk. An old B-picture called *Radio Patrol* (or something like that) yielded a shot of the camera panning up an ultramodern antenna that could pass for a Russian antenna. As this shot came on the screen, "reverb" was added to Nixon's dialogue track so that the illusion was one of his voice coming out of a loudspeaker. Next we cut in about a minute of Russian people listening intently to the important words of the important American; that is to say, we cut in close-ups of people who looked as if they might be Russian and who looked as if they might be listening to radio or watching TV. One advantage of working in 35 mm film is that if you do not have enough close-ups of individual faces to use as reaction shots, the optical lab can take a group scene and rephotograph close-ups of the various faces in it.

TECHNIQUES: DELAYED WRITING, LETTING THE PICTURES SPEAK

Another common failing of campaign films is that they talk too much. They never know when to shut up and let the visual drama of the images on the screen speak in their own symbolic language. One reason for too much talk is that the script is written in advance of production. The sponsor wants to see on paper just what he is paying for before he gives the go-ahead for the big expenses of photography, editing, and lab work. Since an untrained eye usually reads the right-hand, or voice, column of a script, what often gets approved is an endless spiel of words that say everything and relegate the visual to little more than accompanying illustrations. The ideal device is delayed writing, that is, producing the film to amplify a thematic outline and then, after the rough cut, writing only that minimum of talk that serves to enhance, underscore, and clarify the nuances of each sequence. Of course, this is asking candidates and their aides and the producers of their campaign films to realize that visual images have their own peculiarly powerful ability to affect people by stimulating a subrational preliterate vocabulary of symbols that are common to most people in a given culture.

In the unusable version of *Ambassador*, there was powerful footage of a Venezuelan mob attacking Nixon's car. But in this version, the offscreen narrator kept pattering along saying things (such as are italicized below) that were completely and much more eloquently conveyed by the picture.

MOTORCADE STOPPED	NARRATOR (vo): A stalled truck stopped the motorcade from the airport and enabled the mob to *sweep*
MOB ATTACKING CAR	*over the procession. They attacked* the Vice-President's car with stones. They *spat* upon Mr. Nixon, his wife, and his party and *nearly wrecked*
SCENES OF DAMAGED CAR	*his car.* But order was restored before any of the party was injured.

Below is my reconstruction of this mob attack sequence as melodrama, foreshadowing it as a coming evil and then, when it does come, letting the pictures (and music) fulfill the viewer's anticipation of violence.

CLOSE-UPS:
ANGRY STUDENTS IN THE
ASSEMBLY ROOM TRYING
TO BAIT NIXON

(*Music:* OMINOUS STING)

NARRATOR (VO):
At San Andreas University,
a few students were determined
to embarrass their visitor
or at least to provoke him
into a display of temper
that would reflect unfavorably
on the United States.

NIXON ANSWERING STUDENTS

Their thrusts were parried,
their verbal attacks
turned aside by sound
logical answers.

CLOSE-UPS:
STUDENTS GLARING
AT NIXON

Obviously something
more damaging than words
would have to be thrown
at this man.

(*Music*: STING AND FORESHADOW
OMINOUS EVENTS)

CARACAS AIRPORT:
NIXONS DEPLANING

Caracas, Venezuela—
the last stop
on this South American tour.

CLOSE-UPS:
JEERING KIDS
(3 shots)

(*Music:* STRONGER)

The last stop—

MOTORCADE STOPPED
(4 shots)

(*Music:* CARRY ACTION)

CAR STOPPED

LARGE CROWD—
MOB RUNNING AND
THROWING STONES

DAMAGED CAR DETAILS
(3 shots)

(*Music:* SOFTER, SADDER)

VENEZUELAN OFFICIALS
APOLOGIZE

Later,
humiliated and embarrassed,
Venezuelan officials arrived
at the United States Embassy
to bring the apologies
of a shocked nation.

POLITICIANS WITH THEIR
BARE FACES HANGING OUT

Ambassador of Friendship played several times on California
television stations prior to June 7, 1960. Perhaps it did increase
the number of Republicans who came out to cast a vote for
Vice-President Nixon and consequently enhance the aura of his
popularity in advance of the Republican national convention—
although there is little doubt but that he would have gotten the
nomination regardless of what happened in the California primary.

Reaction to the film was gratifying. Republicans and Democrats who had been indifferent about him before reported feeling a great admiration for the candidate after seeing the film.
Apparently by generating a dramatic impression of a world in
turmoil featuring one tireless American who had made endless
rounds of the trouble spots, the film convinced viewers that
Richard Nixon was indeed the man who "understands what
peace demands"—the campaign slogan (coined by Carroll Newton, I think).

Carroll Newton, at the New York office of Campaign Associates, decided to use *Ambassador of Friendship* as a final
emotional jolt to the electorate by holding the film off network
television until a day or so before the November 8 election,
then putting it on in the best available network time.

Coincidentally, the use of *Ambassador* on California television
before the primary taught me something about image material
that I have never forgotten, namely, that you cannot mix it with
unstaged direct-to-camera material on the same program without making the direct-to-camera speakers seem more dull and

pedestrian than they might be. Because *Ambassador* was only two reels long, a bit over twenty minutes, California Republicans Senator Thomas Kuchel and Congressman Bob Wilson were drafted to fill out the remaining nine minutes of the time period with a short discussion about the candidate.

CONGRESSMAN BOB WILSON: . . . and I know this film is going to have its impact on the women of California too, because if you'll notice— if you've watched—in nearly every scene where it showed the Vice-President visiting in foreign countries, that Pat was at his side, and certainly that's been of importance too; the fact that she's been able to see the problems of the women, the problems in the homes of foreign countries, is going to be very important too.

SENATOR THOMAS KUCHEL: She's a gracious lady, and we can be proud of her, and she'll grace the White House with real American dignity.

WILSON: She's going to be one of our real ambassadors when she's in the position of First Lady of the land, I know.

KUCHEL: And I must say, in addition to that, during this campaign I think Pat Nixon will be an admirable asset to the Republican party across the country.

The senator and the congressman are intelligent, competent, and personable. Such men in legislative bodies across the land carry the responsibility of effecting public policies that influence our individual and national destinies. But put them on the home screen after twenty minutes of detachment devices, leitmotifs, reaction shots, musical underscoring, sonorous narration, cheering crowds, and mobs stoning cars and their words seem dull, pedestrian, ludicrous.

This contrast suggested a larger question. Twenty-three hours a day television presents dramatic art much more adept than *Ambassador of Friendship*. What then happens in the twenty-fourth hour, when television, fulfilling its journalistic function as an arm of the American press, presents reality?

NOTES

1. Siegfried Kracauer, *From Caligari to Hitler* (Princeton: Princeton University Press, 1947), pp. 300-303.

CHAPTER

4

___

AN IMAGE OF A PARTY

There is not much time to think about larger questions in the
heat of a campaign.

TED ROGERS (ON PHONE): Campaign Associates is transferring you to
M-E Productions.
GENE: You're not happy with M-Y productions?
TED: M-E is a division of the McCann-Erickson agency. McCann-
Erickson has the Bell & Howell account. Chuck Percy of Bell &
Howell is chairman of the Republican Platform Committee. You're
going to make an hour film for him to narrate at the convention in
Chicago on July 27.
GENE: That's next month!
TED: A real challenge.

On a clear day, you can see a good part of Lake Michigan
from the terrace of the elegant Percy home in Kenilworth, Illinois. I think Saturday, June 25, was clear, but I wasn't considering the view. There was no 1960 Republican platform on

which to base a film. There would not be one until the 103 members of the Platform Committee assembled in Chicago one week before the convention and drafted a document of party principles and goals for the delegates to approve. There were thirty-one days between June 25 and Wednesday night, July 27, when Chuck Percy was scheduled to stand up before the entire convention, and the nation via television, and present his film version of the platform. Those thirty-one days included five Sundays, four Saturdays, and the Fourth of July—ten days on which film libraries, laboratories, and other production facilities would be closed. That left twenty-one days to write and produce a one-hour film about something that did not exist.

CHARLES PERCY: Ted Rogers told me I could have absolute confidence in you.
GENE: Ted is a good friend.

The only possibility was to produce a film version of an imagined platform synthesized from such party documents as the 1956 platform and a recent book about "challenges" for Republicans that had come out of a study committee directed by Percy. The reels of film could have music, effects, and dialogue (such as statements by Nixon and Eisenhower) on the sound track, but could not have the narration. The narration—which would have to give the final twist to the import of the footage so that it appeared to be a visualization of the 1960 platform—really could not be written until there was an approved 1960 platform. This meant that I would have to do it in Chicago, writing the narration as a speech that Percy could deliver from the rostrum while the film was running simultaneously. In Convention Hall, delegates would see the film above and behind Percy on two huge screens. Television would be showing the film with Percy's voice as an offscreen narration.

The big hitch in the scheme was the proper synchronization of a live speech with that much footage. It would mean rehearsal, Percy working hours and hours with his script and each reel of film, adjusting his pace of delivery so that each spoken phrase fell against the proper scene. Percy agreed to this rigor. None of us on the terrace at Kenilworth that day anticipated the turmoil that was going to strike the Platform Committee and upset all schedules in Chicago.

Nixon's feelings about Madison Avenue notwithstanding, I immediately followed the Madison Avenue procedure of hiring an assistant, Mel Stuart, who could be blamed in case things went wrong.

MEL STUART: We need Ross-Gaffney.
GENE: Travel agents?

At the time Ross and Gaffney were two young film editors with a few younger-looking assistants crammed into some tiny offices with a lot of old-looking equipment. Angie Ross had trained as an operatic tenor and applied his talent to make stock music cues fit pictures better than original scoring. Jim Gaffney, besides his round-the-clock endurance at a movieola, was a genius at getting difficult or expensive things done faster or cheaper. He used an international approach: an Irish smile, American five-dollar bills, and Scotch whisky.

For example, Mel Stuart came in with a small reel stashed under his coat: Russian footage of a missile control room and one of their huge rockets taking off. The footage cried out for an authoritarian Russian voice on the sound track counting down to blast off.

JIM GAFFNEY: The night man on the elevator is always cursing us out in Russian.
GENE: So?

So with a bottle of Scotch in one hand and a five-dollar bill in the other, at two o'clock in the morning the elevator operator made like a Russian general. I could only hope that his words on the sound track that fed into 30 million Americans homes as part of convention coverage were really "Three, two, one, blast off!"

Judy Trotsky, a film researcher borrowed from CBS, brought in footage of the Depression dating back to the late 1930s:

maybe we could use it to show life in America before the Eisenhower-Nixon administration took over. After all, we didn't have to say how long before.

I mumbled something about scruples and demurred.

A few days later the Democrats put on their film at their convention in Los Angeles. Their film had that identical Depression footage illustrating how bad economic conditions really were *during* the Republican administration in the 1950s.

Judy also found beautiful footage of Negro and white faces in a mixed audience, a long moody scene that would be perfect visual counterpoint to narration about civil rights. But the film belonged to Charlie Guggenheim, a sensitive documentary-commercial producer and a very ardent Democrat. Guggenheim's office reported that he was out at the Democratic convention and gave us his Los Angeles hotel number. I could just picture his reaction on hearing that we wanted to use some of his footage in the Republican platform film.

JIM GAFFNEY: If you called him right now, it's so early on the Coast that you'd wake him up and he wouldn't know exactly what you were talking about. Offer him a five-dollar bill right off the bat [$5 per foot, or $450 per minute, for rights to use his film]. Just tell him it's for some sponsored film we're making. You don't have to say who the sponsor is.

By July 14, less than two weeks before air, Charlie Guggenheim's footage was one of several hundred scenes and sequences, each ranging from a few seconds to hundreds of feet, that we had on hand and cleared for use. Items ranged from "Khrushchev and Mao shake and hug" (foreign relations) to "Boy eating hot dog" (Americana) to "Werner von Braun saying we have to speed up the missile program" (defense).

For a leitmotif to unify this hodgepodge, I sent a camera crew down to Washington, where the Census Bureau has an animated display board in the lobby of the Commerce Department building. For our filming, the Census people were kind enough to set the big counting device ahead to just what the population would be at eight o'clock on the evening of July 27, when Chuck

Percy would start his presentation. We also filmed the population counter for the predicted figures at 8:01 P.M., 8:02, 8:03, 8:05, 8:10, 8:15, and so on, giving us a selection of demographically accurate scenes to edit into the film as a striking visual transition. For example:

(REEL ONE)

CENSUS CLOCK:	PERCY (CONTINUING; VO):
	This is the speed of change.
ZOOM IN TO FIGURES	There are eleven more Americans
THAT NOW READ	now than there were
180 750 650	two minutes ago.

.   .   .

(REEL FIVE)

CENSUS CLOCK:	PERCY (VO):
	In these few minutes
ZOOM IN TO	while we have talked
180 750 780	of foreign policy and defense,
	our country has grown
	by one hundred and thirty people.

The repeated scenes of the population clock gave the platform film an emphasis that was my own, whatever the opinions of the 103 members of the Platform Committee, who were formulating the actual document. Political leaders, I have concluded, tend to be cowardly about birth control because of the Catholic vote. But population is, in my opinion, the number-one problem behind such pressing and expensive public problems as overcrowded slums, jammed traffic, water shortages and pollution, and double school sessions. Ultimately, I fear, the political cowardice of our elected leaders—abetted by the "do-not-offend" policies of our national press media—will lead us into an era when our easy-to-get natural riches (food, water, air, power, space) are overwhelmed by so many people that, for survival, many more aspects of our daily lives will have to be regulated.

I do not mean to evangelize here but to point out how one propagandist preparing image material that gains national exposure can cause it to leave an impression upon the public that was hardly intended by its sponsors.

TECHNIQUE: CUTTING TO MUSIC

Late in 1952, film editor Elmo Williams—then about to win an Oscar for his work on *High Noon*—showed me the technique that helped to make the climax of that picture so exciting. Rather than editing the scenes together first and then adding music, which is the common practice in film making, the climax of *High Noon* was cut to Dimitri Tiomkin's music so that every few measures, on the downbeat, the scene changed: a close-up of the clock ticking with its hands approaching noon; a closeup of Gary Cooper getting ready to face impossible odds by himself; a close-up of the gunmen coming closer. The rhythm of the music and the rhythm of the scene changes became one, so that—as the music made its hearers anticipate the strong beat at the beginning of each measure—the audience came to sense just when the next change in scene was going to come and when it did come precisely as anticipated, the audience was more and more caught up by the mounting excitement.

I recalled this technique in July, 1960. Film or no film, Percy was going to have to do an awful lot of talking in an hour and somewhere along the line I felt the film should give him a chance to keep quiet and give itself a chance to excite the audience on purely cinematic terms.

One segment of the platform film was supposed to tell about America's prosperity under the Republican Eisenhower-Nixon administration, with the explicit persuasion that the next four years would bring more of the same if Richard Nixon was elected President.

Angie Ross found a piece of stirring "growth" music about two minutes long and stretched it another minute by duping a middle refrain and cutting it in twice. Then a picture editor worked a full week assembling a flow of separate short scenes— industry, schools, homes, roads, libraries, backyard cookouts, concerts, ballet dancers, churches—each scene no more than a few seconds long and each appearing precisely and rhythmically on the beat of every second or fourth measure. (This was the illusion. To be technically accurate, the pictures were edited so as to appear four frames—one-sixth second—before the beat of the music so that the eye of the viewer registers the visual image just as the ear hears the beat.)

This "growth" reel of film was exhilarating to watch. Its long rapid rhythmic montage was impressionism analogous to Seurat's technique with tiny dots of paint that—unseen themselves—blend into an aesthetic experience. I thought to myself that if I got away with using it—and I expected objections from some literal-minded Republican—it would be quite a precedent for the use of image propaganda in national politics. For three minutes, Chuck Percy would be standing up there on the rostrum to tell the nation about the goals of the Republican party in 1960— and he would not be saying a word.

THE CONFLICTING DEMANDS OF PROPAGANDA AND POLITICAL REALITY

On Friday, July 22, five days before the scheduled platform presentation, I was in a Chicago hotel with all the timings, foot by foot, of the film. But there still was no approved 1960 platform to write a script from. Nobody would give me assurance as to when—or if—there would be one.

The Platform Committee was in a turmoil. Supporters of New York's Governor Nelson A. Rockefeller were insisting on a document of *crisis* that would sound an alarm to waken Americans to the *emergencies* that existed with respect to civil rights, defense, and other public problems.

But a document of crisis, alarm, and emergency would be completely contrary to Nixon's basic stance that America had been prospering and doing a good job on public problems under the Republican Administration (of which he was the second man) and more of the same could be expected if he was elected President in 1960. Rumor around Nixon headquarters was that Rockefeller was trying to force a convention floor fight over the platform as a means of entree by which the delegates might be persuaded that the proper Republican presidential candidate should not be Nixon but rather a man who recognized crisis and emergency.

According to author Theodore H. White in *The Making of the President 1960,* Chuck Percy was so desperate to compromise the warring factions in the Platform Committee that he offered to let the Rockefeller people write the script of the platform film presentation.[1]

If Percy ever made that offer to Rockefeller's people in Chicago, I did not know about it, and if I had known about it, I would have advised him to forget about putting the film on. Such rigidity is inherent in the nature of image propaganda: once it is made, it is "locked" to do just what it is supposed to do and—while its meaning may be shaded just the slightest bit by choice of words—the pictures, music, and general production finesse will leave the dominant impressions no matter what the accompanying patter. Further, at that late date in Chicago, every sentence and thought written for the narrator (Percy) to say while the film was running would have to follow the precise timing of each scene lest the talk lop over into irrelevant scenes and just be confusing. And I very much doubt that any of the governor's men in Chicago at that time were walking around with that sort of professional script-writer's skill.

Vice-President Nixon tried to calm things down by flying to New York and meeting with Governor Rockefeller at the governor's apartment on Fifth Avenue. At this news, conservatives on the Platform Committee were enraged. They called the Nixon-Rockefeller meeting the "Munich of the Republican party" and the "Fifth Avenue surrender." All pretense of constructive work by the committee was dropped while emotions raged for a day or so.

At this point I counted the remaining hours until eight o'clock on the night of July 27 and said, "The hell with this. I'm going to write a platform of my own." It took me about twenty-four hours.

On Monday and Tuesday, July 25 and 26, the Platform Committee was still squabbling in their hotel meeting room. The press, with its portable carnival environment of television cameras and floodlights, jammed the hall outside, ready to bring viewers the next bit of platform drama.

But in a little room off the big room, the version of the platform that the nation would see was already in rehearsal. A portable 35mm projector had been installed. Whenever he could, Chuck Percy turned the Platform Committee gavel over to someone else and slipped into the little room to read part of the script against the film footage, over and over again, until he caught the timing and rhythmic relationship between the words, pictures, dialogue, music, and sound effects.

The little room became a bastion of illusion amid a chaos of reality. I cheered up—too soon. Abruptly there was chaos in the bastion.

Peter Peterson, a former McCann-Erickson man then being groomed by Percy for the top job at Bell & Howell, decided that the platform presentation would be greatly improved if his boss showed a series of charts and graphs (prepared by Peterson) to illustrate statistically the growth of gross national product, housing starts, classroom construction, and other economic indicators under the Eisenhower-Nixon Republican administration. What Peterson wanted to cut out of the presentation was—naturally—the strongest thing in it from an image point of view: the three-minute "Growth" musical montage.

Peterson was overruled, thanks to the intervention of Bob Goldwin, who was an adviser to Percy on matters of political science. Dr. Goldwin convinced Percy to leave my work alone because it had its own aesthetic unity, with which the Peterson-type facts-and-figures chalk talk would conflict. But this disagreement between Peterson and myself was not resolved until the situation in that little room off the big room became so sticky as to raise the question of whether the cans of film would simply disappear before Wednesday evening.

I cite this incident not to reopen old scars but because it proved to be an archetype of the most serious obstacle an image specialist is liable to face in preparing his materials for television.

In the entourage of almost every "top man," there seems to be at least one aide who wants to change the work of the television/film professional who has been hired during a campaign. At first I thought this common occurrence was only a matter of everyone's having two businesses, their own and show business—that it was just a variation of the sponsor's wife wanting to pass on the scripts. But sad experience has taught me that it goes beyond that. When an image specialist works with a top man, he must work directly with that man and not through any intermediaries. The specialist is, after all, putting words into the candidate's mouth that must sound natural. And the specialist must know the candidate so well that on cue (in front of cameras) he can elicit from the candidate a selective aspect of personality and demeanor.

This close relationship between image specialist and top man bothers aides and advisers. The top man is the power source in a political staff organization and there are jealousies when the established pecking order of the organization is upset, even temporarily, because of a campaign that may require specialist capabilities that the regular organization does not possess.

The image specialist should be aware that he is an interloper to the candidate's staff and anticipate, as best he can, the one aide or adviser who will step forward with "ideas" regarding image material as a way of demonstrating to his boss that he (the aide) is really a valuable and essential person at all times. Sooner or later, an image specialist may have to make the decision of whether to go along with the amateur advice of the aide and compromise the effectiveness of the material or to be a perfectionist and take his chances against the polite knife-in-the back enmity of the aide and staff.

On Wednesday afternoon, Percy had his dress rehearsal in the empty arena. On Wednesday evening, he went on as scheduled for the delegates and the three television networks. When no film was running, his script was up on a teleprompter in front of him so that he appeared to be looking straight out at the delegates and television cameras as he talked. On cue, the film—two copies of each reel running simultaneously on two projectors so that if one copy broke while on the air the second copy could immediately be "punched up"—appeared on a small television monitor that was concealed in the speaker's rostrum. At that point, Percy could switch from the teleprompter copy to his own personal script, which was very carefully marked with the pacing and inflection cues developed during his work with the film on the preceding two days.

A platform had finally been approved. A few of its pertinent planks, condensed and translated into oral English, were incorporated into the breaks between the presentation. But the rational meaning of those actual platform words seemed so completely overshadowed by the fact of presentation that they were stage waits between the more exciting segments of film.

And the film labored to leave just three impressions upon viewers: (1) "you never had it so good"; (2) the Republican party cares about individual dignity and personal freedom above all things; and (3) the exploding population is the greatest challenge we face and the Republican party is alert to that challenge.

(REEL ONE—OPENING LIFE CYCLE MONTAGE)

(*Music:* NURSERY SONG—
"ORANGES AND LEMONS SAY THE
BELLS OF ST. CLEMENS")

MR. PERCY (VO):
HOSPITAL NURSERY — We start
CU: BABY ON TABLE — with this unchanging belief:
CU: MOTHER WITH BABY — that individual dignity
LITTLE GIRL EATING — and personal freedom
MOTHER WITH SON ON LAP — are precious above all things;
CHILDREN, RING-A-ROSY — that governments exist

YOUNG GIRLS READING
TEEN-AGE GIRLS
YOUNG BOY IN SCHOOL LAB
MAN AT OSCILLOSCOPE
FAMILY PICNIC
WOMAN HANGING WASH
FAMILIES COMING TO CHURCH
MIDDLE-AGED MAN SMILING
MIDDLE-AGED WOMAN
OLD MAN WITH GRANDCHILD
    ON BEACH

not to dominate people,
not to regulate
and run their lives,
but to serve them
and defend them
and nourish their hope
for a better tomorrow.

(*Music:* TENSION STING AND
    CLOCK THEME ESTABLISHES)

CENSUS CLOCK

Our basic faith in people
endures.
Everything else changes,

CLOSE-UP TO ESTABLISH WHAT
    THE CENSUS CLOCK IS AND
    THEN PULL BACK SLOWLY TO
    SHOW IT IN FULL

challenging us
to preserve a country
and a world
where individual freedom
is not submerged
in the course of events.
At this hour
on Wednesday evening,
the 27th of July, 1960,

ZOOM IN TO NUMBERS
    ON TOP OF CENSUS CLOCK
    SO THAT THEY FILL
    THE ENTIRE SCREEN

a device in Washington
counts the population
of the United States
at 180   750   638.

(*Music:* STING)

THE NUMBERS CHANGE

Even as we talk
that number will change
many times.

NOTES

1. Theodore H. White, *The Making of the President 1960* (New York: Atheneum, 1961), p. 195.

CHAPTER

5

CANDIDATE VERSUS IMAGE

Chicago was a fateful city for Nixon in 1960. The peak of his popularity followed the televising of his acceptance speech at the convention. Two months later, his popularity suffered a terrible setback following his first encounter with Senator John F. Kennedy, the Democratic presidential candidate, in a Chicago television studio.

The acceptance speech came on the night after the platform film presentation. I watched it from my hotel room, feeling a million miles away from politics after a day of loafing on the beach at Wake Forest. But watching that speech was like seeing Nixon for the first time. I suddenly had a good feeling about him. And obviously I was not alone in that sort of a response.

Nixon himself sensed that something unusual had happened, some magic connection between himself and those who saw and heard him. Later he wrote:

RICHARD NIXON: In the thousands of speeches I had made in my political career, there had never been a more responsive audience. . . . That speech was to mark a high point of my campaign for the presidency . . . the reaction of the television audience was more favorable even than that of the audience in Convention Hall.[1]

Nixon sensed the magic but apparently could not fathom it. He tried to generate it again—in desperation, I believe—by reviving and reusing the very same words and thoughts on his telecast of Sunday evening, November 6, two days before the election. Nixon has never seemed to grasp the concept why, at that late date, the same theme and words that stimulated such favorable public sentiment at the convention had lost their power to persuade. (See page 57 for further discussion of the November 6 telecast.)

Unquestionably the acceptance speech was excellent. I had the job of cutting down a film of it to a half-hour length that would be suitable for showing by Republican groups around the country. It was very hard to cut, so tightly written were the passages. But ultimately, after watching it fifty times on a movieola, I came to the conclusion that the magic of the speech was its theatrical intensity. The words were fine and right in character. But it had been the power of the moment, the power of the setting, that had lent to Nixon (or enhanced for him) his habitual characterization as the hero-with-humility. Again, what he said beautifully enhanced this character. But it was a mistake to think that the words alone were making the character so intense or the overall experience so theatrically exciting for viewers. Rather, it was the setting and his appearance and his demeanor and his words reinforcing each other that added up to a memorable image.

Evidently, what I was just figuring out for myself about the importance of stage setting, appearance, and demeanor to the impression that a candidate makes on television viewers was not unknown to Ted Rogers and Carroll Newton. Immediately after Chicago, they put me to work researching film footage and blocking out tentative scripts for two half-hour programs, each of which—by its staging—would convey an image of Nixon clearly different from the Kennedy image *regardless of the exact words Nixon might say on these two programs.* One of these half-hours was to be called *Khrushchev as I Have Seen Him.* In this, Nixon was to work with film and videotape elements such as the footage of him confronting the Russian Premier at the American exhibition in Moscow. We had collected more than enough film of Khrushchev indulging his mercurial temperament (such as haranguing the press in Paris over the U-2 spy plane) to visually characterize him in the melodramatic image of an international villain. In juxtaposition, Nixon would be characterized as the American who best understands what peace demands.

The second proposed program of this type was tentatively titled *You and Your Family.* The format called for a remote videotape pickup from the Nixon home outside of Washington, where he could talk about family problems—such as inflation, consumer debt, morality of the younger generation—to humble families (such as his own) in humble circumstances across the nation. Again, implicitly, this context of presentation would heighten viewer perception of Nixon's *character* regardless of exactly what he said (as long as the idiom of what he had to say enhanced this character).

Richard Nixon, however, would have nothing to do with these two proposed programs. It was not that he disagreed with the premise of their persuasive effect. Rather, he seemed not to understand the premise and therefore relegated such television effort to a low priority in his campaign efforts. According to his priorities, his melodramatic vow to campaign personally in every one of the fifty states—and his frantic scurrying to keep that vow —was important, although it exhausted him (and his staff) personally. When a bad infection of the knee hospitalized him for over a week in early September, his state-hopping schedule became so backlogged as to make a full day's rehearsal for a scripted live-and-film television program beyond consideration. And further, whatever Nixon's own attitude toward television's persuasive effect, Nixon's closest advisers—Bob Finch and Herb Klein—were (typically) oriented to newspapers rather than to television as the important medium of communication during the campagin. Finch and Klein made it difficult for Ted Rogers and Carroll Newton to have any time alone with the candidate.

Their heads—Finch's and Klein's—probably came up out of the sand on September 26, when the image lightning struck their candidate a mortal blow. September 26 was the date of the first one-hour televised confrontation between Vice-President Nixon and Senator Kennedy. By all accounts, this one hour made an indelible impression on millions upon millions of American voters. In juxtaposition, Nixon and Kennedy helped characterize each other for viewers with striking clarity. And it was character or image that viewers remembered rather than content of the program. In support of such a conclusion, I refer you to the multitude of studies reported in *The Great Debates*,[2] the paper dustjacket of which conveys a summary of its contents in two close-up photos from the debate kinescope. One photo shows Senator Kennedy looking full of face, handsome, thoughtful but with the slightest nuance of a smile around his lips and in his eyes, reflecting his precious leavening quality of humor. Richard Nixon looks mean, ugly, and haggard.

Unquestionably he was haggard, as any man might be who had been running on nervous energy for three weeks after a wicked bout with staphylococcus. Ted Rogers had vainly tried to get the candidate to break that ungodly schedule and rest before the first debate, but it was like trying to stop a juggernaut. Ted had urged full make-up to cover the deeply etched facial lines and the sickly pallor that emphasized the dark areas of Nixon's heavy beard. The candidate himself overruled Ted on that. Ted tried to ban reaction shots of Nixon listening to Kennedy so that at least whenever Nixon's face did appear on the screen, it would be talking and animated. But CBS director Don Hewitt insisted that reaction shots were part of normal television production technique. (See Chapter 17.) Ted wanted the candidate to come out with some forceful opening in order to establish immediately who was the experienced Vice-President and who was the young untried senator. But Nixon went through the first debate with a subdued agreeable, almost conciliatory demeanor.[3] This low-key performance was probably because Nixon was utterly exhausted, although Theodore White reports, in *The Making of the President 1960,* that Henry Cabot Lodge had urged Nixon to be gentle to contradict an alleged widespread image of Nixon as an "assassin."[4]

Ambassador Lodge, then Republican vice-presidental candidate, should have been the last one to give advice about television images. While his own newspaper or literary-fiction image was about as attractive as any candidate could hope for—after eight years of prominence in the United Nations—once he got out among crowds and once he got on television, something mysterious happened. People did not warm to him. My camera crews, trailing him for footage for a fifteen-minute film, reported difficulty in finding enthusiastic crowds.

To impress viewers with Lodge's "ambassador" image via television, Carroll Newton bought a half-hour on CBS-TV for Monday night, October 3, and had me block out a program called *The Danger Spots.* The format called for film footage—backed by music and effects—that Ambassador Lodge could work with to give viewers the impression that there was serious trouble brewing for America in locations that he knew well. Since Lodge was campaigning on the West Coast at the time, we rented a Los Angeles television studio for Saturday, October 1, in order to tape the program two days in advance of air. A handsome stage setting with a big dimensional map of the world was ordered for the ambassador to work in. A day or so early, I got out to the Coast with all my film segments and a script blocked out for Lodge to work from. (This was not presumptuous: my source material was Lodge's own back speeches adapted into television phrasing.)

But this time there was no amenable Chuck Percy who wanted to put on a good show and who had been warned far in advance of the rigors involved in rehearsal and production. This time there was an imperious palace guard of aides and advisers surrounding the ambassador, to whom television was just one more nuisance. "Just let him sit and talk to the people," they told me.

When he walked into that television studio on Saturday morning, Henry Cabot Lodge was absolutely unprepared for the production complexities that hit him. With facilities and crew probably costing close to $1,000 per hour, he began to argue and pick at the script—which did not contain any thought not his own. And when you begin correcting script that has already been typed onto two or three camera-mounted prompting devices, it takes time. Then, whenever the film came up on his monitor to illustrate one of the trouble spots, he would start to watch it and lose his place in the script.

Dennis Kane was directing. Dennis is one of the most experienced directors of political programs in the country. He tried ingenious methods to get enough usable material on tape, methods such as letting the ambassador talk ad lib about trouble spots, to which the film footage could be added electronically later. But Ambassador Lodge could not or would not perform.

I do not mean to imply that there was any fault on his part for the shambles in that studio on October 1. Lodge was what he was: virtues and shortcomings. The fault rather must be laid at the doors of Carroll Newton and Ted Rogers, who should have known better than to plan this elaborate production without taking into account the realities of Lodge's character, abilities, and campaign schedule. Top candidates usually can be brought to perform in a polished television idiom. Most can do a good job of enacting that selective aspect of their total character that favorably corresponds with publicly held images of what characters should be in high places, but to elicit such a performance can be a very painstaking procedure. This is a lesson that I have learned by trial and error. And few errors were more expensive than the one on October 1, 1960.

By evening, when Ambassador Lodge had left the studio, I had to call Carroll Newton and give him my opinion that the tape was unusable. Production costs had already passed the

$12,000 mark. The half-hour of prime time on CBS television had already been paid for, because all political time purchases must be paid in advance. And it was now less than forty-eight hours away. Carroll told me to bring the tape east on the next jet. By mid-morning Sunday, he and Len Hall had seen it and agreed that it was no good. By Sunday afternoon, I was back on another jet to Los Angeles with instructions to start all over again, this time using a program format that made absolutely no demands on the vice-presidential candidate.

By this time, my "internal clock" was not sure what hour or day it was. We managed to find four professors who knew something about foreign affairs and paid them to sit in a studio for a half-hour and ask Lodge some pertinent questions. The talk was learned, intelligent, and dull. It probably told viewers far more about foreign affairs than viewers wanted to know after a hard day's work, assuming any viewers would tune in to a dry-as-dust panel show when good entertainment programs were available on other channels. There was absolutely no excitement, no mood, no power-of-the-moment staging in the program to enhance the image of Henry Cabot Lodge.

By early October, after this incident and just five weeks before Election Day, gloom pervaded the little advertising agency just off Madison Avenue. Ted Rogers seemed stunned as the dimensions of public-opinion change following the first debate became clear. Nixon staff people were blaming Ted for the sickly, haggard appearance of the Vice-President on television. After the disheartening experience of the Lodge program, Carroll Newton did not want to hear any more about using television in any way except to put on all the direct-to-camera programs and commercial spots that Nixon requested to "get his views across to the people."

The format now was simple. Nothing showed on the screen except the Vice-President's face. A question was asked by an off-screen announcer: "Mr. Nixon, what is the truth? Are we really falling behind the Communists?" or "Mr. Nixon, what is the truth? Is America lagging behind in economic growth?"

The candidate would answer these questions briefly, so briefly in the shorter commercials as to be little more than a few words that did not convey anything of substance to viewers, especially not when you considered that the political commercials might well appear between much more showy and stimulating consumer-product commercials or program material.

RICHARD NIXON (TYPICAL 20-SECOND COMMERCIAL): We must speak up for America—for our strength—for our ideals of peace with justice and equality for all mankind. That's the way to keep the peace.

ANNOUNCER (VO): Vote for Nixon and Lodge November 8th. They understand what peace demands.

A few direct-to-camera film commercials were also made of Ambassador Lodge, showing him at his worst: fidgeting in a chair, squinting at some cue cards that were probably lying on the floor under the camera, and reading as if he was seeing the words for the first time and was not quite sure what they meant.

By this date, I was convinced that the Republican candidates were doing themselves no good on television. Nixon's setback from the first debate was clearly a matter of image rather than content. How could he now think that any amount of direct-to-camera talking he might do could wash away that lingering comparison of the Nixon and Kennedy images in the minds of so many millions of viewers? With Henry Cabot Lodge, the aspect of personal appearance was fine. He looked like what you would expect an American statesman to look like. But when he opened his mouth and when he interacted with people on television, there was something not so attractive—something in his demeanor, a touch of hauteur, arrogance, aloofness, or condescension perhaps. His characterization did not ring true.

Different attributes of Nixon and Lodge seemed to be preventing television viewers from feeling good about them, from feeling that these characters, more so than John Kennedy and Lyndon Johnson, should be at the nation's helm. Clearly—to me —it was time to use more image materials, if not image materials exclusively, in which elements of appearance, demeanor, and presentation added up to an exciting stimulating experience for viewers. The twenty-minute film *Ambassador of Friendship* could do a job for Nixon, but Carroll Newton was holding that off the networks as a matter of strategy until just before the election so that any emotions it generated would not be dissipated too soon.

Necessity—namely, little time and no access to the candidates —was the mother of invention at this point. We turned to the technique of using still pictures, many still photographs passing in rapid sequence, treated under an animation camera to create a sense of motion by a combination of zooming and panning actions. This technique proved to be a campaign gold mine. It was fast: within two weeks, we had completed *Meet Richard Nixon* and *Meet Mr. Lodge,* each 4:16 in length for five-minute time periods. It was cheap: what the candidates' scrapbooks and family albums did not yield, one good still photographer could get. And it was extraordinarily suitable for conveying an impression of heroic image, perhaps because each still photograph in itself is a slightly unreal impression, a moment frozen from life, that makes it easier for viewers to accept and be moved by an illusion of the candidate's heroic dimension. (See Chapter 13 for the complete script and further discussion of *Meet Mr. Lodge.*)

Actually, the hardest ingredient to find for these two films was the voice of President Eisenhower lauding Nixon and Lodge. I have no doubt that the President would have recorded this specially for the sound track, but presidential Press Secretary Jim Haggerty told us that Eisenhower would not do any active campaigning until he was asked by the Vice-President and for reasons of his own, Nixon was not yet asking. Fortunately, all public utterances of a President are recorded. Back issues of *The New York Times* helped us locate the date of a dinner speech during which the President had praised the Republican candidates in detail. Haggerty's office provided a tape of this speech. After a few hours of editing to clear up the President's diction by snipping out mispronounced words and replacing them with properly pronounced words from other portions of the speech, we had quite an acceptable film narration by Eisenhower.

One of the unique circumstances of a national campaign, as differing from a state or local campaign, is that the networks will provide five-minute time periods for "paid politicals" during good viewing hours. Their practice is to shorten regularly scheduled game shows, panel shows, musical and variety programs—almost any format except dramatic programs whose replay value might be hurt by shortening.

Campaign Associates had purchased about thirty of these five-minute time periods, mostly for two direct-to-camera talks by Nixon that had been made in that length. I wanted the two still-picture image films to start playing in these periods. Carroll Newton was reluctant. It might mean more trouble with the candidates and his inner circle.

It was Ruth Jones, Campaign Associates' time buyer (on loan from J. Walter Thompson) who finally prevailed on Carroll to let these two image films start playing on our daytime five-minute periods, which had a smaller audience than the evening periods. A favorable response was almost immediate. Reports came filtering back through Nixon headquarters that something on television was making the Republican candidates look good again. Within a week, the two five-minute image films were replacing the Nixon direct-to-camera films in the evening prime-time periods as well as in the daytime.

Carroll Newton's enthusiasm for the use of image materials on television seemed to revive. He persuaded Len Hall to come up with the money for a prime-time exposure of *Lodge for Vice-President,* a fifteen-minute image film that dramatically juxtaposed some excerpts from Lodge's best United Nation speeches with newsreel footage illustrating his words. The ABC-TV network shortened its very popular *Lawrence Welk Show* by fifteen minutes to provide air time for this film.

Keeping his promise to let the powerful *Ambassador of Friendship* play in the best possible prime time, Carroll preempted the *General Electric Theatre* for Sunday evening, November 6, two days before election. "Preemption," the canceling of regularly scheduled programs for political programs during a campaign period, is a stipulation made to stations by the Federal Communications Commission. Candidates (or their agents) are required to pay the production costs of the programs they preempt and generally try to pay "repeat" (second showing) production costs, which can be less than half of first-showing production costs, a difference largely due to the fact that residual payments to talent are less than the first-performance rates.

The *General Electric Theatre* time period (CBS-TV, 9 P.M., E.S.T.) enjoyed a tremendous carry-over audience from the top-rated *Ed Sullivan Show*, which preceded it. In that spot millions of viewers/voters would at last have a chance to be impressed with a rousing hero image of Dick Nixon, *Ambassador of Friendship*.

But it never happened. We had reckoned without the candidate.

NOTES

1. Richard Nixon, *Six Crises* (New York: Doubleday, 1962), pp. 318-319.
2. Sidney Kraus (ed.), *The Great Debates* (Bloomington: Indiana University Press, 1962).
3. Possibly to get it off his chest, Ted Rogers wrote a fictional version of his trials with that first debate, which is quite revealing of campaign practices. Edward A. Rogers, *Face to Face* (New York: Morrow, 1962).
4. Theodore H. White, *The Making of the President 1960* (New York: Atheneum, 1961), p. 285.

6

LET ME GO ON AND TALK
TO THE PEOPLE

Vice-President Richard Nixon had failed to understand the exact nature of the cruel lightning that struck him down on the first of the four television debates with Senator Kennedy. People around him were honest enough. They said it had been his appearance, that he had looked sick and weak and mean. So he went on a malted-milk diet and scheduled more sleep. His face began to fill out. The sharp lines of exhaustion disappeared. He used full face make-up on television. His shirt collars began to look as if they belonged to him. On the second, third, and fourth debates the visual contrast between the two seemed less pronounced. In an image sense, Nixon did not appear to be losing more ground to Kennedy. But neither did he appear to be gaining back the ground he had lost.

The first debate had evidently been a strongly disillusioning experience for viewers who tended to prefer Nixon because of an image of Nixon derived largely from common knowledge about Nixon's greater experience in high public office. Now these viewers suddenly saw a new image of Nixon, a less desirable image, an image less congruent (than the image of Senator Kennedy) with commonly held stereotype images of what the President of the United States should be like.

To compensate for this disillusioning exposure, what television viewers should have seen in the campaign from that date on was a presentation of Nixon designed to reestablish and reimpress the favorable image illusion. ("Illusion" is not an unfair word to apply to deliberately staged image material because it is presenting only a selective view of the candidate's most attractive attributes.) What viewers should have seen extensively after the first debate was more of Nixon as he was the night of the acceptance speech or as he appeared in *Ambassador of Friendship* or the five-minute still-picture commercial or as he finally began to appear on rally platforms before frantically cheering crowds attracted by the personal magnetism of President Eisenhower. Viewers needed strong impressions of Vice-President Nixon as a man to remember before one could expect them to remember anything he said. And they did not get those impressions, not nearly often enough or pervasively enough. Nixon did not comprehend such emotional needs. He knew a better way to regain his leading position in the campaign. "Let me go on and talk to the people," he told his television aides. "I have to get my views across to them."

Talking directly with "the people" had worked for him before, or so he thought.

In September, 1952, the intensely Democratic *New York Post* had started an editorial howl about a fund that had been raised in Southern California to help defray Nixon's political expenses. Other newspapers picked up the cry, speculating about what contributors to the fund were getting in return and about the propriety of a vice-presidential candidate (which Nixon was at the time) accepting such monies. Even the benign Eisenhower seemed to doubt whether Nixon should stay on the Republican ticket.

Nixon had broken off his campaign schedule and flown back to Los Angeles. He was alone in the noise-filled cocoon of a plane when he jotted down his first ideas for a televised explanation directly to the people of the nation. He was alone for hours in the Ambassador Hotel while he fleshed out his notes. He was alone on the stage of the El Capitan Theatre when he took his place behind a desk and waited for the red tally lights on the television cameras to tell him that he was on the air.

NIXON (SEPTEMBER 23, 1952): Not one cent of the $18,000 or any other money of that type ever went to me for my personal use. . . .

I am going at this time to give this television and radio audience a complete financial history: everything I've earned; everything I've spent; everything I owe. [Enumerates family finances.]

. . . .   .   .

. . . That's what we have and that's what we owe. It isn't very much but Pat and I have the satisfaction that everything that we've got is honestly ours. I should say this—that Pat doesn't have a mink coat. But she does have a respectable Republican cloth coat. And I always tell her she'd look good in anything.

One other thing I probably should tell you because if I don't they'll probably be saying this about me too. We did get something —a gift—right after the election.

A man down in Texas heard Pat on the radio mention the fact that our two youngsters would like to have a dog. And, believe it or not, the day before we left on this campaign trip we got a message from Union Station in Baltimore saying they had a package for us. We went down to get it. You know what it was?

It was a little cocker spaniel dog in a crate that he had sent all the way from Texas. Black and white spotted. And our little girl— Tricia, the six-year-old—named it Checkers. And you know the kids love that dog and I just want to say this right now, that regardless of what they say, we're going to keep it. . . .

Public reaction had been overwhelming. More than a million letters, wires, and calls said, "Keep Nixon on the Republican ticket." And Ike himself had come out to the airport when Nixon's plane had landed at Wheeling later. Ike had said to him, "You're my boy."

That had been in 1952. In 1960, at the convention, a similar sort of magic had occurred. The new Republican candidate for President had been alone out there on the rostrum, alone after a hero's entrance and ovation, alone talking to the people.

NIXON (JULY 28, 1960): . . . When Mr. Khrushchev says our grandchildren will live under Communism, let us say that his grandchildren will live under freedom. . . .

. . . I believe in the American dream because I have seen it come true in my own life. . . .

. . . Abraham Lincoln was asked during the dark days of the tragic War Between the States whether he thought God was on his side. His answer was, "My concern is not whether God is on our side, but whether we are on God's side."

On each weekday, Monday through Friday, of the week before Election Day, 1960, Campaign Associates purchased fifteen minutes of prime television time (CBS-TV, 7 P.M., E.S.T.) for Nixon to go on and talk to the people. In addition, he was appearing on many one-minute and twenty-second direct-to-camera spots and a few of the five-minute spots. In addition, with President Eisenhower now making a belated start on the campaign trail and attracting huge crowds to Republican rallies, Nixon was seen via "paid-political" and news coverage of the rallies: from the New York Coliseum on Wednesday night, November 2; and from the Pan Pacific Auditorium in Los Angeles on Saturday night, November 5. In addition, Campaign Associates bought local television time for "paid-political" coverage of rallies that were not big enough for network coverage. In addition, a four-hour telethon was scheduled at the last minute to replace all of the regular programming on the ABC-TV network on Monday afternoon, November 7, four more hours of Nixon talking directly to viewers. In addition, he was scheduled for an election-eve telecast to be carried first by CBS-TV and then repeated by both of the other networks around midnight.

On Saturday afternoon, November 5, without notice (because the candidate had given him little notice), Carroll Newton shipped me out to WXYZ-TV in Detroit to help put together the four-hour telethon that was scheduled for Monday afternoon.

Sometime on Saturday, November 5, or Sunday, November 6, Richard Nixon made a decision about television that Carroll could not or would not oppose. Nixon canceled the one showing of *Ambassador of Friendship,* which was scheduled for 9 P.M., following Ed Sullivan. Nixon wanted to go on the air for still one more half-hour and just talk to the people.

Later, writing in his book *Six Crises,* Nixon recalled that Sunday evening telecast of November 6.

RICHARD NIXON: I returned to the theme of my acceptance speech at Chicago. I did this deliberately, to complete the circle of three months' effort. I restated the one great and overriding issue of the campaign: how to keep the peace without surrender of principle, and how to preserve and extend freedom everywhere in the world.[1]

Nixon did not conceive that it might not have been his words or his theme so much as the fundamental dramatic situation of the acceptance speech that generated such a favorable sentiment about him. He did not conceive that the dramatic setting of that moment in Chicago's Convention Hall imparted an heroic stature to his character (image) before he opened his mouth. There is little doubt but that his masterful phrasing and delivery of the text exploited the moment exquisitely. But it was *exploitation* of the moment, of the setting, of the character delineation established by the situation.

Since Nixon did not comprehend this concept of television's influence upon voting, he saw no reason not to deliberately restate the theme of his acceptance speech in a barren television studio on Sunday, November 6. He saw no reason why the same words and ideas should not prompt the same viewer reaction to him.

Similarly, I doubt that he has ever come to realize why that "Checkers" telecast of 1952 was so persuasive. His words were exquisitely in character on that occasion, as he reduced the candidacy of Vice-President of the United States of America to a matter of his wife's "Republican cloth coat" and a little cocker spaniel "black and white spotted." But what had truly given the persuasive power to that character? In essence, was it the words or was it the melodrama of the moment that had been created in the public consciousness: the honest, humble hero baring his modest means to defend himself against slander, vowing to give up his political career rather than take Checkers away from Tricia?

Richard Nixon was wrong not so much in believing that his televised words had unusual power to persuade as in his failure to comprehend *why* they had that power and *when*. Again, the power in his words lay in the way they characterized him for viewers—humble and modest, yet strong and forthright—rather than in the rational political substance of what he said. His intimate-conversation style of delivery also worked to enhance this characterization. His appearance, usually, did not contradict it. And when the stage setting or manner of presentation was dramatic enough, he could make that character he was playing come across with great intensity.

Looking back at the 1960 campaign, Nixon himself belatedly acknowledged the visual aspect of television.

RICHARD NIXON: I believe that I spent too much time in the last campaign on substance and too little on appearance: I paid too much attention to what I was going to say and too little to how I would look.

Again, what must be recognized is that television has increasingly become the medium through which the great majority of voters get their news and develop their impressions of the candidates. . . . One bad camera angle on television can have far more effect on the election outcome than a major mistake in writing a speech which is then picked up and criticized by columnists and editorial writers.[2]

But it is not a matter of one bad camera angle. It is a much larger matter, of which camera angles are a slight part. It is a matter of the human dimensions of candidate character that viewers perceive on television. While what they *see* on the screen apparently conveys more intense clues to character than what they *hear*, what they see involves much more than camera angles.

There are still prints of *Ambassador of Friendship* around. Although like yesterday's newspaper the film has lost its immediacy, it still seems to generate a feeling in viewers that Richard Nixon was a great man. But the millions of voters who might have seen it when it was timely, on that Sunday evening just before the 1960 election, never did. What they saw was the man himself, still one more time trying so hard to get his views across to the people.

NOTES

1. Richard M. Nixon, *Six Crises* (New York: Doubleday, 1962), p. 371.
2. *Ibid.*, p. 422.

PART THREE

A Case Study of
Candidate Images

CHAPTER

7

___

NEW YORK CITY, 1961

It was a year of quiet panic. In April, the CIA-engineered invasion of Cuba was a tragic comedy. At an early summer meeting in Vienna, Premier Khrushchev gave President Kennedy six months to get American soldiers out of Berlin. Kennedy promptly went on United States television and rashly implied that nuclear conflict seemed imminent and that every family should consider methods of survival. Homeowners began to burrow underground and to arm their shelters against any neighbors who might also want to survive. Far above the troubled planet, the second Soviet cosmonaut, Maj. Gherman Titov, was making our space-hardware scientists eat crow with his cries of "I am Eagle!"

This was the summer of newsreels showing the building of the Berlin wall and frantic refugees being garroted by barbed wire or cut down by East German bullets. Even baseball declined to reassure Americans that a touch of sanity prevailed. The Yankees' Roger Maris and Mickey Mantle were both demolishing existing home-run records.

Russia began setting off multimegaton bombs in Siberia. Our newspaper headlines announced "poisoned clouds" drifting toward the West Coast, and television newscasts presented prophets of doom: Herman Kahn predicting that "40 to 50 million Americans will die on the first day of attack"; Ralph Lapp describing the devastation of Washington that would follow a nuclear bomb attack on the White House; and Linus Pauling computing the number of defective children that would be born because of strontium 90 from the Soviet fallout.

BEN GRAUER (WNBC-TV): What do you think is the key issue to be decided in this primary election? I'll start with Mayor Wagner.

MAYOR WAGNER: . . . whether we're going to have an independent government here for the next four years in the City of New York or whether we're going to have a boss-dominated government where the bosses have chosen the candidates on their ticket and I believe this is the opportunity for the Democratic voters to see that: (1) the party is returned to the rank and file in the party; that decisions are given to—are made after consultation with the people who are members of the party in free discussions in their various organizations and—eh—also that the members elected—the ticket elected rather—in this primary election which will go on to fight in the general election will be one that will be absolutely free to be able to move ahead for four years that are an important and crucial four years for the City of New York. . . .

In 1961, the sensitivities of New Yorkers were also being buffeted by an unusual political turbulence. It was one of those years when a prominent Democrat was rebelling against the "bosses" of the big city's regular Democratic organization (which is usually responsible for nurturing such rebels to their prominence). The rebel in 1961 was Robert F. Wagner, two-term mayor seeking a third term and a more glorious political future. The organization immediately put up New York State Controller Arthur Levitt to contest Wagner for the Democratic mayoral nomination.

BEN GRAUER: Controller Levitt—the key issue to be decided in this primary?

ARTHUR LEVITT: You ask a very simple question and you have just evoked a rather complex answer [from Mayor Wagner].

I can answer that in very simple terms. I think the key issue is a determination by the Democratic voters as to which of the two candidates is best fit—best qualified to fulfill the responsibilities of the Democratic candidate for the very important office of mayor.

Now I suggest that the—the experience of the incumbent mayor is a significant item to be considered but truly the last four years at least, his administration has been characterized by an ineptness, a lack of leadership, a fumbling, a bumbling attitude with the result that he has lost the confidence of the people.

Now I point particularly to his complete unwillingness to face what is the real issue in this campaign and that is his own record in office.

I point too to his recently announced disposition to resort to a series of outrageous and vicious falsehoods in support of a faltering campaign.

This dialogue, taken from the one face-to-face television appearance of Wagner and Levitt prior to the September 7 primary election, conveys the contrast in their television characterizations or television "images."

Mayor Wagner's dialogue was bland rather than sharp, rambling rather than concise, with a perceptible undertone of good will. He appeared to be a sincere man who, if not sharp enough to be revered, was not sharp enough to be feared. The mayor was able to sustain this affable façade in the face of charges that might have made another man's blood boil. For example, City Controller Lawrence Gerosa (himself an independent candidate for mayor) charged that the mayor's lavish household expenses and use of city employees in the Wagner summer home violated the City Charter. When the mayor was informed of this charge on a television newscast, he just smiled.

MAYOR WAGNER: Well, this is the kind of thing that happens in a—eh—a political campaign and—eh—they dig around and I suppose this is the best they can do. After all, a man in the position of the mayor to have all that power is pretty small potatoes, isn't it?

Arthur Levitt's blood, in contrast, appeared to be boiling all the time, as his dialogue, quoted on the preceding pages, suggests. To the mayor's face, Levitt slashed away: ". . . his administration has been characterized by an ineptness, a lack of leadership, a fumbling, a bumbling attitude. . . ." According to Levitt, the man sitting next to him was a liar who would resort to "a series of outrageous and vicious falsehoods in support of a faltering campaign."

And viewers could see (and feel for?) Mayor Wagner smiling and enduring.

What impression might such intense acrimony, in close-up, have given to viewers about Levitt's own character?

Throughout the campaign, Levitt seemed unaware of any difference in effect upon voters between a political rally, where wrathful indignation might be necessary to project across the open spaces between speaker and crowd, and the privacy of a viewer's living room, where vituperation can be so close as to be offensive. On those rare occasions when the mayor leveled an accusation against the state controller, Levitt had no safety valve on his temperament. The mayor's charge, he snarled into a newsfilm camera, "was a contemptible despicable attempt to get cheap publicity. It was an outrageous and cowardly slander. . . ."

Television also emphasized the unattractive quality of evasiveness in Levitt's image. The medium intimately revealed his inability to extricate himself gracefully when called to account for some of the flimsy charges he was making. (He was not the only candidate making flimsy charges.) For example, apparently nettled by the Transport Workers Union endorsement of Mayor Wagner, Levitt released a statement implying a "deal" between the mayor and TWU president Mike Quill.

TV REPORTER: In other words, you *suggest* that an arrangement has been made. Could you amplify that for us?

LEVITT: Well, the statement speaks for itself. It says very clearly that there are circumstances such as the Transport Workers' help for Mayor Wagner in this campaign in the form of securing signatures to his petitions—the promise—eh—perhaps the actuality of financial help—eh—suggests that—eh—there may be some understanding—eh

—that—eh—the mayor would be sympathetic—to—eh—a—eh—wage increase for the transport workers. Eh—I—eh—indicated—eh—these circumstances and—eh—called upon the mayor and—eh—Mr. Quill either to affirm or deny the conclusion.

TV REPORTER: Well, are you asking them to affirm or deny something about which you are not quite sure of?

LEVITT: I think I have already informed you adequately on the position I have taken.

Levitt did not seem to realize that campaign coverage on television might appear to viewers as a political drama, one consequence of which would be the magnification of "implied" charges into plot incidents of personal conflict between the drama's protagonists.

For example, when Levitt came across an anonymous leaflet— allegedly being distributed by Department of Sanitation workers —that urged voters to support Mayor Wagner to prevent the city from falling into the hands of a "Levitt" or a "Lefkowitz" (the Republican mayoral candidate), Levitt went on television newscasts with this sort of accusation.

LEVITT: We've received reports that the Wagner forces have now resorted to a tactic of injecting the religious issue. . . . I think this is a most—eh—deplorable outcome and—eh—eh—it's my conviction that it stems from a feeling of desperation on the part of the Wagner forces.

In no time at all, prominent Wagner supporters were abstracting an implication from this charge that Arthur Levitt was accusing the mayor of being anti-Semitic, thus blackening Levitt's character as the sort of despicable person who would try to blacken the mayor's character with such an untruth. And, true to form, on television Levitt proved unable to extricate himself gracefully from the mud that he had started slinging. On television, he appeared to be both evasive and imperious in refusing to discuss the charge.

LEVITT: . . . I was merely pointing out an outrageous situation that had been brought to my attention. And I was invoking the mayor's denunciation of this practice.

REPORTER: Have you any indication where these anonymous pamphlets originated?

LEVITT: All of this information is now in the hands of the attorney general. . . . I don't think we ought to pursue this any further at this time.

Mayor Wagner and Arthur Levitt might have been the stars of the political drama seen by television viewers prior to the September 7 primary, but they were by no means the entire cast. Aligned with the mayor were three attractive "characters" whose personal auras may well have enhanced the mayor's image: Mrs. Eleanor Roosevelt, widow of FDR; former senator and governor Herbert Lehman, who enjoyed the esteem of the city's sizable Jewish vote; and Mike Quill of the TWU, who made better use of an Irish brogue than Barry Fitzgerald.

Aligned against the mayor for reasons apart from the immediate primary contest were State Attorney General Louis Lefkowitz, the Republican candidate for mayor, and City Controller Lawrence Gerosa, who became an independent candidate for mayor after being dropped from Mayor Wagner's 1961 ticket.

Aligned with Arthur Levitt was the strongest character in the primary contest, Carmine G. De Sapio, chairman of the New York County Democratic Committee, but more commonly called —especially by Mayor Wagner—the "master boss" of Tammany Hall.

Beyond his reputation as a political manipulator, four singular personal attributes contributed to the usual strength or intensity of De Sapio's character and the viewer/voter emotions it may have generated.

1. *His name.* Good guys are not named "Sap" in the popular literature of the mass media that conditions Americans from an early age. By definition, a "sap" is either a stupid person or a blackjack used to knock people unconscious. In image terms, "De Sapio" seems as evocative a name for a sinister political boss as the name "Killer Kane" was for the interplanetary archenemy of Buck Rogers. Shakespeare, Goldsmith, Sheridan, and

Congreve—all purveyors of popular drama in their day—similarly used adjectives for names of characters.

2. *His dark eyeglasses.* Due to an inflammation of the cornea known as "tritis," Carmine De Sapio constantly wore eyeglasses with tinted lenses. For the big close-ups of television, this shadowing of his eyes seemed as striking a visual characterization as the hemiplegic limping of Dick Deadeye in *H.M.S. Pinafore* or the black hats worn by the "heavies" in Western movies.

3. *His overly ornate vocabulary.* According to columnist Murray Kempton, De Sapio used big words even when "Puerto Ricans in public housing projects were dropping garbage on the heads of his canvassers."[1]

CARMINE DE SAPIO (ON A TELEVISION NEWSCAST): Unfortunately, in a campaign of this magnitude and importance, it's always important for the opposition to seek out a scapegoat for the purpose of camouflage—diversionary tactics in order to obscure the real facts so that the public generally will be confused.

4. *His lisp.* De Sapio spoke his big words with just a whisp of a lisp, the sort of speech defect that some comedians affect when telling jokes about homosexuals.

The political significance of personal contrasts in this cast of characters seemed to be a fascinating premise for a case study of what New York City's television stations would do, if anything, in their campaign coverage to influence the vote by manipulation of images.

NOTES

1. Murray Kempton, "What It All Boils Down to Is: The Mayor Vs. Himself," *Life*, September 1, 1961, p. 31.

BIAS IN TELEVISION COVERAGE
OF THE PRIMARY CAMPAIGNS

In its youth, the vigor of the American press was directed largely toward political causes: the colonies versus the crown; the Federalists versus the Republicans; the Democrats versus the Whigs; the abolitionists versus King Cotton. Our founding fathers expected organs of the press to be partisan and to try to influence votes. They also expected political balance in the press to be an inevitable consequence of any dissenting group's constitutionally guaranteed right to publish a newspaper of their own.

Public expectation of nonpartisanship in the American press is a twentieth-century phenomenon traceable in part to conditioning by modern newspapers, which tend to subdue their partisanship in the interests of greater circulation and advertising revenues, but traceable much more so to the two greatly pervasive electronic media of modern journalism—radio and television—which are required by federally issued station licenses to be nonpartisan and balanced in matters of public controversy.

This requirement was formulated by Congress in 1927 and has been supported by the courts over the years because of the limited nature of the broadcast spectrum. Since only a few stations in each area could broadcast without interfering with each other's signals, the reasoning went, exclusive licensing of a station or stations to use the available channels would abridge the right of any other parties to use those channels and thus to "publish" dissenting views by means of radio or television. To compensate for this necessary exclusivity, Congress stipulated that each broadcast station must offer equal opportunities for the use of its facilities to all candidates for the same public office if use was granted to one candidate for that office. This statute, Section 18 in the Radio Act of 1927, which became Section 315 in the Communications Act of 1934, became known as the equal-time law. Stations were soon informed that the phrase "equal time" referred only to speaking appearances of the candidates themselves and not to anyone speaking on behalf of candidates. "Equal time" sounded like a meaningful standard to prevent the privileged licensees of broadcast stations from promoting their favored political candidates and causes. Perhaps this standard served its purpose with respect to radio when radio was the only pervasive broadcast medium. I do not know about that. My own curiosity focused on New York City's seven television stations during the 1961 mayoral campaigns. Were they practicing "image" techniques of persuasion, similar to the techniques I had begun to use in the 1960 national campaigns? Were they using other techniques to influence the vote? One thing I knew for sure: Section 315 had been amended in 1959 to *exclude* from the equal-time requirement certain bona-fide regularly scheduled news programs produced by the stations.

For seventeen days before the September 7 primary and for twenty-one days before the November 7 general election, I lined up seven television receivers and patched their audio circuits to seven tape recorders. From 7 A.M. to midnight (excluding the weekday hours of 9 A.M.–6 P.M., when only a very few, very brief newscasts were scheduled), I watched and recorded and timed with a stopwatch and typed out transcripts of anything related to the mayoral candidates or campaign issues. I was not concerned with "paid-political" programs or commercials in this study, only with mayoral campaign coverage that appeared on programs produced by the stations.

Mayoral campaign coverage appeared on two clearly different types of program: *newscast* and *news-feature*. News-feature formats mostly were scheduled once a week, mostly were 30 minutes or an hour in length, and mostly consisted of a mayoral candidate being questioned by an "impartial" panel.

Prior to the September 7 primary, Mayor Wagner and Arthur Levitt, the only two mayoral candidates competing for the Democratic nomination, received approximately equal time on news-feature programs. (Actually the mayor received an all-station total of 165 minutes to 135 for Levitt, who defaulted on one scheduled WCBS-TV appearance.) But this measure of equal exposure seemed unreliable as an indication of bias or balance if one looked a bit further and closer at some of the stations' news-feature programs.

Betty Furness, for example, on her weekday evening program, *At Your Beck and Call* (WNTA-TV, Channel 13), gave Wagner and Levitt equal time before the primary, but on other evenings she also invited two top municipal aides to come on her program who spoke well of the Wagner administration. Just two days before the primary, she invited the ebullient Mike Quill on her program from which he reiterated his ardent support of Mayor Wagner.[1] And she had no comparable supporters of Arthur Levitt on her program during this period.

This sort of superior exposure for the supporters of one candidate might be termed "conventional" bias in that it did not utilize the singular image-projecting qualities of television. In contrast, certain news-feature programs on WNBC-TV, Channel 4, suggested that someone may have been (a) aware of how candidates' televised images can influence voters, (b) aware of the sharp television image contrast between Wagner and Levitt, and (c) prone to help the cause of Mayor Wagner. On WNBC-

TV and only on WNBC-TV out of New York's seven television stations did Mayor Wagner and Arthur Levitt appear on the same news-feature program before the primary and thus facilitate viewer comparison of their images. This did not happen once, but twice. For an hour on Saturday evening, August 26, they sat side by side and answered similar questions. For the first half of a half-hour program on Sunday morning, September 3, Arthur Levitt answered questions posed by a panel. Then he left the studio and Mayor Wagner entered to answer similar questions. These two tandem appearances on the one station only may have been strictly coincidence, due to many other reasons than intent to promote image contrast between Wagner and Levitt. Yet the possibility of intent must be mentioned not so much because it finds support in the extensive findings about mayoral campaign coverage on the same station's newscasts, but because it does suggest that the promoting or avoiding of candidate image contrasts on television news-feature programs can serve as a manipulative technique working independently of equal-time measurements.

This is a touchy matter: being specific about campaign coverage that may have influenced voting for a favored candidate. It is touchy because my presumptions of effect are no more than educated guesses. The influence of any one medium of mass communication during an election campaign still defies scientifically precise measurement. But more than this, it is the inescapable implication of *intent* that will touch on the sensitivities of the cited newscasters and stations. The implication is inescapable because television, justifiably, prides itself on being a profession and professionals are commonly reputed to know exactly what they are doing in exercise of their specialty. The reader, if he so wishes, can judge intent, but neither the above nor the following citations should be construed as direct accusations of deliberate bias on the part of newscasters and stations named, since the main focus of this study remains the types of biased television material that can be broadcast under existing regulations, and not the newscasters and stations involved.

Because a station *can* load its news-feature programs with supporters of one candidate and because a station *can* promote or avoid tandem appearances of prominent candidates on its regularly-scheduled (315 exempt) news-feature programs, measurement of how much time each candidate was given on a station's news-feature programs hardly seems a reliable measure of the overall influence of that station's news-feature programs upon voting. With respect to *newscasts,* measurement of candidate exposure may not only be meaningless, but also misleading as to which candidate is being favored by the newscast coverage.

Table 1 reports how many speaking appearances and how much total air time in minutes and seconds each mayoral candidate received on the newscasts of New York City's television stations between August 21 and September 6, the day before the primary. The abbreviation "SOF" literally means "sound-on-film." It is used in television script writing to differentiate footage that carries its own dialogue from silent footage over which a newscaster's or narrator's voice will be heard.

The figures in Table 1 might suggest to someone applying the equal-time standard (if indeed the standard still applied to newscasts) that WCBS-TV was slightly favoring Mayor Wagner, that WNBC-TV was treating Wagner and Levitt about equally, that WNEW-TV's newscasts were impartial, that WABC-TV was favoring Levitt, and that WPIX was impartial.

But every one of these conclusions would be wrong according to further findings. Consider the 7:10 P.M. newscast of August 24 conducted by John Tillman on WPIX, Channel 11. Table 1 includes the measurement that Arthur Levitt got 2:05 SOF on this particular newscast to charge that there was a "deal" between Mayor Wagner and Mike Quill in return for the Transport Workers Union endorsement of Wagner. Table 1 also includes the measurement that Mayor Wagner received no SOF exposure on this newscast. What Table 1 does not show is what Tillman did with that Levitt SOF footage. What Tillman did was call Mike Quill on the telephone and make sure that Quill was watching a television set while the Levitt SOF was being shown.

TABLE 1
SOF FOOTAGE OF MAYORAL CANDIDATES ON TELEVISION NEWSCASTS

Station	Wagner NO.	MINS.	Levitt NO.	MINS.	Lefkowitz NO.	MINS.	Gerosa NO.	MINS.
WCBS-TV (Ch. 2)	10	8:05	8	6:50	4	3:15	6	7:30
WNBC-TV (Ch. 4)	25	18:50	26	17:10	11	6:00		none
WNEW-TV (Ch. 5)	(no SOF coverage of mayoral candidates)							
WABC-TV (Ch. 7)	2	1:50	4	2:15		none		none
WOR-TV (Ch. 9)	(no newscasts)							
WPIX (Ch. 11)	3	3:00	2	4:30		none	2	5:10
WNTA-TV (Ch. 13)	(no SOF coverage of mayoral candidates)							
All Stations	40	31:45	40	30:05	15	9:15	8	12:40

JOHN TILLMAN: Did you see and hear Mr. Levitt?

MIKE QUILL (ON PHONE, UNSEEN BY VIEWER, THICK IRISH BROGUE): Yes.

TILLMAN: And what's your answer to Mister . . .

QUILL: Well, Mr. Levitt takes a very good picture. He sounds very nervous and ill at ease. Now Mr. Levitt definitely said yesterday that there was collusion between the mayor and myself on the question of a higher fare. . . .

Mr. Levitt tried to smear our union as he tried to smear the entire labor movement yesterday, because 80% of the labor movement is supporting Mr. Wagner and not Mr. Levitt.

TILLMAN: Just one final question, Mr. Quill. Would you be willing to take an oath to the effect that there is no deal between you and Mayor Wagner?

QUILL: I certainly would take an oath now or at any time. I again issue the challenge to Mr. Levitt to *put up or shut up!*

TILLMAN: Thank you very much, Mr. Quill.

"Put up or shut up." Who got the last word in this scene from the continuing political drama? Who was characterized as a cowardly slanderer? Whom did the coverage favor—Arthur Levitt, who received 2:05 air time, or Mayor Wagner, who did not appear at all?

The only numerical measurement of bias or imbalance in television campaign coverage that seems fairly reliable—and there is always someone who wants to reduce everything to terms that a computer can play with—is the amount of *comprehensive coverage* afforded to each candidate on newscasts. Comprehensive coverage is simply the total air time [2] used for news items, SOF or reported by newscasters, that informs viewers about a candidate's opinions, activities, charges, rebuttals, and (or SOF of) supporters.

For example, Mayor Wagner's comprehensive coverage included all SOF or reported items of/about the mayor himself, former Governor Lehman, Mrs. Eleanor Roosevelt, Mike Quill, Ed Cavanaugh (the mayor's campaign manager), Louis Kaplan (City Investigation Commissioner), John J. De Lury (president, Uniformed Sanitation Men's Association), John Bailey (chairman, Democratic National Committee), and sidewalk passers-by who had something good to say about the mayor.

A similar small army of supporters contributed to the figures for Arthur Levitt's *comprehensive coverage* reported in Table 2.

By way of explanation, the "Official Activity" column in Table 2 reports news items about Mayor Wagner as mayor of New York rather than as a candidate for reelection, news that probably would have received similar coverage if the campaigns had not been in progress. The column labeled "Other Non-Wagner Coverage" reports news items of or about Lefkowitz, Gerosa, and certain other people mentioned as possible mayoral candidates. Prevalent in this "Other Non-Wagner Coverage" was critical opinion of the incumbent. Thus, the figure of 43:25 for WCBS-TV's "Other Non-Wagner Coverage" suggests a consistent emphasis in the station's campaign coverage on criticism of Mayor Wagner, an emphasis that further findings (see Chapter 11) confirmed and clarified.

The figures in Table 2 suggest that newscasts on WABC-TV

TABLE 2

COMPREHENSIVE COVERAGE OF/ABOUT MAYOR WAGNER
AND ARTHUR LEVITT ON TELEVISION NEWSCASTS

Station	Wagner Comprehensive Coverage	Levitt Comprehensive Coverage	Other Non-Wagner Coverage	Miscellaneous Coverage	Total Mayoral Primary News	Wagner Official Activity Coverage
WCBS-TV (Ch. 2)	29:40	34:30	43:25	22:05	129:40	8:05
WNBC-TV (Ch. 4)	42:20	31:55	20:20	14:15	108:50	3:40
WNEW-TV (Ch. 5)	1:45	none	none	0:45	2:30	1:10
WABC-TV (Ch. 7)	6:40	6:30	2:00	3:35	18:45	1:40
WOR-TV (Ch. 9)	(no newscasts)					
WPIX (Ch. 11)	17:50	14:20	17:00	7:05	56:15	2:50
WNTA-TV (Ch. 13)	0:55	1:05	0:45	1:00	3:45	0:35
All Stations	99:10	88:20	83:30	48:45	319:45	18:00

and WNTA-TV were balanced, and no evidence was found to the contrary. The figures indicate that newscasts on WCBS-TV, WNBC-TV, WNEW-TV, and WPIX were unbalanced to favor or derogate Mayor Wagner, and further evidence corroborated this imbalance. But, to the extent that candidate images are the essential ingredient in television's influence on voting, comprehensive coverage measurements give no suggestion of what techniques were being used to create the imbalance on the newscasts.

The combination of slight mayoral campaign coverage and complete imbalance in favor of Mayor Wagner on the newscasts of WNEW-TV seemed to be a simple and accidental consequence of the station's taking its news copy and visuals from a syndicate that relied on City Hall for its New York news source whether or not political campaigns were in progress. Thus, the first "news" WNEW-TV conveyed to its viewers about Lawrence Gerosa's charge against the mayor was the mayor's reaction to that charge.

WNEW-TV NEWSCASTER (VOICE OVER STILL PICTURE): Mayor Wagner answered Controller Gerosa's charge of City Charter violations.
The mayor said that the three employees whom the controller said should be working at Gracie Mansion and not at Wagner's home in Islip were transferred for the summer and Wagner employed them, not the city.
He also added: "I pay my own food bills at Gracie Mansion."
And in conclusion, he decided that the current political campaign was becoming a sordid one.[3]

WCBS-TV's imbalance, its newscasts emphasizing comprehensive coverage of Levitt and "Other Non-Wagner" coverage more so than other stations, was more in the television idiom than WNEW-TV's coverage but still did not emphasize "political drama" and image-conflict juxtaposition between the opponents. As a matter of fact, the editorial slant of WCBS-TV's newscasts was quite unclear during the preprimary period. A viewer might certainly get the impression that the station had no high regard for Mayor Wagner, but then again it seemed to have no regard for Arthur Levitt either. The "intros" to mayoral campaign items were larded with snide little gibes at what—for 8 million New Yorkers—was a pretty serious matter.

VARIOUS NEWSCASTERS, WCBS-TV: Politicians, like women, must be given the prerogative of changing their minds. . . .[4]
The witches' brew of New York politics continues to boil and bubble this morning. . . .[5]
Mayor Wagner was campaigning in the Bronx today. A delicatessen owner gave him a salami and a baker gave him a coconut layer cake.[6]

It was on the newscasts of station WPIX and, to a greater extent, on the newscasts of WNBC-TV that candidate images appeared in such a manner as to properly exploit television's unique abilities to influence voting. Campaign coverage was presented with a strong sense of political drama on these two stations. Personal characterization of—and personal conflict between—Mayor Wagner and Arthur Levitt was intensified by dramatic juxtapositions of them and their supporters. Campaign coverage on these two stations seemed more exciting to watch than coverage on other stations' newscasts.

Without attributing cause and effect, there was one significant production factor operating in the newscasts of WNBC-TV and WPIX that did not operate in production of other stations' newscasts. The on-the-air newscaster on WNBC-TV and WPIX was also the man with the microphone who had treked around during the day with a camera crew making the filmed interviews with people prominent in the news. WNBC-TV had Gabe Pressman, a human dynamo who apparently spent six days a week *running* between City Hall, the Tombs, Bellevue Hospital, and political rallies in the garment district. Gabe Pressman presented his own film on his own ten-minute newscasts Monday through Saturday. (On Sunday he may have rested, but the station carried his appearance as permanent panelist on a public-service interview program.) WPIX had its news director, John Tillman, who had fifteen minutes five nights a week for local news and a prestige sponsor to provide the budget for extensive location news-film sequences.

By accident or design, Gabe Pressman seemed to use the four image "techniques" described below and John Tillman seemed to use the first three to enhance the television image and candidacy of Mayor Wagner. Please note that although the description of the Pressman and Tillman newscasts is accurate, the terminology of image techniques such as *evaluation, rebuttal and topping, popularity coverage,* and *hero imagery* is more or less my own and not common jargon of television.

TECHNIQUE: EVALUATION

No mayoral candidate was openly endorsed by a New York television station in 1961. On occasion WNBC-TV's Gabe Pressman said things that seemed to reveal a personal preference for Mayor Wagner. For example, he introduced some Levitt SOF footage by figuratively dismissing it: "And of course the regular Democratic candidate, State Controller Arthur Levitt, also had something to say." [7]

But on Pressman and Tillman newscasts, opinions about the candidates by men in the street appeared in such a manner as to leave a stronger favorable evaluation of Mayor Wagner. Pro-Wagner opinions appeared last on a Tillman newscast, first and last on a Pressman newscast. Scholarly findings, let alone show business savvy, indicate that the first and last items in a sequence make the deepest impression and are remembered best. [8] Educators talk about the U-curve of recall.

Sequence of Sidewalk Opinions of a WPIX Newscast:
1. Lady prefers Levitt because he is a friend of Abe Stark [prominent Brooklyn Democrat] and Abe Stark is a neighbor of the lady.
2. Man has no preference between Wagner and Levitt. Thinks he might vote for Gerosa in November.
3. Man thinks Wagner has been doing a good job in office and should be kept in City Hall.

4. Girl believes Wagner was "really sincere in trying to get rid of the bosses." [9]

SEQUENCE OF SIDEWALK OPINIONS OF A WNBC-TV NEWSCAST:
1. Wagner supporter cites bossism.
2. Wagner supporter decries Levitt's anti-Semitism charge.
3. Dissident: both candidates are no good.
4. Levitt supporter: Levitt has a good record.
5. Levitt supporter: Levitt would be an active mayor.
6. Levitt supporter: Wagner's bossism issue is false.
7. Wagner supporter: will bet anyone $1,000 that Wagner will be reelected because "he's one of the finest guys in the world." [10]

TECHNIQUE: REBUTTAL AND TOPPING

Rebuttal, as a propaganda technique, calls for giving the favored candidate the last word or last news item in a sequence of campaign coverage items on the assumption that the last word or item leaves the strongest impression on viewers. Topping is a sophisticated form of rebuttal peculiar to show business and television newscasts, which represent the closest commingling of journalism and show business in the American press. In show business lingo, one act or appearance "tops" another when it is more theatrically intense and capable of generating a greater excitement in audiences.

Topping, as an image propaganda technique, may not require any literal rebutting of an item that has preceded it. For example, on his newscast of August 25, 1961, Gabe Pressman showed SOF footage of Levitt denouncing Wagner's campaign charge that linked Levitt with the windfall profits of the Lindenwood Housing Project in Queens. Viewers saw and heard Levitt call this charge a "vicious, contemptible lie."

The next item on this newscast was SOF footage of Pressman and Mayor Wagner riding on the Staten Island Ferry. A classic view of the New York skyline was in the background. Pressman did not mention the Lindenwood charge in asking the mayor about the progress of the campaign. The mayor did not mention it in his answer.

MAYOR WAGNER: Well, eh—I must say that as I look back at that sky-line, I—eh—wasn't thinking really of the campaign, Gabe—of what a great city we have and what a great ride this is on the Staten Island Ferry—still for a nickel.

And—eh—as I look back, too, and you bring up the subject of the campaign, I want to see that—that skyline as—eh—as representing a picture that many people have of New York that—that New York is going to be the kind of city that we are going to be proud of with no bosses trying to run this city.

The sound track did not pick up the romantic sounds of water

TABLE 3

REBUTTAL AND TOPPING OF OPPOSITION COVERAGE BY
WAGNER COVERAGE ON WNBC-TV NEWSCASTS

Pressman Newscast Date	First SOF in Sequence	Middle SOF in Sequence	Last SOF in Sequence	Compensating Factor If Wagner SOF Was Not Last in Sequence
8/25	Levitt	————	Wagner	
8/26	Levitt	Lehman	Wagner	
8/29	Wagner	Levitt	Lefkowitz	Followed by three items of reported news about Wagner
8/31	Levitt	Lefkowitz, Sharkey	Wagner	
9/4	Wagner	Levitt, Rockefeller	De Sapio	Wagner SOF while marching in Labor Day Parade could not be topped by remarks of others, as onlookers, in reviewing stand
9/5	Wagner	Lefkowitz	Levitt	Followed by Pressman "editorial" that all candidates are really better men than their campaign behavior would indicate
9/6	Lefkowitz	Levitt	Wagner	

lapping under the prow or a sea gull circling overhead and certainly there was no distant organ grinder playing "Sidewalks of New York," but the theatrical effect was there. This was pure image juxtaposition. Whether or not Levitt had been literally answered on his "outrageous-contemptible-vicious-lie" dialogue about the Lindenwood charge, he clearly had been *topped* by the mayor's ferryboat serenade.

On two of his newscasts during the preprimary period, Gabe Pressman showed SOF footage of Levitt, but no Wagner SOF. On both of these programs, Pressman followed the Levitt SOF with reported news items favoring Mayor Wagner. On two other newscasts, Pressman had SOF coverage of Wagner, but not of Levitt. On neither of these two programs did Pressman follow the Wagner SOF with reported items about Levitt. On seven other newscasts, Pressman had SOF items of Mayor Wagner and of Arthur Levitt. As shown in Table 3, the mayor's SOF item was placed last in sequence four times. Levitt's SOF was last only once. For each of the three instances when Wagner SOF items were not placed last in sequence, there was some factor of topping that helped Wagner to leave the strongest favorable impression.

TECHNIQUE: POPULARITY COVERAGE

Enhancing the favored candidate's characterization as the people's choice is known as popularity coverage.

GABE PRESSMAN (VO): The mayor is drawing crowds wherever he stops. . . . In Riverdale today, the usual sidewalk handshaking and then an unusual side trip. The mayor was invited to visit a beauty parlor and the ladies came out from under their dryers and clustered around him.

LADIES (CALLING OUT): Hello, Mayor!

MAYOR WAGNER (SOF): This is the first time I've ever been in a beauty parlor and I enjoy it.

PRESSMAN (VO): Outside, more handshakes—Mr. Lehman the object of many greetings. And then we stopped Mr. Lehman and the mayor to talk about the campaign.

PRESSMAN (SOF): Governor, what do you think of the results of this campaigning so far?

FORMER GOVERNOR LEHMAN: Well, I think they've been very very satisfactory. I've been with the mayor on a number of his campaign tours throughout the different boroughs of the city. Last night we were down over in Brooklyn and we had fabulous crowds, really touching.[14]

Popularity coverage of Mayor Wagner appeared mainly on Pressman's WNBC-TV newscasts and to a lesser extent on Tillman's WPIX programs. Tables 4 and 5 show the popularity coverage by the four stations that were using film coverage of local news.

TABLE 4

POPULARITY COVERAGE: SOF ITEMS SHOWING CANDIDATES SPEAKING TO AND BEING APPLAUDED BY A CROWD

Station	Mayor Wagner		Arthur Levitt	
	NO.	MINS.	NO.	MINS.
WCBS-TV (Ch. 2)	0	0	0	0
WNBC-TV (Ch. 4)	6	3:00	0	0
WABC-TV Ch. 7)	0	0	0	0
WPIX (Ch. 11)	2	2:00	0	0

All stations ignored coverage of Arthur Levitt with crowds except WNBC-TV, which gave him two items of this nature totaling just 0:25 (see Table 5).

TECHNIQUE: HERO IMAGERY

With one exception, Table 5 does not include any station's film of Mayor Wagner at the Labor Day Parade because such an item should rightfully be considered coverage of the mayor's "official activity" and not campaign coverage at all. The one exception was WNBC-TV, whose footage of Mayor Wagner at the parade was not only popularity coverage but also a first-class example of hero imagery.

PRESSMAN (VO): Mayor Wagner was Grand Marshall of the parade. (FILM SHOWS LABOR DAY PARADE ON FIFTH AVENUE WITH BANDS PLAYING AND CROWDS CHEERING. MAYOR WAGNER IS SEEN STRIDING ALONG, WAVING TO THRONGS OF WELL-WISHERS WHO LINE THE CURBS AND CALL OUT GREETINGS TO HIM AS HE PASSES.)

PRESSMAN: And at St. Patrick's Cathedral, the Mayor kissed the ring of Francis Cardinal Spellman. (FILM SHOWS MAYOR WAGNER KISSING THE CARDINAL'S RING WHILE STIRRING MUSIC IS HEARD IN THE BACKGROUND, MARTIAL MUSIC YET WITH A DEFINITE OVERTONE OF RELIGION, A MARCH VERSION OF "ADESTE FIDELES"—"O COME, ALL YE FAITHFUL.")

PRESSMAN: It sounded like Christmas on September 4th. . . . We caught up with some of the candidates and other interested parties in New York's mayoral campaign. Mayor Wagner was caught on the run. (FILM NOW SHOWS GABE PRESSMAN, HOLDING A MICROPHONE, WALKING IN THE PARADE ALONGSIDE MAYOR WAGNER. WE HEAR THE MAYOR'S VOICE ANSWERING THE FRIENDLY CALLS FROM THE SIDEWALK CROWDS.)

MAYOR WAGNER (SOF): . . . just about halfway—and—I think we're very thrilled at the outpouring. (CALLS OUT) Thank you! Hi, there! Hello!

PRESSMAN (SOF): I guess this is the biggest Labor Day Parade in the city's history.

MAYOR WAGNER: I guess so. Well, each one has been bigger than the next one and I'm sure this will top—probably top them all, Gabe.

PRESSMAN: Any political thoughts today?

MAYOR WAGNER: I don't think so. This is a Labor Day Parade.

PRESSMAN: You don't think you're marching ahead to victory?

MAYOR WAGNER: Well, I—if we have to talk about politics—yes.[12]

During the seventeen days before the primary election, Gabe Pressman managed to use two hero-image sequences commonly found in propaganda films: the grand entrance and the high place. The Labor Day Parade gave him the raw materials for grand entrance, which requires that the hero walk through crowds of cheering admirers while bands play a familiar stirring

TABLE 5

POPULARITY COVERAGE: NEWS ITEMS SHOWING CANDIDATES WITH,
BUT NOT SPEAKING TO, ADMIRING CROWDS

Station	Mayor Wagner			Arthur Levitt		
	NO.	MINS.	TYPICAL LEAD-IN COPY BY STATION NEWSCASTER	NO.	MINS.	TYPICAL ACCOMPANYING DESCRIPTIVE COPY BY STATION NEWSCASTER
WCBS-TV (Ch. 2)	1	0:10	Mayor Wagner was campaigning in the Bronx today. A delicatessen owner gave him a salami and a baker gave him a coconut layer cake.	0	0	——
WNBC-TV (Ch. 4)	7	4:05	In the largely Jewish section of Williamsburgh, Brooklyn, the mayor was cordially mobbed this afternoon. Perhaps in response to Levitt's bigotry charge, a tremendous crowd turned out.	2	0:25	Levitt made the accusation during handshaking tours of the Bronx and Brooklyn, where he made use of Yiddish in trying to win the votes of orthodox rabbis.
WABC-TV (Ch. 7)	1	0:10	ABC's Ed Silverman accompanied the mayor on a walking tour of the Lower East Side to get his answer to the charge.	0	0	——

| WPIX (Ch. 11) | 1 | 1:30 | TILLMAN (SOF): Mr. Mayor, quite a wonderful crowd here at Cropsey Avenue and Twentieth Avenue. I believe it is a wonderful reception. I wanted to ask you, as you head into the home stretch, how do you feel? | 0 | 0 |

air. Pressman's grand-entrance sequence was complete to the point of having the hero reveal his true humility by stopping en route to pay homage to the hallowed wise man, usually played by C. Aubrey Smith or Finlay Currie.

(In the spring of 1960, Spyros Skouras, then president of Twentieth Century Fox, showed Richard Nixon a collection of newsreels that had been made for presidential candidates Truman, Dewey, Eisenhower, and Stevenson by Fox-Movietone News. Skouras offered to make a similar campaign film for Nixon. In accepting the offer, Nixon singled out the 1948 Truman reel as his favorite and particularly noted one sequence in that reel where Truman had been shown marching along in a parade, acknowledging cheers of the crowd.)

The Staten Island Ferry (see pages 81–83) was the setting for Pressman's high-place sequence, which requires that the hero be shown in a location where he has a symbolic overview of the world so that his words convey the impression that he has a touch of the poet in his character.

Two other findings about television coverage of the mayoral primary campaigns gave additional insight into the singular nature of the medium's influence on voting.

First, I could not find any correlation between the emphasis on certain campaign issues and the presence (or absence) of bias in a station's newscasts. The "bossism" issue was the subject of just about the same amount (relatively) of coverage on the pro-Wagner newscasts of WNBC-TV, WNEW-TV and WPIX as it was on the anti-Wagner newscasts of WCBS-TV or the neutral newscasts of WABC-TV. This finding underscored the probability that treatment, not subject matter, is the important factor in persuasion by television.

Second, I found a remarkable difference between subjects of campaign coverage that were emphasized on news-feature programs and newscasts. For example, the following six subjects received 28 percent of the total mayoral campaign coverage on news-feature programs and only 5.1 percent of the total campaign coverage on television newscasts: (1) significance of the primary—if Wagner wins, will Levitt support him? (2) Wagner's "miserable" record—who else can be blamed for alleged failures of City Hall? (3) slum clearance and housing; (4) crime in the streets; (5) consolidation of city departments; and (6) city employees—do they need political pull for promotions? In contrast, as Table 6 shows, the ten most prominent subjects of mayoral campaign coverage on television newscasts, consuming 81.7 percent of total newscast time given to the campaigns, received only 46.2 percent of the time given to mayoral campaign coverage on news-feature programs. Note, in Table 6, the sharp newscast–news-feature prominence contrast between such subjects as the Gerosa charge about Wagner's household expenses, the Wagner-Sharkey (a Democratic organization leader) dispute, and the Wagner-Levitt-De Sapio dispute over "bossism."

This contrast in subject emphasis between newscasts and news-feature programs may be greatly magnified for television viewers by common scheduling practices of the stations. Local newscasts, with their emphasis on the action and conflict and drama of the campaign, may appear once or twice every day of the week in prime or near-prime time periods, "prime" in this sense referring to those hours (such as 7–11 P.M.) when the maximum number of viewers will be tuned in. Local news-feature programs, with their emphasis on exploration of the more substantial campaign issues, are usually scheduled, if at all, in the worst possible time periods, such as Saturday afternoon or Sunday morning, and usually just once a week. With the rare exception of prime-time preemption of entertainment programming for a face-to-face confrontation between two or three leading candidates, the appearance of local news-feature programs in prime time is usually a matter of noble gesture—that is, the entertainment programs in that time period on competing stations have proven so popular as to virtually monopolize the available audience and the station on the low end of the rating scale might as well put on a sustaining local news-feature program, which will look good to the FCC at license-renewal time. (Sta-

TABLE 6

COMPARISON OF CONTENT EMPHASIS:
NEWSCASTS AND NEWS-FEATURE PROGRAMS

Subject of Coverage (INCLUDING REBUTTALS AS WELL AS CHARGES)	Newscasts		News-Feature	
	PROMI-NENCE	PERCENT-AGE	PROMI-NENCE	PERCENT-AGE
SCHOOLS: Legislature fires NYC Board of Education. Blue-ribbon panel to select new nominees.	1	17.4	2	13.6
WAGNER'S HOUSEHOLD EXPENSES AND SERVANTS: was the City Charter violated (Gerosa charge)?	2	16.5	0	0.0
ANTI-SEMITIC CAMPAIGN LITERATURE: was it being distributed by Wagner campaign workers (Levitt charge)?	3	10.7	6	4.2
WAGNER-QUILL "DEAL": did the mayor agree to raise subway fares in exchange for TWU support (Levitt charge)?	4	6.8	14	2.6
LINDENWOOD "WINDFALL" PROFITS: were Levitt and Gerosa culpably involved (Wagner charge)?	5	6.5	9	3.5
GENERAL CAMPAIGN ACTIVITY: what candidates are doing to woo voters.	6	6.1	0	0.8
WAGNER-SHARKEY DISPUTE: variation on bossism issue (Wagner charge).	7	5.6	0	0.7
BOSSISM: applied to—and called a "phony" issue by—Levitt and De Sapio (Wagner charge).	8	5.5	1	19.9

Subject of Coverage (INCLUDING REBUTTALS AS WELL AS CHARGES)	Newscasts		News-Feature	
	PROMI-NENCE	PERCENT-AGE	PROMI-NENCE	PERCENT-AGE
DISCRIMINATION: did Wagner administration bar Negroes and Puerto Ricans from policy-level jobs (charge by Levitt and Adam Clayton Powell)?	9	3.5	0	0.7
PERSONAL FAVORS: did Wagner "freeload" on firms doing business with the city (De Sapio and Mackell charge)?	10	3.1	17	1.2
Totals		81.7		46.2

tions are obligated to put on local public-service programming as part of their federal license to use a certain wavelength of the public's broadcast spectrum.)

Thus, to the extent that most viewers most often may see the campaign presented as political drama, they may be encouraged to perceive the candidates as players in that drama and to substitute hero-villain appraisal of these candidate-players for thoughtful consideration of the political viewpoints embodied in the images.

NOTES

1. *At Your Beck and Call,* WNTA-TV, 8:30–10 P.M. Anna M. Kross, Commissioner of Correction, appeared on August 22, 1961; Hortense W. Gabel, director of Neighborhood Conservation, August 29; and Mike Quill, September 5.
2. Since newscast items are generally quite short, the measure of total air time accurately reflects the frequency of news items of/ about a candidate.
3. *Newsreel Five,* WNEW-TV, August 22, 1961, 11 P.M.; repeated on the station's 7:15 A.M. newscast of August 23.

4. Peter Thomas, *The Morning Report,* WCBS-TV, August 21, 1961, 7:10 A.M.; repeated.
5. Peter Thomas, *The Morning Report,* WCBS-TV, September 6, 1961, 7:10 A.M.
6. Harry Reasoner, *Seven O'Clock Report,* WCBS-TV, August 26, 1961, 7:05 P.M.
7. *Gabe Pressman and the News,* WNBC-TV, September 5, 1961, 6:30 P.M.
8. Carl I. Hovland and others, *The Order of Presentation in Persuasion* (New Haven: Yale University Press, 1957), p. 136.
9. *New York News,* WPIX, August 29, 1961, 7:10 P.M.
10. *Gabe Pressman and the News,* WNBC-TV, September 2, 1961, 7 P.M.
11. *Gabe Pressman and the News,* WNBC-TV, August 26, 1961, 7 P.M.
12. *Gabe Pressman and the News,* WNBC-TV, September 4, 1961, 6:30 P.M.

CHAPTER

9

NEWSPAPER COVERAGE OF THE
PRIMARY CAMPAIGNS

The 1961 mayoral campaign in New York City was a good
opportunity to broaden one's understanding of what may be
unique about television's influence on voting by comparing television and newspaper coverage of the same campaigns. Newspapers, in our history, have been the traditional medium for
conveying political opinion and information—including candidate
images—to voters. In 1961, New York City had seven daily papers
with city-wide circulation, down from a total of fifteen in 1900
and twelve as recently as 1930, but still significantly more than
the three remaining papers that were publishing in 1967.

Examination of 1961 mayoral campaign coverage in these
seven newspapers suggested two major differences between the
influence of the two media on the outcome of an election. First,
there is a matter of image differences: where candidates' television images seem largely to be appearance, demeanor, and
style of presentation, their newspaper images are conveyed by

(often biased) descriptions of candidate reputation, candidate position on issues, and the sociopolitical importance of those issues. Second, there is the matter of whom the images reach: whereas Republicans, Democrats, and politically unsophisticated voters alike may be exposed to candidates unexpectedly on newscasts or unavoidably on face-to-face confrontations, newspapers' (often biased) images of candidates tend to reach self-segregated communities of readers who are generally in agreement with the partisan views of the paper to which they subscribe and hence are less prone to vote for the opposition candidate because of anything about the opposition that appears in the paper to which they subscribe.

Before the September 7 primary, four papers took editorial positions on the mayoral candidates. The *Times* endorsed Mayor Wagner over Arthur Levitt because Wagner had "declared his independence of disreputable Tammany Hall and of party bosses De Sapio, Buckley and Sharkey." The *Times* noted that this endorsement was for the primary only because it found the Wagner administration to be "full of glaring disappointments [and] an accumulation of defects and scandals." (The *Times* subsequently endorsed Republican candidate Lefkowitz before the general election in November.) The *New York Post*, habitually favoring Liberal and Democratic candidates, was intensely pro-Wagner. The New York *Herald Tribune* and the *World-Telegram & Sun* published numerous anti-Wagner editorials, but although the overall thrust of their primary coverage favored Levitt over Wagner, they did not go so far as to praise Levitt in editorials. The *Herald Tribune* (habitually Republican) and the *World-Telegram & Sun,* both staunchly endorsing Louis Lefkowitz before the general election, wanted Levitt to beat Wagner in the primary in order to split the huge Democratic vote in November.[1] This would happen because whether or not Wagner won the primary, his name would be on the November ballot as the Liberal party's candidate for mayor.

In addition to presenting opinion identified as opinion in editorials and by-line columns, most of the seven papers tended to emphasize favorable news about favored candidates. The more highly partisan papers tended to emphasize negative news about the opposition as well. Some techniques by which this selective emphasis was accomplished are listed below.

TECHNIQUE: PROMINENT PLACEMENT

Many more people read the front page and the first page of the second section of a newspaper than read an average interior page.

Example 1. "CANDIDATE LEFKOWITZ VOWS 15¢ FARE AND MODERN CARS" was a front-page headline in the pro-Lefkowitz *Herald Tribune* of August 27. The only comparable item in any of the other papers on August 26–27–28 appeared on page 3 of the neutral (at this date) *Journal-American*: "LEFKOWITZ AGAINST INCREASE IN SUBWAY FARE."

Example 2. The intensely pro-Wagner *New York Post* published two editorials on its front page: "BEAT THE BOSSES" (August 23) and "IT CAN BE DONE" (September 1). No other newspaper put political editorials on its front page.

TECHNIQUE: SLANTED OR "LOADED" HEADLINES

Adjectives are used to help readers perceive a certain version of the news.

Example 1. The *Herald Tribune* would have its readers believe that the Republican mayoral candidate was "warmly" received by the public: "LEFKOWITZ WARMLY HAILED IN TOUR OF GARMENT CENTER" (August 29, page 1). *The New York Times* told its readers the facts: "LEFKOWITZ TOURS GARMENT DISTRICT" (August 29, page 22).

Example 2. In the *Herald Tribune*, the simple fact that summer vacation was over for the city's schoolchildren became a front-page reminder for the paper's readers that the city's schools were inadequate and that Mayor Wagner was to blame for the inadequacies: "1,000,395 KIDS UP AGAINST IT." On the same day, September 5, the same news appeared on page 5 of the neutral *Daily News* as simply "MILLION KIDS TO HEAR SCHOOL BELL" and on page 5 of the neutral *Mirror* as "MILLION BACK TO SCHOOL."

TECHNIQUE: EXCLUSIVE NEWS

The more partisan papers found items of campaign news—sometimes praising the favored candidate but more usually aimed at discrediting the opposition—that other papers did not feature as prominently or did not publish at all.

Examples. The intensely pro-Wagner, anti-Levitt *Post* published the following exclusive news prior to the primary election: "PROBE LEVITT'S ROLE IN 2ND QUEENS CO-OP" (August 27, page 5); "LEVITT 'UPSET'—SKIPS TV SHOW" (August 27, page 8); and "LEVITT SENT LOAN SEEKERS TO SHARKEY KIN'S FIRM" (September 1, page 4).

TECHNIQUES: SUBDUED CHARGES, SUBDUED REBUTTALS

Campaign charges by the opposition candidate against the favored candidate receive subdued, if any, coverage. Rebuttal by the opposition to charges made by the favored candidate receives subdued coverage.

Example 1. The pro-Wagner *New York Post* carried this story head: "WAGNER DENIES DEAL WITH QUILL TO RAISE FARES AFTER ELECTION (August 24, page 5). This item of rebuttal by the *Post*'s favored candidate was not preceded by coverage of Levitt's charge lest such a charge, standing by itself, cause any doubts about Mayor Wagner in the minds of *Post* readers.

Example 2. "LEHMAN CALLS LEVITT CHARGE 'FOUL BLOW'" was the *Post*'s first coverage of the Levitt charge that Wagner supporters were allegedly distributing anti-Semitic leaflets (September 1, page 4).

A major difference between selective emphasis in newspaper

and television coverage of a campaign is revealed by the relative amount of space concerned with specific issues in the newspapers. In the television coverage, I had found no significant variation in the amount of time given to campaign issues among the stations, that is, no variation such as more time given to pro-Wagner issues (such as "bossism") on the pro-Wagner stations, WNBC-TV, WPIX, and WNEW-TV.

With respect to the seven newspapers, there was an obvious variation, as it is reported in Table 7 in terms of the relative amount of space given to four key issues. At the top of the table, the seven newspapers are named, left to right, in order of decreasing partisan intensity, with the most intensely partisan *New York Post* on the left and the neutral (before the primary) *Journal-American, Mirror,* and *Daily News* on the right. The figures in Table 7 are the percentages of each newspaper's total mayoral campaign coverage that were primarily concerned with a certain issue. For example, the figure of 15 under the *New York Post* for the "bossism" issue indicates that out of all the column-inches used by the *Post* to publish coverage of the mayoral compaigns between August 21 and September 6, 15 percent of that total space was mainly about the "bossism" issue that Mayor Wagner was using to convince Democratic voters to rebel against Carmine De Sapio's puppet candidate, Arthur Levitt.

Not every figure in Table 7 is significant, but most of them are and—to single them out—the significant figures are marked with an asterisk (°). These are the figures which, in the partisan papers, differed predictably and exceptionally from the emphasis that more neutral papers placed on the same campaign issue.

In combination, selective emphasis on certain issues, prominent placement, exclusive news, slanted headlines, and subdued charges or rebuttals added up to a biased description of candidate deeds and reputation. For example, durnig the week beginning August 21, headlines on front pages of the *World-Telegram & Sun* added up to an unrelieved indictment of Mayor Wagner.

TABLE 7

SELECTIVE EMPHASIS ON CERTAIN CAMPAIGN ISSUES EXPRESSED IN PERCENTAGES OF EACH NEWSPAPER'S MAYORAL CAMPAIGN COVERAGE

Campaign Issue	Post	World-Telegram	Herald Tribune	Times	Journal-American	Mirror	Daily News
WAGNER'S HOUSEHOLD EXPENSES (Gerosa's anti-Wagner charge)	0.8*	13.6*	6.3	3.4*	6.6	5.4	8.0

*The pro-Wagner *Post* and *Times* gave less space to this anti-Wagner issue than did the three neutral newspapers listed on the right. The intensely anti-Wagner *World-Telegram* gave this issue much more emphasis than did the three neutral papers.

LINDENWOOD "WINDFALL" PROFITS (Wagner's anti-Levitt charge)	10.4*	3.2*	3.1*	4.8	4.5	6.2	7.4

*The pro-Wagner, hence anti-Levitt, *Post* gave this issue considerably more emphasis than did the neutral newspapers. The anti-Wagner *World-Telegram* and *Herald Tribune* subdued coverage of an issue that might do Mayor Wagner any good.

BOSSISM (Wagner's main charge against Levitt)	15.0*	0.0*	1.8*	9.9*	3.0	3.2	2.9

*The neutral newspapers gave an average of 3 percent of their mayoral campaign coverage to this issue. The *Post*, intensely pro-Wagner, gave 15 percent of its mayoral campaign coverage to the bossism issue, or *five times* the emphasis placed upon it by the neutral papers. The moderately pro-Wagner *Times* gave better than three times the neutral newspaper average, and the intensely anti-Wagner *World-Telegram* and *Herald Tribune* played down or omitted coverage of this issue, which—by hurting Levitt's chances to win in the primary—would eventually hurt Louis Lefkowitz's chances to win in November. (See explanation of this strategy on page 94.)

ANTI-SEMITIC CAMPAIGN LITERA-   3.2*   1.6*   3.5*   3.0*   4.2   4.8   5.2
TURE (Levitt's charge)

*This issue was clearly a hot potato to the more partisan newspapers. They did not know what to make of it or which candidate would be hurt the most by it so they played it safe and subdued coverage of it. The three neutral newspapers gave the issue an average of 4.7 percent of their mayoral campaign coverage; the four partisan papers only gave it an average of 2.8 percent, considerably less.

August 21: "MAHONEY WOULD REMOVE WAGNER IN SCHOOL
SCANDAL"

August 22: "WAGNER ACCUSED OF USING CITY LABOR AT HIS
LONG ISLAND HOME"

August 23: "RELIES ON BAR GROUP, SAYS MAYOR, BUT HE'S
REMINDED HE IGNORED IT IN NAMING O'DWYER KIN" AND
"GEROSA'S OFFICE BARES WAGNER CHARGE DATA"

August 24: "WAGNER SAYS AILING HOUSEKEEPER IS NOT
ELIGIBLE FOR CITY SICK PAY"

August 25: "LEVITT LABELS WAGNER 'UNFIT,' WITHDRAWS
PLEDGE OF UNITY"

August 26: "LEVITT URGES UNION TO 'BURY' THE MAYOR"

Strangely enough, photographs or cartoons of the mayoral
candidates were not consistently used as an extension of selective
emphasis. There were a few obvious examples of partisan selection at work in pictures chosen for publication: the biggest photograph of any mayoral candidate was of Louis Lefkowitz in
the Republican *Herald Tribune*; the most unflattering shot of
Mayor Wagner—stuffing a sloppy wedge of pizza in his mouth—
was predictably published by the *World-Telegram & Sun*.
But since anti-Wagner papers were found to publish occasional
flattering pictures of the mayor and pro-Wagner papers printed
some flattering pictures of Levitt and Lefkowitz, it seems reasonable to conclude that newspapers do not include distortion of
candidate appearance in their current catalog of propaganda
techniques.

In summary, then, newspaper coverage—including consider-
able (if biased) appraisal of candidate positions on public
problems—seems to characterize candidates by a description of
deeds and reputation in contrast to television coverage, which
seems to characterize candidates mainly in terms of appearance
and demeanor. Further, candidate images conveyed by newspapers must be termed more derivative, or secondary, than television images because the newspaper images must be derived

in the mind's eye of the reader from consideration of the published description, whereas the television image is perceived directly.

Generally, in terms of influence on voting, the television image appears to dominate the newspaper image of a given candidate, the television image working on the viewer-voter much in the manner of the old axiom that holds "What the eye rejects, the mind dismisses." However, there are exceptional cases in which newspapers can so convince readers' minds that their eyes will dismiss an attractive appearance and demeanor in much the same manner that we do not find a rosy red apple attractive when we know for sure that its insides are ridden with worms. But these exceptional cases tend to involve fairly universal condemnation of a candidate by all newspapers.

SELF-SEGREGATED COMMUNITIES OF READERS

While techniques of newspaper bias may be fascinating to contemplate, they probably have very little influence upon the outcome of campaigns for our highest public offices. In fact, there are reasons to suspect that the *most biased* campaign coverage has the *least influence* upon voting. Those reasons relate to the finding that newspapers—differing from television stations —tend to have *singular journalistic identities,* which attract differing groups of habitual readers who like the style and editorial views of one paper more than another. (Television journalism, in contrast, was found to differ in the quantity of news programs and personalities of the newscasters.) Some variables in this identity are format, tabloid or full size; number of pictures; emphasis on sensationalism, such as violent crime, gory accidents, marital scandal, gossip about celebrities, human oddities, and female cheesecake; selection of columnists; completeness of coverage; news background features, such as pertinent biographies of public figures; financial news; advertising; emphasis on sports coverage, such as horse-race information; use of proper

English or slang in headlines; entertainment features, such as comic strips, contests, and serialized fiction; and editorial attitudes—moral, social, and political.

Each of New York City's seven leading daily newspapers in 1961 had a singular journalistic identity. Thumbnail sketches of these seven identities are listed below, along with the mid-1961 circulation figures for each paper. In reading these sketches, one is impressed by the very definite correlation between circulation and degree of political intensity.

Daily News (1,980,000)

Morning tabloid. New York's picture newspaper. The news in the *News* was about people: about public leaders and their families, about celebrities and others caught in provocative situations, and about pretty girls. Mayor Wagner was "Bob" in *News* story heads. Governor Rockefeller was "Rocky." Coverage of the mayoral primary campaigns often read like a serial entitled "The Adventures of Mayor Bob": "SCHOOL BOARD FIRED—BOB GETS PICK"; "LEVITT SAYS BOB 'N' MIKE PLOT BUS 'N' SUBWAY HIKE"; "BITTER LEVITT DENIES BOB'S WINDFALL RAP;" and—to be continued.

Of the seven newspapers, the *Daily News* gave most space to biographies of the mayoral candidates, heavily illustrated, of course, and showing the candidates with pretty girls when possible. Arthur Levitt actually smiled in his *News* photo. If readers were not also television viewers, the *News* biography might have left an impression that Arthur Levitt, was a fairly pleasant fellow.

The *Daily News* was the only one of the seven papers studied that did not endorse any candidate for mayor either before the primary or before the general election, on November 7.

New York Mirror (841,000)

Morning tabloid, started in 1923 by William Randolph Hearst to challenge the success of the *Daily News,* by 1961 had matured into a garish caricature of the *News,* emphasizing sensational sex and crime coverage and the sporting life, particularly horse racing and boxing news.

During the week beginning August 21, 1961, the *Mirror's* front pages were concerned with: "TEENER TELLS HOW HE KILLED TWO LITTLE BOYS"; "ALTAR BOY SLAIN IN NEW JERSEY ROBBERY"; "OWN MOB PUTS GALLO ON THE SPOT—POLICE ARREST TRIGGERMAN"; "SUES TO REGAIN 'CAPTIVE BRIDE'"; and "SEIZE SLAYER OF LONG ISLAND DOCTOR." None of these stories appeared on the front pages of *The New York Times* and probably were not missed by habitual *Times* readers.

Mayoral campaign coverage in the *Mirror* appeared in sporting lingo: "THE CANDIDATES: ROUND BY ROUND"; "THE CAMPAIGN: BLOW BY BLOW"; "THE CANDIDATES ARE IN THE STRETCH." The *Mirror* remained neutral in the primary contest and endorsed Wagner over Lefkowitz before the general election, mentioning that endorsement only in two editorials. No other techniques of bias could be found in an examination of the *Mirror's* campaign coverage.

The New York Times (745,000)

The newspaper of record: all the news fit to print; more background information than other papers; original texts of important statements such as candidate platforms; editorial endorsement of Wagner over Levitt in the primary and Lefkowitz over Wagner before the general election. The *Times* editorial page, however, published long letters that disputed and deprecated the paper's editorial position on mayoral candidates.

Journal-American (639,000)

Afternoon, full size, the big city's self-ordained hell-fire-and-brimstone evangelist. Readers could find a daily text from the Bible on the editorial page and inspiring quotations from "great" Americans. The selection of columnists, including Barry Goldwater and George Skolsky, reduced world affairs to the sort of simplistic statements that appealed to fundamentalists. Westbrook Pegler smeared red-white-and-blue patriotism with a trowel: "I have come to realize that William Randolph Hearst was one of the greatest patriots in our history." Columnist William S. White used typical ultraconservative jargon in describing Mayor Wagner's prominent supporters as the "rule-or-ruin ultra-liberal reform element." Bishop Sheen's columns considered such fundamental topics as "True Prayer Seeks God."

In the *Journal-American*, sensationalized crime coverage was presented as a fervent crusade for law and order. "HE GAVE HIS LIFE," an editorial eulogy to a young policeman who had been shot down by a hardened criminal out on parole, and a large photo of the dying policeman on his knees in the gutter where he had fallen mortally wounded, the blood streaming down his face, was pure righteousness. But it was also compelling argument for a change in public attitudes about law enforcement, the sort of argument rarely found in television journalism.

The *Journal-American* did not endorse any mayoral candidate before the primary election. It endorsed Wagner over Lefkowitz before the general election, but was fairly mild in this editorial position and by its continued emphasis on crime in the streets actually contradicted its own editorial position in the sense that Republican mayoral candidate Lefkowitz was using the crime issue as his main example of Wagner failure.

World-Telegram & Sun (478,000)

Afternoon, full-size newspaper, the *World-Telegram* was trying to pull a "fast one" before the primary election, deprecating Mayor Wagner in editorials and front-page biased coverage without revealing its pro-Lefkowitz (Republican) position.

The honorable crest of the Scripps-Howard newspaper chain appeared on the *World-Telegram* editorial page: a lighthouse with the motto "Give Light and the People Will Find the Way."

Before the mayoral primary election, that light was being secretly manipulated in a not-so-honorable fashion to help Democratic voters choose Levitt over Wagner and thus sail onto some political shoals (see page 94) at the November election.

Herald Tribune (368,000)

Morning, full-size newspaper. In its coverage of the 1961

mayoral campaigns, a perceptive reader could detect inherited journalistic traits of liberal Republicanism that had come down from Horace Greeley (New York *Tribune*) and news-making sensationalism of the James Gordon Bennetts, Senior and Junior, (New York *Herald*).

The *Herald Tribune*'s front pages were splashed with attacks on Democrats in general and Mayor Wagner in particular, headline features spanning the whole eight columns and set above the masthead itself: "GEROSA'S TARGETS—MAYOR'S SUMMER HELP, A NICE CONTRACT FOR IN-LAW"; and "THE MAYOR UNFIT, ANGRY LEVITT SAYS."

On the front page of the *Herald Tribune*, coverage of a joint Wagner-Levitt television appearance appeared under the "loaded" headline: "REGULAR CANDIDATE FACE TO FACE WITH WAGNER IN TV FLOP." A large photo of Mayor Wagner, Arthur Levitt, and other dignitaries standing solemnly with their hands on their hearts as a flag passes by in the Labor Day Parade became the illustration for a front-page headline: "GRIMLY AWAITING THE VERDICT—CITY'S DIRTY PRIMARY IS NEARLY WASHED UP."

It hardly seems likely that regular readers of the *Herald Tribune* could be unaware of their paper's ritualistic stoning of Democrats prior to an election. Rather, it seems likely that the *Tribune*'s habitual readers relished what they read and preferred its bias to the bias (or lack of it) in New York's other newspapers.

New York Post (309,000)

Afternoon tabloid. The *Post*, in 1961, seemed to be a minority-group paper but oriented to a minority group so large in New York as to give the paper a city-wide circulation not too much below that of its more general-appeal competitors. The *Post*'s advertising, selection of columnists, lack of sensational crime and sex coverage (it had less crime coverage than the other six papers in this study), and other editorial features strongly suggested that the paper was largely intended to be attractive to New York's middle- and lower-class Jewish-American families.

Editorial endorsement of Mayor Wagner in the primary and later over Louis Lefkowitz in the November election was inevitable once the mayor became the clear choice of two public figures revered by *Post* readership: former Governor Lehman and Mrs. Roosevelt, whose column appeared regularly in the *Post*.

The *Post's* coverage of the 1961 mayoral campaigns was more blatant and intensely biased than that in the other six newspapers. In fourteen issues published between August 21 and September 6, the *Post* included thirteen editorials pro-Wagner or anti opposition. In eighteen issues between October 18 and November 6, 1961, it published fourteen editorials in a similar vein, many more than any of the other papers published in the same period. In column-inches given to mayoral campaign coverage, the *Post* placed selective emphasis on pro-Wagner/anti-opposition news consistent with its editorial position.

The correlation between partisan intensity and circulation figures of these seven newspapers came out to be near-perfect mathematically in this study: the more biased the coverage, the fewer readers it reached. Moreover, it reached those readers who, by and large, tended to be in agreement with the newspaper's partisan position in advance of the campaign and thus who probably would have voted for the candidate endorsed by their newspaper regardless of the biased coverage. Since the early "classic" studies of American voting behavior in the 1940s, political scientists have known that "Voters somehow contrive to select out of the passing stream of [communications] stimuli those by which they are more inclined to be persuaded. So it is the more they read and listen, the more they become convinced of the rightness of their own position."[2]

In context of understanding more about television's influence on voting, there may be several points worth remembering about this (inverse) correlation between partisan intensity and circulation in newspapers.

1. It underscores the supposition (Chapter 1) that habitual public identification with or loyalty toward a particular political

party is weakening. In 1961, the vast majority of New York newspaper readers were subscribing to the neutral or near-neutral newspapers, apparently having no strong political viewpoints that needed to be reconfirmed by what they read in the papers.

2. The partisan intensity/circulation correlation will stand as a warning to television stations not to become blatantly political, lest ratings drop.

3. Newspapers, in order to increase circulation (in order to raise advertising base rates in order to survive increasing production costs), will modify their partisan intensity and thus present candidate images in more nonoffending shades of gray rather than as traditional black-and-white literary-fiction characterizations. Thus, newspaper readers may increasingly get, from their papers, no clear image of political candidates. Therefore, their minds may be, more than ever, receptive to the appearance-demeanor-presentation candidate images seen on television.

With respect to the third point, we should note that by the middle of 1967, less than six years after this study was performed, the *Herald Tribune, World-Telegram & Sun, Journal American,* and *Mirror* had gone out of business. *The New York Times,* the *Daily News,* and the *New York Post* survived. But, interestingly, the *Post* may be beginning to transform itself into a general-appeal paper. It now carries the column of William F. Buckley, Jr., an eloquent conservative.

In summary, then, the influence of candidate images conveyed by newspapers is probably less than television images of the same candidates because (1) readers *derive* candidate character from descriptions of deed and reputation whereas viewers judge character from directly perceived appearance and demeanor; (2) the most intense descriptions of candidate character reach the fewest reader/voters; and (3) the surviving mass-circulation newspapers tend to be bland about candidate character, describing candidates in terms of nonoffending shades of gray rather than the black-and-white literary-fiction characterizations of yesterday's newspapers.

Newspapers probably influence the outcome of an election more than television when (1) there is little personal contrast between the television images of the major candidates and (2) there is a contrast in their reputations or positions on important issues.

One further note: biased or balanced, New York's newspapers were providing a wealth of opinion about and background information for the 1961 mayoral campaigns. Even the garish sports-crime sensation-oriented *New York Mirror* managed to publish a three-part series tracing the fluctuations of Tammany Hall's power and establish a political perspective not only for Mayor Wagner's rebellion against the Democratic "bosses," but also for the anti-Tammany role that Mrs. Eleanor Roosevelt was playing in 1961. Murray Kempton, the only dissident in the *Post*'s pages who seemed to prefer anybody to Robert Wagner, wrote such columns as: "WAGNER IN THE BRONX," a sensitive essay about a professional politician at work in the streets; "POLITICAL LUNCH," describing the relationship between city-wide candidates, who could deliver lofty statements at local meetings, and a typical district leader, whose year-round job was to persuade voters to support the organization's candidates; and "DE SAPIO H.Q.," which was the only bit of coverage trying to portray the beleagured "boss" as other than a melodramatic villain.

This sort of political perspective and appraisal was conspicuously absent from television coverage, which tended to present a here-and-now personal conflict between here-and-now characters rather than a current confrontation between conflicting political forces.

To the extent that the demise of newspapers in the age of television leaves the electorate relatively less exposed to political perspective and appraisal, the act of voting may less represent the intelligent exercise of consensus on matters of public controversy.

NOTES

1. In 1961, Democratic voter registration in New York City was 2,202,162, almost triple the number of registered Republicans, 767,526. The Liberal party had a registration of 67,541 that year. There were no other "regular" political parties—"regular" by virtue of having polled a certain number of votes in the preceding gubernatorial election. Other mayoral candidates could be nominated by petition.

2. Paul F. Lazarsfeld, Bernard Berelson, and Hazel Gaudet, *The People's Choice* (New York: Duell, Sloan, and Pearce, 1944), p. 82.

10

AFTER THE PRIMARY

On August 7, 1961, petitions were filed with the New York City Board of Elections on behalf of mayoral candidates whose names were to appear on the September 7 primary ballot. Arthur Levitt's petition had 283,304 signatures, a number so far in excess of the legal requirement (5,000) and so far in excess of the 64,831 signatures on Mayor Wagner's petition as to suggest that the Democratic organization was trying to demoralize Wagner's campaign workers and let the mayor know that he could not possibly reach enough registered Democrats before September 7 in order to bring out the less-active less-organization-oriented party members.

(It is a well-known fact of political life that the more active, more organization-oriented members of a party tend to vote in primary elections. The less-active party members stay home on primary day, but come out for the November elections.)

Furthermore, thousands of New Yorkers were vacationing,

escaping the frightful August ovenlike heat of the city by fleeing to beaches or parks or out-of-town resorts. How could the mayor reach a significant number of a party registration that totaled 2,202,162 in 1961? Assuredly not by the conventional methods of street campaigning. And he could command no army of campaign workers as could the organization.

Secure in their organizational strength, De Sapio and Democratic leaders in the city's four other boroughs played it cool, "following a strategy of maintaining a low gear campaign to permit a 'controlled vote.'" The organization leaders counted on each of the 5,000 Democratic district captains to bring out an average of 80 "safe" votes for Arthur Levitt.[1]

Largely because of television—which could project the images of the candidates into every home as well as outlying resorts within fifty or sixty miles of the city—their strategy came apart at the seams.

TV Guide or some similar television program might well have sketched the following synopsis of the primary plot:

MAYOR BOB, sincere, bumbling but affable incumbent, steadfastly strives to save City Hall from LEVITT, acid-tongued henchman of DE SAPIO, powerful political boss. MAYOR BOB's crusade is further endangered by harassing actions of LITTLE LOUIE LEFKOWITZ, agent of THE GOVERNOR and his Albany gang.

American television viewers have seen these characters, under various guises, play their parts to a predictable end in countless dramatic programs. It was hardly likely that viewers would use their votes in any way but to bring political reality in congruence with television fantasy. Some 742,000 Democrats came out on primary day: 451,000 voted for Mayor Bob; 291,000 for De Sapio's creature, Levitt. Newspapers called it a landslide.

The *Herald Tribune* of September 9 provided an interesting footnote about the image of the vanquished Levitt.

ANGRY LEVITT ALMOST QUIT RACE
HERE'S REASON WHY

. . . Chief source of the Levitt anger . . . was what he considered the mismanagement of his campaign by some strategists at his Hotel Biltmore offices.

"I'm going to walk out," Mr. Levitt said to his friends. "Those b——s at the Biltmore are putting words into my mouth that I do not want to say."

A similar report about Levitt had appeared in the *Daily News* of September 3: "This quiet usually soft-spoken man is reported writhing inwardly over the harsh words his organization-assigned speech writers have placed in his mouth."

Before television, newspaper readers might have no reason to doubt that Arthur Levitt was indeed a soft-spoken man who had unwillingly been turned into a tiger by back-room strategists. But television viewers had many opportunities to see Levitt in action and to hear the cutting rasp of his voice. Viewers could see for themselves that no one was making Levitt call Mayor Wagner "contemptible, cowardly, vicious, fumbling, and bumbling" on the air.

NAMES ON THE NOVEMBER BALLOT

Louis J. Lefkowitz (Republican, Civic Action, and Nonpartisan parties)

Republican image makers of the old literary-fiction school soon revealed their strategy. Page 1, Section 2, of the *Herald Tribune* displayed an illustrated piece of candidate description in its issue of September 11.

"LOUIE" LEFKOWITZ TAKES A SENTIMENTAL JOURNEY
. . . yesterday to the lower East Side, scene of his birth and his early election triumphs, in his bid to become Mayor of all the sidewalks of New York.

It was a day of reunion for "Louie" and many of his childhood friends. He threaded his way past push-carts on Avenue C and mingled with the Sunday shoppers of fruits, vegetables and clothing. Sweet plums were selling for 20¢ a pound.

. . . He looked up at the grimy face of a six-story tenement where he had been born fifty-seven years ago. . . . A white and red banner,

"Welcome Home Our Own Louie Lefkowitz," was suspended across the width of the street.

In his campaign oratory, our-own-humble-Louie-from-the-grimy-tenement-near-where-sweet-plums-are-20¢ emphasized that he was a regular guy and that what he had to say was terribly important to regular-folks-like-you-and-me.

> LOUIS LEFKOWITZ: Incredible as it may seem, murder and savage assaults are more rampant today than when Murder Inc. was operating twenty years ago. . . . And they are killing and assaulting decent law-abiding citizens—people like you and me.[2]

Republican propagandists also tried to characterize Lefkowitz as "The Son of Fiorello." Mrs. Marie La Guardia, a widow of New York's last Republican mayor (1933–1945), was brought forward to smile on Lefkowitz for the press because, as she said on cue, "This city desperately needs a return to good strong government." "LEFKOWITZ HAILS LA GUARDIA AIMS—," announced a headline on September 28, "—SAYS HE WILL 'STAND OR FALL' ON A SIMILAR REGIME." Huge billboards asking voters to "REMEMBER HOW GREAT CLEAN GOVERNMENT USED TO BE? IT'S YOURS AGAIN WHEN YOU ELECT LEFKOWTIZ FINO GILHOOLEY" were illustrated only with a recognizable caricature sketch of the late and great Fiorello.

LEFKOWITZ—FINO—GILHOOLEY, shades of WINTERGREEN FOR PRESIDENT, SENATOR CLAGHORN, and every other theatrical caricature of politicians that have provoked mirth for American audiences. The Jewish-Italian-Irish identification of the Republican ticket was too obvious. And Republican publicists emphasized the caricature by incessantly playing a musical-comedy type campaign song on roving sound trucks.

> You'll be safe in the park
> Any time after dark
>   With Lefkowitz, Gilhooley and Fino
> That fine City Hall
> Will be open to all
>   With Lefkowitz, Gilhooley and Fino.

Unfortunately, the television image of candidate Lefkowitz

probably heightened the sense of caricature implied by the jux-taposition of the three names. His appearance and demeanor on television, marked by a receding chin, receding forehead, thick-lensed spectacles, and a lower East Side dialect reminiscent of the late Willie Howard, probably encouraged viewers to dismiss the substance of what he had to say on public issues as comic dialogue.

Some years later, I got to know Lefkowitz on a conversational basis and was struck by the marked difference between the man himself and the television image that I remembered from 1961. The man is intelligent, perceptive, and soft-spoken—qualities that never emerged on television. In exchanging views with him personally, I was hardly aware of his looks or his dialect.

Lawrence E. Gerosa (Citizens party)

From his newspaper coverage, City Controller Lawrence Gerosa—dropped by Mayor Wagner and running as an independ-ent candidate for mayor—appeared to be a man of narrow ex-perience who viewed the world through a dollar sign: "GEROSA'S PLATFORM PLEDGES 3% CUT IN EXPENSE BUDGET—CALLS FOR PROGRAM THAT PROMISES SAVINGS OF $75,000,000 IN YEAR"; "GEROSA PREDICTS NEW WAGNER TAX—CALLS LEVY INCREASE IF MAYOR IS ELECTED"; "GEROSA HITS COST OF REGISTRATION." His television image conveyed a similar impression of narrowness, along with a crudeness of character completely alien to "good-guy" characters on television's predominant escapist fare.

As a fiscal conservative and a regular organization Democrat, Gerosa might be expected to attract the votes of conservative Democrats who were concerned about the growing cost of muni-cipal government and/or who could not bring themselves to vote for Mayor Wagner after the primary fracas, in which the organ-ization had been defeated.

Vito P. Battista (United Taxpayers party)

Vito Battista took pride in proclaiming himself to be a self-made man, an architect by trade, who wanted to stop New

York from destroying itself by encouraging "problem people" to come and take advantage of too-liberal welfare programs and public housing.

VITO BATTISTA: I believe that we are destroying ourselves. I believe in the private enterprise principles. I believe that a person is responsible to himself, not to the state. And I believe in the policies and principles of Barry Goldwater. I'm a conservative. I'm the only conservative running. All the others are liberals.[3]

According to the Citizens Union, a nonpartisan association interested in municipal affairs, Battista was no more than a "zealous gadfly" who primarily represented the interests of small home-owners.[4]

In campaigning, Battista was inclined to showy demonstrations in front of City Hall and other public buildings. He sought to contrive a singular visual image of himself by always dressing in a dark business suit and a black broad-brimmed hat of the sort made popular by the late Mayor La Guardia.

Eric Hass (Socialist Labor party)

Hass, editor of his party's newspaper, *Weekly People*, sought to promote a very special vision of a socialist utopia in the United States, a society in which a congress of representatives from workers' unions would run the country and decide "how many pairs of shoes do we need next year, how many new school-rooms, how many of this and that and the other thing . . . practical questions that working men's representatives can answer."

ERIQ HASS: In this new society for which I stand, for which the Socialist Labor party stands, we're going to vote—not from where we live as we do today for politicians whom we do not know except for the image they project in television—we're going to vote for people that we know in the industry where we work. . . .

We're going to elect our foreman in the shop, our management committee in the plant, our representatives to all the higher administrative councils—right up to the Socialist Industrial Union Congress that takes the place of that temple of palaver down there on the banks of the Potomac.[5]

Richard Garza (Socialist Workers party)

The Socialist Workers party, descended from a Trotskyite group that was expelled from the Communist party in 1928, contends that it—and not the Communists—is the true defender of Karl Marx's ideology. The Marxian concept of history as a matter of class struggle was evident in Richard Garza's 1961 mayoral campaign speeches. He appealed to voters by group, trying to make Negroes, Puerto Ricans, workers, and even old people more aware of their status as a "class" so that they might vote as a class and collectively influence government to better provide for their special needs. The banning of nuclear-bomb tests was a prime issue for Garza because "testing is an insane policy of our government leading to war. The people of this city are a prime target and should be able to decide whether they want to be wiped off the map or not." [6]

Garza was under no delusions that he could win the mayoral election. Rather, he regarded his campaign as public education: "... police brutality, Jim Crow practices in New York City, the problems of the poor, the urban revolution in Cuba and its application to New York ... many people would not believe that conditions in New York were as bad as we pictured them." [7]

Robert F. Wagner (Democratic, Liberal, and Brotherhood parties)

According to some political reporters, Lefkowitz, Gerosa, Battista, Hass, and Garza were going to meet a revitalized Mayor Wagner during the final weeks of campaigning.

THE NEW YORK TIMES (SEPTEMBER 25, P. 37): Instead of showing the strain, Mr. Wagner seems more affable than ever before. He acts like a man who enjoys making decisions and wielding power, rather than one who shrinks from these responsibilities.

Those who hold that the new Wagner is only a temporary phenomenon are of the opinion that long-settled habits cannot be easily changed.

The contrary view is that real power, once tasted, has a headiness that is irresistible.

HERALD TRIBUNE (SEPTEMBER 7, P. 3): The new Wagner image—

though some suspect that it may be just another election year mirage—comes after years of City Hall foot-dragging.

IN SEARCH OF AN ISSUE

At his opening campaign rally, Louis Lefkowitz said that "the basic issue of this campaign is one-party rule and the corruption and incompetence that goes with it." To another audience, he said: "The real issue is whether the city is to become solvent or go broke."

What he was really saying, by omission, was that he did not have a single fresh vital issue that might either arouse the sentiments of a large bloc of voters because of particular significance to them or arouse voters generally to the alleged *evil failures* of the incumbent. Consequently, he was playing for a protest vote, trying to focus the general discontent that usually exists with the way things are upon the incumbent mayor. For example—

Re crime issue: "MAYOR ASSAILED ON CRIME 'CRISIS'—LEFKOWITZ CALLS HIM 'TOO BUSY' TO SHOW CONCERN."

Re racial discrimination: "LEFKOWITZ SAYS NEGROES IN CITY ARE SHORTCHANGED BY WAGNER—HE TERMS MAYOR'S CIVIL RIGHTS RECORD ONE OF INACTION AND INDIFFERENCE."

Re problems of the aged: "LEFKOWITZ URGES BAN ON AGE BIAS—SAYS HE WOULD PRESS FOR LAW ON EMPLOYMENT."

Re public housing, slum clearance: "LEFKOWITZ SEES HOUSING 'FAILURE'—HE PROMISES WAR ON SLUMS AND OTHER STEPS TO CORRECT 'DISMAL' WAGNER RECORD."

Some of the Republican charges were downright silly, such as the one coming from Paul A. Fino, candidate for City Council President on the Lefkowitz ticket, after the Americans for Democratic Action endorsed Mayor Wagner: "FINO CHALLENGES WAGNER ON RED CHINA—ASKS IF MAYOR WOULD ADMIT REDS TO UNITED NATIONS." The ADA favored the admission of Red China to the United Nations.

Briefly, at the end of September and for a week or so thereafter, Lefkowitz appeared to have a fresh dramatic issue that could serve to characterize Mayor Wagner as a *bad guy*. On September 27, the mayor attended a luncheon at Sakele's Restaurant in Brooklyn.

CITY BOARD OF ETHICS REPORT (OCTOBER 5, 1961): At some time during the luncheon bank checks were handed out to each guest. [The guests were builders and real-estate men who regularly did business with the city.]

Those checks were made out to the Citizens Committee for Wagner, Beame, and Screvane . . . with the amount and the signature left blank.

Thereafter each guest was, or most of them were, called upon by name . . . to, and did, announce publicly how much each guest would contribute to the Committee's efforts.

The "Shakedown at Sakele's" was political drama smacking of scandal and corruption.

The mayor's immediate response was a counterattack. With the same political cunning that made him go for De Sapio rather than Levitt before the primary, Wagner aimed beyond Lefkowitz at the Republican hierarchy around Governor Nelson A. Rockefeller in Albany. Newspaper headlines reported that "WAGNER CHARGES G.O.P. CHEATS CITY ON STATE AID"; "WAGNER SAYS CITY IS PAWN TO G.O.P.—ASSERTS ROCKEFELLER, NIXON EYE IT FOR POLITICAL GAIN"; and "WAGNER IMPLIES G.O.P. SHAKEDOWN OF 35 COMPANIES—CITES ADVERTISEMENTS IN FUND-RAISING JOURNAL FOR CITY CAMPAIGN—EXPLANATION DEMANDED."

Sure enough, state-level Republican leaders rose to the bait and began fighting with state-level Democratic leaders over Wagner's charges, thus obscuring the Sakele's luncheon incident. By mid-October, Lefkowitz had naught to do but pick up his protest-vote blunderbuss and begin aiming more broadsides at City Hall.

A NOT-SO-GREAT DEBATE

Immediately after the primary, Louis Lefkowitz began challenging Mayor Wagner to debate on television "the record of the Wagner administration and the 'positive' program for improvements that the Republicans advocate."

Station WNEW-TV, Channel 5, offered Wagner and Lefkowitz prime time for a "series of television debates or discussion programs" *on the condition* that Congress waive Section 315 (Communications Act of 1934), the so-called "equal-time" statute that would obligate the station to include or give equal time to Gerosa, Battista, Hass, and Garza. Since Congress was then rushing to adjourn, there was no chance for such a waiver of Section 315 to be considered, not that it would have had the barest chance of passage regardless of the date. (Congress' rigid attitude toward Section 315 is described in Chapter 20.)

WPIX, Channel 11, offered a prime-time hour for a Wagner-Lefkowitz confrontation with no strings attached. News director John Tillman said that WPIX would comply with Section 315 by granting one half-hour of time to each of the four minor mayoral candidates on another night, a half-hour each approximating the time that Wagner and Lefkowitz would be on the air during their one-hour program.

Independent candidate Gerosa was infuriated with this arrangement. He paid $850 for one minute of commercial time on WPIX shortly before the Wagner-Lefkowitz program went on the air and denounced his exclusion from the program as "unfair discrimination."

According to a Nielsen rating, about a million viewers watched Mayor Wagner and Attorney General Lefkowitz have at each other while answering questions from a panel of reporters. *The New York Times* television critic Jack Gould concluded that Mayor Wagner was easily the more attractive candidate, but that it was impossible to tell where the truth lay in the candidates' disagreement on campaign issues.[8] *Time* magazine reported that although "spot surveys next day indicated the debate had changed few minds, Lefkowitz was eager to try again. Not so Bob Wagner. Said he: 'I'm not going to give him any free publicity.' With a 3–1 Democratic registration working for him, and a sorry two-term record working against him, it was one of his wisest decisions." [9]

NOTES

1. "Political Round-Up," New York *Journal-American*, August 27, 1961, p. 12.
2. *The New York Times*, September 25, 1961, p. 37.
3. *Meet Your Candidates*, WABC-TV, October 29, 1961, 12:30–1 P.M.
4. *Voters Directory* (New York: Citizens Union, 1961), p. 14.
5. *Meet Your Candidate*, WABC-TV, October 29, 1961, 12:30–1 P.M.
6. *Ibid.*
7. Letter from Richard Garza to the author, August 7, 1965.
8. *The New York Times*, October 11, 1961, p. 95.
9. *Time*, October 20, 1961, pp. 26–27.

11

THE LAST THREE WEEKS
BEFORE ELECTION DAY

Instead of building to a climax, the mayoral campaigns of 1961 seemed to run downhill toward November 7.

JOHN CROSBY (NEWSPAPER COLUMNIST): This is a very dull election. As a matter of fact the candidates seem almost unreal. The Republicans seem to be running the ghost of Mayor La Guardia rather than a real man and the Democrats, of course, are running Mayor Wagner who for eight years has avoided anything resembling city government.[1]

Due to political agility and luck, it was Mayor Wagner who dominated the news toward the end of the campaign. He was able to ride through the streets of New York in an open car at the side of President Kennedy as a visual display of the President's endorsement. He was able to take a brisk morning walk with the venerable Harry Truman and a small army of the press, who duly recorded that presidential endorsement. He was able to intervene in negotiations of the strike by milk-truck drivers, which cast him in the role of the dynamic public leader struggling against time and political enemies to get milk for crying babies. All this Wagner activity relegated Louis Lefkowitz to the role of a sidelines critic.

NEWSCASTER (RE KENNEDY ENDORSEMENT OF WAGNER): Lefkowitz said that Democratic desperation was bringing President Kennedy to the city. . . . He described the Mayor as sending a frantic S.O.S. to the White House.[2]

LOUIS LEFKOWITZ (SOF, RE MILK STRIKE): [Mayor Wagner] knew in advance that this strike was going to take place. He should have moved in prior to the strike and made every conscientious effort . . . to have avoided the thing.[3]

The most prominent campaign issue in the final weeks originated with Mayor Wagner and put Lefkowitz on the defensive. The mayor accused Albany Republicans of rushing a "sleeper" amendment to the rent-control law through the closing hours of the State Legislature session, an amendment that would permit thousands of New York City landlords to file for rent increases.

This charge definitely had the two necessary qualities of an issue that can influence votes: (1) it was new and specific; and (2) it was of intimate concern to a very large group of voters, namely, tenants.

NEWSCASTER: The G.O.P. candidate [Lefkowitz] got an angry reception last night. . . . Members of the audience jeered and shouted hostile questions about rent increases under the legislation.[4]

Just as Mayor Wagner would have wanted (to help characterize Louis Lefkowitz as a pawn of the Albany Republican "bosses"), Governor Rockefeller acted promptly to freeze rent increases under the disputed legislation. This left Lefkowitz to try to wriggle out of the situation as best he could, such as by pleading on television that he "had nothing to do with the bill, nothing to do with the preparation. . . ."[5]

TELEVISION COVERAGE

In the last twenty days before the November 7 election, television newscasts actually gave 17.5 percent *less* time to the mayoral campaigns than had been given during the seventeen-day period prior to the September 7 primary. On news-feature programs, where drama or dullness were not factors influencing amount of coverage, the mayoral campaigns received 23.8 percent more air time during the final than during the pre-primary period.[6]

WNBC-TV's indefatigable Gabe Pressman seemed to do his best to keep up the drama of a personal struggle between the two leading candidates. When no immediate conflict presented itself, he asked Wagner or Lefkowitz the sort of questions that directed their attention to each other's personal failings: "Is there any coolness between you and Wagner?"[7] "I noticed you didn't shake hands after the debate. Any coolness between you and Lefkowitz?"[8] "What do you think is the chief weakness of your opponent's campaign?"[9]

On WPIX, the other station where one newscaster-reporter dominated local newscasts, the drop-off in drama caused the most striking decrease in campaign coverage. During the seventeen days before the primary election, the mayoral campaigns received 56:15 on WPIX newscasts (Table 2). During the twenty days before the November 7 general election, the mayoral campaigns received 36:05 on WPIX newscasts, some twenty minutes, or 36 percent, less (Table 9).

An extreme example of the way that drama can determine newscast coverage was illustrated by the difference in air time given to items of/about Lawrence Gerosa before the primary and before the general election on WPIX. Before the primary, Gerosa had taken a dramatic personal slash at Mayor Wagner, charging that the mayor's "lavish" household expenses and use of city employees at the Wagner summer home were violations of the City Charter. In the last weeks before the November election, Gerosa was making statements and accusations about the high cost of municipal government under Wagner, snow removal costs, and Wagner's failure to obtain adequate state aid for city problems. However important as campaign issues, these subjects were not the stuff of personal conflict between candidates that constitutes political drama. Gerosa received a total of 15:45 comprehensive coverage on WPIX newscasts, including two SOF exposures for himself and three SOF exposures for prominent Gerosa supporters, before the primary, when his name was not on the ballot and nobody could vote for him. Before the general election, when his name was on the ballot as a mayoral candidate, Gerosa received a total of 3:20 comprehensive coverage on WPIX newscasts, about 21 percent of his pre-primary exposure on the station's newscasts.

The Case of Station WCBS-TV

Mayoral campaign coverage on newscasts of WCBS-TV, Channel 2, appeared to be weighted against the reelection of Mayor Wagner. This coverage did not involve the use of image techniques so much as a general emphasis on favorable coverage of/about Lefkowitz, coverage often critical of Wagner. It seemed to be part of a station-wide editorial attitude about the coming election rather than flowing from the preferences of an individual newscaster. Also, the coverage was extraordinary because CBS President Frank Stanton has publicly argued that, should the federal regulation of political broadcasting be abolished, stations would determine how much coverage each candidate should receive strictly according to "the flow of the news." [10] But newscasts have been exempt from Section 315 since 1959 and between October 18 and November 6, 1961, WCBS-TV's newscasts—if their mayoral coverage reflected flow-of-the-news—differed significantly from the other New York television stations in interpreting the flow-of-the-news. Table 9 shows that WCBS-TV gave Louis Lefkowitz 40 percent more comprehensive coverage than Mayor Wagner: 41:45 total for Lefkowitz to 29:55 total for Wagner.

WCBS-TV's selective emphasis on news of/about Louis Lef-

TABLE 8

COMPREHENSIVE COVERAGE OF/ABOUT MAYORAL
CANDIDATES ON TELEVISION NEWSCASTS

Station	WAGNER	LEFKOWITZ	GEROSA	BATTISTA	HASS	GARZA	Misc.	Total
WCBS-TV	29:55	41:45	3:55	–	–	–	18:35	94:10
WNBC-TV	38:35	31:50	6:45	1:50	–	–	7:55	86:55
WNEW-TV	3:05	0:40	0:20	–	–	–	–	4:05
WABC-TV	9:20	7:55	6:15	4:50	4:50	4:15	2:30	39:55
WOR-TV	2:00	0:50	–	–	–	–	0:20	3:10
WPIX	11:25	10:50	3:20	0:15	–	–	10:15	36:05
WNTA-TV	(no regularly scheduled newscasts during this period)							
All Stations	94:20	93:50	20:35	6:55	4:50	4:15	39:15	264:20

kowitz did not seem to flow from particular admiration for Lefkowitz or from latent Republican preferences in the news department. Rather, the bias seemed to flow from genuine concern for bad conditions in New York City: crime in the streets, traffic jams, dilapidated and unsafe subways, inadequate housing and schools, slums, archaic zoning laws, lack of fallout shelters, and so forth.

WCBS-TV newsmen may have shared a common point of view that New Yorkers ought to consider *issues* as a basis of voting rather than voting just because of habitual party loyalties or because one candidate's personal image seemed more attractive. This editorial attitude seemed evident in the nature of questions that WCBS-TV reporter Tom Costigan asked of onlookers at a Republican street rally.

TOM COSTIGAN (SOF): Have you changed you mind after hearing the arguments today?
FIRST ONLOOKER: I might have. I might.
COSTIGAN: In other words, the Republican arguments have caused you to do a little more thinking, huh?
FIRST ONLOOKER: I think so. Yes.

SECOND ONLOOKER: I'm from Brooklyn. I work for Lefkowitz. My man. Best man there is.

COSTIGAN: Had you made up your mind before?

SECOND ONLOOKER: Made up my mind before. A long time ago.

COSTIGAN: Nothing anybody says will change your mind?

COSTIGAN: How about you? You look happy at the arguments today. Have you been listening to them to a great extent?

THIRD ONLOOKER: Nice talk, you understand, but I still believe that Wagner will do the job.[14]

"Nice talk, you understand, but . . ." As such flat dismissal of campaign issues by voters became clear to those concerned with news at WCBS-TV, the overall tone of genuine concern turned more to genuine cynicism. This cynicism was the theme of a one-hour documentary program, *Vote for Whom?*, which WCBS-TV scheduled in prime evening time on Thursday, November 2, five days before the election. The leitmotif of the hour was a series of sequences showing the people of New York lamenting.

MAN (SOF): The candidates that's up for office at this time are about as straight as a pretzel.

WOMAN: I feel we should have a choice of better qualified men to run for office of our city.

ANOTHER MAN: It's my opinion that we are running short on all types of material for every public office in the country.

ANOTHER WOMAN: I'm very blah about the election this year.

CBS newsman Harry Reasoner, whose style tends toward cynical wit, opened the program by calling 1961 the year of "midgets for mayor." He quoted *Life* magazine's opinion that "New York's political zoo is open again. The voter's problem is why settle for a hack or a bungler when you can get an incompetent?"[12] Reasoner blamed candidate mediocrity upon New York City's antiquated political clubhouse system, which attracts organization-type politicians and eventually rewards them with nomination for high office.

WCBS-TV newscasts did not consistently project Republican Louis Lefkowitz as less mediocre than the other mayoral candidates. Some items that seemed to reflect harshly on Lefkowitz appeared.

NEWSCASTER: . . . some of the roughest campaign language to date. . . . Lefkowitz denounced city school conditions. He said that when Wagner found a rat in a Harlem school last May, the rat turned away and fled into his hole.[13]

Nevertheless, apparently because of a genuine concern for bad city conditions, WCBS-TV may have begun to favor Lefkowitz as the mayoral candidate of the major "out" party who offered the only reasonable hope of bringing political change to City Hall.

By accident or design, between October 18 and November 6, WCBS-TV newscasts carried items of/about Lefkowitz's "official activities" as attorney general of New York State totaling 5:20 and including two SOF items. In contrast, all the other stations together during this period had Lefkowitz-official-activity items totaling 0:25, a figure that included no SOF. Official activity items may help viewers see the "official" involved in a positive and responsible role.

Any station seeking to promote the cause of a candidate with an unattractive television image will have some special problems, namely to minimize viewer comparison of the favored candidate with the more attractive image of the opposition candidate. By accident or design, although WCBS-TV gave Louis Lefkowitz 40 percent more comprehensive coverage than it gave to Mayor Wagner (see Table 9), that greater amount of coverage did *not* include giving Lefkowitz more SOF items. Between October 18 and November 6, Mayor Wagner received ten SOF news items totaling 8:00 of air time, to Lefkowitz' six SOF items, totaling 4:35. What WCBS-TV newscasts did emphasize was various supporters of Lefkowitz, especially the personable Governor Rockefeller, talking for the candidate.

A column by James Reston in *The New York Times* of November 3 may have suddenly clarified for WCBS-TV the uneasy partisan position it appeared to be following with respect to Louis Lefkowitz. In this column Reston referred to Lincoln Steffens' classic exposé, circa 1902, of graft and corruption in some of the nation's biggest cities.

JAMES RESTON: Mr. Steffens made the point very clearly over half a century ago. . . . "If our political leaders are to be always a lot of political merchants, they will supply any demand we may create. All we have to do is establish a steady demand for good government."

Steffens' conclusion was: Vote by all means, vote for the more promising ticket, regardless of party; and when in doubt, throw out the "ins."

"If we would vote in mass on the more promising ticket, or, if the two are equally bad, would throw out the party that is in, and wait till the next election and then throw out the other party that is in—then, I say, the commercial politician would feel the demand for good government and he would supply it."

WCBS-TV lost no time in trying to introduce the Lincoln Steffens concept into its mayoral campaign coverage. But the merit of the concept was quickly overwhelmed by the personality of crusty old Harry Truman.

HARRY TRUMAN (OUT FOR A BRISK WALK, SOF): Come on. Let's walk here!

WCBS-TV REPORTER DAVE DUGAN: Mr. President, Lincoln Steffens once said that when people are in doubt about voting in a camp—in a party—in a particular election, they should vote for the "outs" rather than the "ins."

Do you think that's a good idea?

TRUMAN: No, I don't. Never did think so. He didn't know what he was talking about either—any more than Ike did.

Turn left here! [14]

Coverage of the Minor Candidates

Table 9 showed how little coverage minor candidates for a top office can expect to receive on television newscasts unless they are—as Lawrence Gerosa was—a dissident normally identified with one of the major parties. Except for a deliberate attempt of one station, WABC-TV, to achieve a more balanced news coverage of the mayoral campaigns by inserting two short interviews with each minor candidate into its weekday evening local newscast, the all-station totals for the minor candidates would have been negligible.

It was on the longer news-feature programs that the minor candidates received substantial amounts of air time. As Table 10 shows, in the last few weeks of the campaign, Lawrence Gerosa ended up with more news-feature program time than either Mayor Wagner or Louis Lefkowitz. The explanation is relatively clear. Section 315, the "equal-time" law, still applies to programs that are not (1) regularly scheduled; (2) originated and produced by the station; and (3) similar in format to *Meet the Press, Youth Wants to Know, New York Forum, Searchlight,* and certain other programs specifically mentioned in congressional debate preceding the 1959 amendment to Section 315 that excluded various bona-fide news programs from the equal-time requirement.

TABLE 9
AIR TIME GIVEN TO MAYORAL CANDIDATES ON TELEVISION NEWS-FEATURE PROGRAMS

Station	WAGNER	LEFKOWITZ	GEROSA	BATTISTA	HASS	GARZA	Misc.*	Total
WCBS-TV	3	33	33	3	3	3	42	120
WNBC-TV	25	25	10	10	10	10	–	90
WNEW-TV	–	30	30	–	–	–	–	60
WABC-TV	25	25	10	10	10	10	15	105
WOR-TV	(no news-feature coverage of the mayoral campaigns)							
WPIX	–	–	30	30	30	30	–	120
WNTA-TV	–	–	30	22	–	–	–	52
All Stations	53	113	143	75	53	53	57	547
Percentage of Total Received by Each Candidate	9.7%	20.7%	26.1%	13.7%	9.7%	9.7%	(10.4%)	100.0%

* Miscellaneous news-feature coverage consisted of portions of two documentary programs about the mayoral campaigns when the mayoral candidates were *not* on the screen.

In order to stay out of trouble with the Federal Communications Commission at license-renewal time, stations may also feel a certain general pressure—related to their general obligations for serving the public interest—to give all candidates for a top public office at least token exposure.

This general pressure and the specific pressures of Section 315 notwithstanding, in 1961 most of New York's television stations followed a number of practices that shunted presentation of the minor candidates away from the mainstream of campaign coverage. The slighting or exclusion of minor candidates on the more frequent, more heavily watched newscasts (with the exception of WABC-TV) has already been noted. Also, two of the stations practiced *tandem appearance*, a way of simulating the exciting face-to-face confrontation between major candidates without incurring an obligation to give the minor candidates equal time, by inviting the two major candidates to appear on the same regularly scheduled Section 315-exempt news-interview program. Mayor Wagner and Louis Lefkowitz made such 315-exempt tandem appearances on WNBC-TV (*Searchlight*, November 5, 1961, 11 A.M.) and WABC-TV (*Youth Wants to Know*, October 29, 1961, 12 noon). Moreover, a number of stations practiced *separate packaging*, giving the minor candidates equal time, but time quite removed from appearances of the major candidates. Two prominent examples of this practice are cited below.

Station WPIX, on Tuesday evening, October 10, brought Mayor Wagner and Louis Lefkowitz together for a one-hour confrontation that attracted about a million viewers. To satisfy Section 315, WPIX "packaged" the four minor mayoral candidates into a two-hour televised confrontation on Saturday night, October 28. Ratings for this two-hour program were not found, but chances are that they were minimal, because the competition on that Saturday night included some of television's most popular programs: the *Lawrence Welk Show* on WABC-TV, *Have Gun—Will Travel* and *Gunsmoke* on WCBS-TV, and Marilyn Monroe in a feature film on WNBC-TV.

Station WNBC-TV, on November 5, put the three most minor candidates by themselves in the second half-hour of a one-hour program intended to bring all six mayoral candidates together for public inspection. Mayor Wagner, Louis Lefkowitz, and

Lawrence Gerosa answered questions from 2–2:30 P.M. Vito Battista, Eric Hass, and Richard Garza gave their answers to the same questions from 2:30 to 3 P.M. Candidate Hass did not like this arrangement.

ERIC HASS: I register my emphatic protest against the arbitrary segregation of the mayoralty candidates on this program and the disparagement that such segregation clearly implies.[15]

Answering Hass, on behalf of the station management, program moderator Vic Roby explained the practical reason for separate packaging (he did not use that term) when there are more than two or three candidates for an office; namely, the more alternative answers to the question presented in a row, the greater the chances that the viewers would be unable to differentiate one from another and would end up more confused than informed.

In addition to making it easy for viewers to avoid minor candidates, separate packaging may also have the unintended effect of making the minor candidates seem like comic caricatures. This distortion appears because the minor candidates are usually ardent spokesmen for more extreme political positions and when they are presented together the contrast can be ludicrous. For example, in the second half-hour of the WNBC-TV program referred to above, pugnacious Vito Battista, a self-styled "Goldwater conservative" and an ardent advocate of free enterprise, found himself sandwiched in between socialists Eric Hass and Richard Garza. While Hass and Garza could not agree on which one of their parties was the true defender of Karl Marx, their horrified reactions to Battista and their fervent proclamations that capitalism and free enterprise were the great enemies of mankind constituted the most delicious comedy.

Who Asks the Questions?

Some members of Congress have voiced their suspicion that television stations try to influence the outcome of an election by controlling the subjects that candidates discuss on news-interview programs.

SENATOR RALPH YARBOROUGH: In *Meet the Press,* the network decides what issues it wants to discuss and asks those questions . . . seizing from the political parties and candidates the direction of the campaign.[16]

This suspicion is groundless if one judges from the news-feature coverage of the 1961 mayoral campaigns. Typically, the stations protected themselves from just such an accusation by producing the programs under the auspices of some respectable nonpartisan citizen organization and/or allowing individuals who were *not* employees of the station to ask the questions. Between October 18 and November 6, 1961, mayoral candidates appeared on ten news-interview type programs, totaling nine hours of air time.

NEW YORK FORUM............WCBS-TV, 10/21/61, 2–2:30 P.M.
Lawrence Gerosa questioned by three lawyers representing the New York City Bar Association.

AT YOUR BECK AND CALL......WNTA-TV, 10/24/61, 8–9:30 P.M.
Lawrence Gerosa answering questions phoned in by viewers.

NEW YORK FORUM............WCBS-TV, 10/28/61, 2–2:30 P.M.
Louis Lefkowitz questioned by three lawyers representing the New York City Bar Association.

DEBATE—PART TWO...............WPIX, 10/28/61, 9–11 P.M.
Candidates Gerosa, Battista, Hass, and Garza questioned by WPIX News Director John Tillman, but Tillman made it clear that he was using the same questions that had been asked of Mayor Wagner and Louis Lefkowitz by three newspaper reporters during the one-hour Wagner-Lefkowitz "debate" put on by WPIX on October 10.

YOUTH WANTS TO KNOW......WABC-TV, 10/29/61, 12–12:30 P.M.
Mayor Wagner and Louis Lefkowitz questioned by high school students.

THE RACE FOR MAYOR.......WNEW-TV, 10/29/61, 8–8:30 P.M.
Lawrence Gerosa questioned by representatives of the Citizens Union, League of Women Voters, and Citizens Budget Commission.

AT YOUR BECK AND CALL......WNTA-TV, 10/30/61, 8–9:30 P.M.
Vito Battista answering questions phoned in by viewers.

SEARCHLIGHT................WNBC-TV, 11/5/61, 11–11:30 A.M.
Mayor Wagner questioned by Milton Bergerman, Citizens Union; Murray Davis, *World-Telegram and the Sun* reporter; and Gabe Pressman, WNBC-TV.

DIRECT LINE.................... WNBC-TV, 11/5/61, 2–3 P.M.
All six mayoral candidates answering questions selected by the
League of Women Voters.

RACE FOR MAYOR............. WNEW-TV, 11/5/61, 8–8:30 P.M.
Louis Lefkowitz questioned by representatives of *Manhattan East*
magazine, City Club of New York, Women's City Club, and United
Neighborhood houses.

In all of these programs, the only station employee who was
in a position to "decide what issues to discuss and seize from the
political parties and candidates the direction of the campaign"
(to paraphrase Senator Yarborough) was Gabe Pressman on
WNBC-TV's *Searchlight* program of November 5. A thorough
scrutiny of that program's transcript did not reveal the slightest
suggestion that Pressman, in his questioning, was treating Mayor
Wagner and Louis Lefkowitz unequally. He challenged the as-
sertions of both candidates. He did not introduce any new subject that had not already been raised by another member of the
questioning panel.

If we assume for the sake of argument that all the image techniques apparent in Pressman's newscasts were not accidental but
rather a reflection of pro-Wagner bias, then Pressman's neutrality
in asking questions on news-feature programs becomes doubly
significant. Even a practitioner of image techniques who inten-
tionally wished to influence the public would be neutral in asking questions *because he is unconcerned about the influence of
the answers on voting*, that is to say he knows the rational substance of the answers may have little influence.

Senator Yarborough's fear of television stations determining
the direction of a campaign by deciding what issues should be
discussed on panel programs seems not only groundless, but
naïve and old-fashioned in an era of image candidates.

NEWSPAPER COVERAGE OF THE
FINAL CAMPAIGN PERIOD

Toward the end of October, six of the seven leading newspapers had editorially endorsed a mayoral candidate. The *Times*,
Herald Tribune, and *World-Telegram & Sun* recommended the

election of Louis Lefkowitz. The two Hearst papers, the *Mirror* and the *Journal-American,* and the *Post* urged readers to reelect Mayor Wagner to a third term. "And as for the *News,* it is an independent newspaper and refuses to be forced to choose one of two or more candidates whom it considers unacceptable. It believes, further, that New York City voters should demand higher-calibre candidates in the future." [17]

Much in the manner that it had given prominence to Arthur Levitt as a source of charges against Mayor Wagner before the primary, the *Herald Tribune* gave unusual prominence to Lawrence Gerosa as Election Day neared: "SINISTER FORCE BACKING WAGNER, GEROSA CLAIMS"; "GEROSA RAPS 'RED TAPE' IN SCHOOLS—SAYS WAGNER NEVER COPED WITH PROBLEM"; "GEROSA SEES WAGNER MAN 'IN CONFLICT' "; "GEROSA QUIZ: HOW ABOUT WAGNER'S ETHICS ON FREE TRIPS, HOTEL BILLS?" The *Herald Tribune* also seemed to step up its use of using "loaded" verbs in headlines to characterize Mayor Wagner as a man who "bows," "explodes," "shifts," "boasts," and "meddles"—for example, "MAYOR BOWS—POLICE GO INTO STUYVESANT TOWN"; "MAYOR 'EXPLODES' ON CRIME—'EVERYBODY KNOWS MOB OPPOSES ME' "; "WAGNER SHIFT: PROJECT PATROL PUT UP TO POLICE"; "WAGNER BOASTS OF HOUSING"; and "MILK STRIKE—SAY WAGNER IS MEDDLING."

The *World-Telegram's* coverage provided an excellent example of exclusive news being published to arouse a partisan vote, in this case against Mayor Wagner. From November 1 through to Election Day, the *World-Telegram* published a series of front-page articles entitled "THE TOUCH OF TERROR" and illustrated with some frightening photographs of sidewalk bums badgering passers-by. Day by day, this series generated headlines such as "NEW WAVE OF DERELICTS POSES MENACE IN PARKS AND STREETS"; "VICIOUS PANHANDLERS ROAM CITY"; "MAYOR ACCUSED IN SWITCH ON BOWERY PLAN"; "WINE-SODDEN BUMS BURDEN HOSPITALS"; "MAYOR ASSAILED FOR TRAMP PERIL"; "BUMS MAKE CITY A BARBARY COAST"; and "LEFKOWITZ HAILS SERIES ON BUMS."

Again, we see the double aim of biased newspaper coverage: (1) to arouse reader sentiment about selective issues that reflect well on the favored candidate and poorly on the opposition; and (2) to describe a repugnant character of the opposition candidate by associating him with bad public (or personal) incidents. Appearance and demeanor of the candidates barely figured in the newspaper coverage.

NOTES

1. John Crosby, a filmed statement on *Vote for Whom?* WCBS-TV, November 2, 1961, 10–11 P.M.
2. *The Morning Report,* WCBS-TV, November 1, 1961, 7:10 A.M.
3. *Report to New York,* WABC-TV, October 30, 1961, 6:15 P.M.
4. *The Morning Report,* WCBS-TV, November 1, 1961, 7:10 A.M.
5. *Searchlight,* WNBC-TV, November 5, 1961, 11–11:30 A.M. Excerpts repeated on 11 P.M. newscast.
6. Between August 21 and September 6, the all-station total of air time given to coverage of the mayoral campaigns on newscasts was 319:45. Between October 18 and November 6, a period three days longer, the all-station newscast coverage total was 246:20, 55:25 or 17.5 percent less than the pre-primary period. Between August 21–September 6, the all-station mayoral coverage total on news-feature programs was 442:00. Between October 18–November 6, the comparable news-feature total was 547:00, up 105:00 or 23.8 percent in the final period. Taking newscasts and news-feature figures together, total television coverage of the mayoral campaigns was up 49:35 or 10.8 percent in the final period. But in contrast, as an indication of the relative importance that newspapers and television may attach to local elections, it should be noted that coverage of the mayoral campaigns was up 21.8 percent in New York's seven newspapers during the final campaign period, twice the increased emphasis that television had seen fit to give the campaigns during the final period.
7. *Gabe Pressman and the News,* WNBC-TV, October 19, 1961, 6:30 P.M.
8. *Ibid.*
9. *Gabe Pressman and the News,* WNBC-TV, November 1, 1961, 6:30 P.M.
10. Testimony of Dr. Frank Stanton, Senate Subcommittee on Communications, June 28, 1963, *Hearings,* p. 227.
11. *The Late News,* WCBS-TV, October 30, 1961, 11 P.M.

12. Quotation read by Harry Reasoner from *Life*, September 1, 1961, pp. 24–25.
13. *The Morning Report*, WCBS-TV, October 18, 1961, 7:10 A.M.
14. *Saturday News*, WCBS-TV, November 4, 1961, 1 P.M.
15. *Direct Line*, WNBC-TV, November 5, 1961, 2–3 P.M.
16. Senator Ralph Yarborough (D., Tex.), member, Senate Subcommittee on Communications, May 19, 1960, *Hearings*, p. 281.
17. New York *Daily News*, November 3, 1961, p. 41.

CHAPTER

12

THE PEOPLE'S CHOICE

By coincidence or cunning, Mayor Wagner convinced the milk-truck drivers to settle their strike and go back to work on Election Day.

Right in character, the *Herald Tribune* assessed the political implications of the settlement in a front-page article "MILK—IT'S OVER ON ELECTION DAY." The front page of the *World-Telegram & Sun* that afternoon featured charges by Louis Lefkowitz and Lawrence Gerosa that the mayor had been "double-dealing...with Teamster bosses to stall negotiations until a dramatic election eve settlement could be announced shortly before the polls opened." The front page of the pro-Wagner *New York Post* translated the whole affair into a simple matter of family finances: "MILK WILL COST MORE."

In the evening, the three network stations (WCBS-TV, WNBC-TV, WABC-TV) had their usual frantic competition to see who could announce the winner first. Mayor Robert F. Wagner had been elected to a third term.

Table 10 reports the mayoral vote in 1961 and compares that vote to the amount or proportion of television newscast time and total television time (newscasts plus news-feature programs) that each candidate received. Remember that the newscast figures are *comprehensive coverage*, which includes all time given to items of/about a candidate and all of his supporters, not just the amount of SOF time given to the candidate himself.

TABLE 10

COMPARISON OF 1961 MAYORAL VOTE WITH SHARE OF TELEVISION AND NEWSPAPER COVERAGE

Candidate	Vote * (in thousands)	Percentage of Vote	Percentage of TV Newscast Coverage	Percentage of Total Television Coverage	Percentage of Newspaper Coverage
HASS	3	0.1%	1.8%	7.1%	negligible
GARZA	7	0.3	1.6	7.0	negligible
BATTISTA	20	0.8	2.6	10.1	1.8%
Subtotal: Three Minor Candidates	30	1.2%	6.0%	24.2%	under 2%
GEROSA	322	13.0%	7.8%	20.2%	8.3%
LEFKOWITZ	836	33.9	35.5	25.5	not computed
WAGNER	1,237	50.2	35.7	18.1	not computed
Misc. Votes †	43	1.7			
Misc. TV Coverage			14.9	12.0	
Totals	2,468	100.0%	100.0%	100.0%	

* Vote reported by the New York City Board of Elections, rounded to the nearest thousand.
† Valid votes cast, but with no choice for mayor.

SUMMARY:
INFLUENCES ON THE 1961 VOTE

In 1961, there were 2,202,162 Democrats registered in New York City, 767,526 Republicans, and 67,541 Liberals. Robert

Wagner was the Democratic and Liberal candidate on the November 7 ballot. Considering the influence of party loyalty alone, his vote should have been about three times greater than that given to Louis Lefkowitz, the Republican. But the mayor emerged with a 3-to-2 superiority instead. It seems probable that factors cutting down his odds were the presence of Lawrence Gerosa as a dissident organization Democrat attracting votes from organization-minded Democrats who resented the mayor's "reform" movement and an abstention from voting of other organization-minded Democrats who resented the Wagner "reform" but could not bring themselves to vote for Gerosa. At the same time, Republican Lefkowitz got the votes of his party plus a certain number of protest votes influenced by bad city conditions and directed at Mayor Wagner as a two-term incumbent.

During the final weeks before Election Day, television probably had little influence on (changing) the outcome. It showed, in Mayor Wagner and Louis Lefkowitz, two candidates who were not dramatic contrasts in appearance and demeanor, although the mayor was somewhat more personable and physically attractive. Democratic viewers—and they were in the vast majority—could hardly be impressed enough by the image of Lefkowitz to contravene their habitual tendencies to vote for a Democrat.

It seems improbable therefore that the slight and naïve bias toward Lefkowitz on WCBS-TV newscasts influenced many votes, because the heart of television's influence appears to be a matter of personal images and not issues. Issues, subject to (sometimes biased) description in literary form, are probably more persuasive as presented by newspapers. In 1961, the relatively nonpartisan *New York Times, Mirror,* and *Journal-American* probably helped rouse the protest vote based on campaign issues—the two Hearst papers doing so accidentally as they, in spite of their editorial endorsement of Mayor Wagner, continued to stress crime and violence in New York City, which turned out to be Louis Lefkowitz's main issue against Wagner toward the end of the campaign. (The habitually Republican *Herald Tribune* and the *World-Telegram* were probably reaching readers who would tend to vote Republican regardless of the specific campaign issues.)

Because the lopsided party registration figures practically guaranteed that the Democratic mayoral nominee would win in November, the crucial election was the September 7 primary. There was good reason to believe that television had played an important role in the outcome of this election. Democratic organization candidate Arthur Levitt had approached the primary with the advantages of a tremendous political organization and the sure knowledge that the more active, hence more organization-minded, party members tend to vote in a primary while the less active members stay home. Mayor Wagner had approached the primary as a dramatically superior *image candidate,* the clear hero of this political drama not because he himself was a paragon of virtue or masculine beauty but because his opponents were so clearly characterized as undesirable characters. There was nothing unattractive about Arthur Levitt's appearance, but his on-camera demeanor was bitter, aggressive, and imperious. And "Boss" De Sapio, lurking behind Levitt, was a rich caricature of a character in this campaign drama, a villainous image in the best tradition of television's *The Untouchables.*

The pro-Wagner *Post,* and to a lesser extent *The New York Times,* were writing this Wagner-vs.-the-bosses story before the primary. The other newspapers were not. Short of reflecting favorably on Levitt or De Sapio, the *World-Telegram* and the *Herald Tribune* were busy trying to delineate Mayor Wagner as the villain of the piece. The *Journal-American* was also giving big play to Levitt and Gerosa attacks on the mayor, but out of a simple love for sensational news rather than a calculated attempt to influence voting. (The Hearst papers later got around to endorsing Mayor Wagner.) The mayor looked fine to the *Daily News,* but then all candidates looked fine—if less than ideal—to the *News.* With the newspapers, it was a case of voters paying their money and taking their choice.

It was television that set up the primary campaign as a clearly delineated hero-villain drama for all voters, as viewers, to see. Because of the sharp personal contrasts between the two sets of characters, Wagner/Mrs. Roosevelt/Lehman on one hand and Levitt/De Sapio/Sharkey/Powell on the other, all the stations on which the candidates and their supporters appeared probably contributed to the "landslide" primary victory of Mayor Wagner. But the WNBC-TV newscasts of Gabe Pressman and the WPIX newscasts of John Tillman particularly presented the drama and probably heightened viewer awareness of the image contrast. Because of what happened on primary day, because great numbers of less-active Democrats came out to the polls to vote for Mayor Wagner and because the less-active members of a party normally do *not* tend to vote in primary elections and do *not* tend to vote against the party's regular candidate, it seems reasonable to conclude that heightened awareness of intense image contrast between Wagner and Levitt aroused their sentiment against the Levitt forces strongly enough for them to come out and vote in this primary.

One final note with regard to the influence—or lack of influence—that television appeared to have on New York City's mayoral election in 1961. As Table 10 showed, the three most minor candidates for mayor—Vito Battista, Eric Hass, and Richard Garza—received all together just over 1 per cent of the vote. Yet, these three candidates had been given air time totaling 24.2 percent of the television campaign coverage, a quantity largely due to the strictures of the federal "equal-time" law regulating broadcast appearances of political candidates.

With all that time on the air, why did Battista, Hass, and Garza not persuade more than one out of a hundred voters to cast a ballot for them?

One answer to this question, of course, would be the extreme nature of their political doctrines. But, since these three candidates also received negligible newspaper coverage and since we are advancing the thesis here that television does not convey much rational comprehension of what is being said by the candidates, how did 99 percent of the voters know that these three were undesirables?

According to the image-candidate concept, Battista, Garza, and Hass persuaded nobody to vote for them—via television—because they were not image candidates. Because of their exclusion from television newscasts that focused mainly on the drama of the campaign and because of their exclusion from real or simulated confrontations between the major mayoral candidates, Battista, Hass, and Garza—in all probability—were not recognized by voters as characters (let alone as desirable or undesirable characters) in the political drama being presented on the home screen. They just were not in the running.

Some day, to test this concept, all the television stations covering a given election might agree to give the candidate of an obscure, politically insignficant party full billing and equal treatment in newscasts and face-to-face confrontations. Let the minor party's doctrine be as extreme as that of New York City's Socialist Workers. But if the minor candidate is as personable and sincere as the Socialist Workers' Richard Garza was in 1961, it would seem reasonable to expect that his vote might be many times more than his party's vote had been heretofore, not because many more voters were suddenly subscribing to the Socialist Workers' doctrine, but because so many voters—as television viewers—use their emotions toward image candidates as their main reason for voting one way or the other.

PART FOUR

Further Adventures

CHAPTER

13

THE CANDIDATE WHO
WASN'T THERE

☆——☆

On June 16, 1963, Henry Cabot Lodge publicly removed himself from the arena of national politics. "I am not running for anything in 1964," Lodge told viewers who were tuned in to NBC-TV's *Meet the Press*. Within a few weeks, President Kennedy had appointed Lodge to head the United States legation in Vietnam, and off went the ambassador to the other side of the world.

In December, 1963, the newspapers reported that (1) General Eisenhower had asked Lodge to make himself available for the 1964 Republican presidential nomination; (2) Lodge had answered, from Saigon, that while he thought he could make his most useful contribution to his country by remaining on the job in Vietnam, he would "consider seriously anything the general asked" of him; and (3) a national "Draft Lodge" organization was announced by Robert R. Mullen, a Washington public relations man who had previously had some association with General Eisenhower.

I remember reading about these political rumblings and wondering if the pattern of the 1960 campaigns was going to be repeated, whether Henry Cabot Lodge would come back and damage his own image by campaigning on television and letting viewers pick up those unfortunate undertones of arrogance and disdain in his personality. As long as he stayed in Vietnam, actively engaged in the diplomatic front of the cold war, newspapers and magazines would be building his literary-fiction image as a courageous American statesman. But if he came back and exposed himself on a medium where appearance and demeanor count heavily, his demeanor might count against him. "There is something vaguely sniffish about Henry Cabot Lodge," wrote *New York Times* columnist James Reston (March 13, 1964), "as if he were vaguely annoyed with the human race and this has prevented him, despite his good looks, from being a wildly popular character."

But Ambassador Lodge did not come back from Vietnam in 1964, not until considerably after he *in absentia* defeated Governor Nelson A. Rockefeller and Senator Barry M. Goldwater in the New Hampshire Republican presidential primary election.

The sidewalks of New York were slushy during the last week of January, 1964, not because an early taste of warm spring air had begun to thaw out the frozen city but because the millions of feet and tires turn winter snow to slush almost as soon as it hits the ground. We had just left a borrowed projection room, Walter Thayer's friend and I, and were trudging through the slush carrying three or four cans of film about Henry Cabot Lodge.

I remember the slush better than Walter Thayer's friend. Thayer ran the Whitney Communications Corporation for John Hay Whitney. His company published the *Herald Tribune* and owned some radio stations. He was an active Republican whom I had met in connection with the 1960 Nixon-Lodge campaigns.

Walter Thayer's friend was a fellow from Boston by the name of Paul Grindle. And Paul Grindle had a conviction that Henry Cabot Lodge should be the next President of the United States.

The first and most crucial step toward this end, as Grindle saw it, was for Ambassador Lodge to win the first of the Republican presidential primary elections, namely, the one scheduled for New Hampshire on March 10. The two announced Republican presidential candidates, New York's Governor Rockefeller and Arizona's Senator Goldwater, would be campaigning hard in New Hampshire. If Henry Cabot Lodge could win that election without even setting foot in the state or in the country, it would be a public rejection of Rockefeller and Goldwater that the Republican national convention could hardly overlook when choosing their 1964 presidential nominee.

Paul Grindle, then in his early forties, was introduced to me as "an importer from Boston." Later I learned that with a background as a newspaper reporter and public relations man, he had started and built a highly successful mail-order house that sold scientific instruments. Unquestionably he was an admirer of Ambassador Lodge, but I think it was the challenge of trying to upset the heavily financed Rockefeller and Goldwater organizations and the larger challenge of maneuvering a presidential nomination that were most intriguing to him. Somehow he had found his way to Walter Thayer and somehow from Walter Thayer to me. Grindle's request was quite simple. He just wanted to see my 1960 Lodge campaign films on the chance that they would give him some ideas on how to promote Lodge on television in New Hampshire.

I showed him the quarter-hour film that had been made primarily from United Nations footage and newsreels, the five-minute still-picture impressionistic treatment of Lodge that I had produced in desperation during the early part of October, 1960 (see Chapter 4), and a number of one-minute spot commercials, including the unused ones that show Lodge at his worst, dully reading some direct-to-camera platitudes.

Of this material, it was the five-minute still-picture film that was most exciting, that played like a tight little drama in which Henry Cabot Lodge was a man to remember. As a piece of persuasion, the film also gained power from the unmistakable voice of President Eisenhower, praising Lodge's virtues and achievements: "It is upon such a record that we acclaim Cabot Lodge as our vice-presidential candidate."

I don't think I told Grindle that the Eisenhower narration was just a pilfered after-dinner speech, because it never occurred to me that Grindle was going to do more with the film than "show it to a few friends," which is what he said he wanted to do when he asked for the loan of a print.

What Grindle and/or his associates did in a matter of days was to hire a film editor and make some changes in the film, changes just subtle enough to give audiences the idea that President Eisenhower was endorsing Ambassador Lodge as the Republican presidential candidate. The first clue I got to this was in the March 6 issue of *Time* magazine, which noted that Lodge's "eager New Hampshire workers were busily buying television time for a five-minute Lodge campaign film that was made in 1960—and narrated by Dwight Eisenhower."

Later, Sam Phillips, manager of station WMUR-TV in Manchester, advised me that this film had been shown no less than thirty-nine times between February 17 and March 10. That is quite a dose for New Hampshire viewers when you consider that WMUR-TV was the only commercial television station located in New Hampshire.

Just as a kibitzer who suddenly finds that he has been dealt a poker hand becomes more keenly aware of the game, I began to study the New Hampshire situation closely, trying to predict the outcome on the basis of the three major influences upon voting: party loyalty, campaign issues, and candidate images.

Party loyalty would be a nil factor in the New Hampshire primary because (1) all the qualified voters were Republicans and (2) the state Republican organization did not have a chosen candidate who was being challenged. (If there had been a Republican presidential nominee somehow chosen, designated, or favored by the state party organization prior to the primary election, the influence of "party loyalty" would have worked in his favor, because the more active members of a party tend to vote in a primary and the more active members tend to be more party-organization-minded.)

The influence of campaign issues was probably going to hurt Senator Barry Goldwater quite badly. New Hampshire Republicans could read in local and national publications of the unusually clear and unusually "extreme" pronouncements that Goldwater was making on public questions that touched the closest interests of many voters. Goldwater had proposed that Social Security payments be made voluntary, a proposal the press immediately interpreted as spelling doom for the Social Security system. There are large numbers of retired people in New Hampshire.

Barry Goldwater advocated that the United States get out of the United Nations if Red China was admitted. New Hampshire, as a state, was on the record as endorsing and encouraging the United Nations.

Barry Goldwater made clear, and frightening, statements about military action: that the United States Marines in Cuba should use force to turn on the water for the Guantanamo base that Fidel Castro had turned off; that certain NATO commanders should have discretion in the use of nuclear weapons; and that nuclear weapons should be used to defoliate the rain forests of Vietnam.

It was not only *what* Barry Goldwater was saying that seemed to send shock waves through the press and hence through the voters, but his offhand manner of making rash and impulsive remarks about very important public questions that appeared to be an influence on New Hampshire Republicans. After all, New Hampshire is part of the Eastern Seaboard and Barry Goldwater was the man who had said, "Sometimes I think this country would be better off it we could just saw off the Eastern Seaboard and let it float out to sea."

Prior to March 10, Senator Goldwater appeared to be driving

votes away with *what* he said, the content of what he said. This content, communicated to New Hampshire Republicans via newspapers, magazines, and printed campaign propaganda (from the Rockefeller organization), may have been so shocking as to largely negate the appeal of Goldwater's personable appearance and demeanor on television.

The television image of Goldwater's main opponent in New Hampshire, Governor Rockefeller, promised to be equally impotent as an influence on voting, although for a very different reason.

"Image" is a Madison Avenue word for the *character* of a candidate. Usually appearance and demeanor, perhaps enhanced by presentation, of a candidate are the main clues that stimulate television viewers to characterize candidates as more or less desirable. Upon occasion, however, a candidate can be so strikingly characterized by other media prior to his exposure on television that personable appearance and demeanor add up to naught.

Shortly before this New Hampshire primary election, Nelson A. Rockefeller had gone through some highly publicized readjustments in his love life that may well have characterized him—in the eyes of many people—as a moral libertine. First, he had divorced a loyal wife of thirty years, Mary, on tenuous grounds. Then he had remarried a much younger woman. To the public it appeared that his new bride, Margaretta ("Happy") Fitler Murphy, in order to gain her own marital freedom surrendered legal custody of her four children to their father, Dr. Robin Murphy.

"The public has a short memory," a leading political figure once told me. But New Hampshire voters hardly had time to forget the luckless Mary Rockefeller and Happy Murphy's four children when Nelson Rockefeller began appearing before them on television in February and March, 1964.

The Rockefeller organization, vast, resourceful, precise, and professional in matters political, was evidently at a loss as to how to cope with the libertine characterization. They made that typically futile gesture of standing their candidate up before a camera and letting him "go on and talk to the people" as if the people were hearing words and not seeing character.

ROCKEFELLER (TYPICAL TV SPOT COMMERCIAL): Senator Goldwater has repeatedly said he wants to make Social Security "voluntary." Now he says he wouldn't make it "voluntary" right away—perhaps not until the 1970s.

Whether we follow Senator Goldwater's idea now or later, it would still bankrupt the Social Security system and be a personal disaster to millions of Americans.

I worked with President Eisenhower when I was Undersecretary of the Department of Health, Education, and Welfare to extend Social Security benefits to 10 million more Americans and to increase their benefits.

I want to help our senior citizens, not hurt them.

ANNOUNCER (VOICE OVER CAMPAIGN FOOTAGE): Vote for Nelson Rockefeller.

In his book *The Making of the President 1964,* author Theodore H. White provides an eye-witness account of what was uppermost in the minds of New Hampshire voters when they heard and saw Governor Rockefeller. He describes a rally in a school gymnasium where Happy Rockefeller waited while her husband talked.

THEODORE WHITE: Her husband stood beside her; she sat—the only seated person in the hall—as if in a witness chair; the townspeople gathered in a semi-circle somewhat apart from the candidate and the seated woman as if they were a jury. And then, as he spoke—excellently that day on the subject of leadership and responsibility in a world at war—I watched the audience.

Whether or not they were listening to him, I cannot say, but their eyes were all staring unnervingly at the handsome woman with bowed head and curled legs who sat in the spot of light. They might have been a gathering of Puritans come to examine the accused.[1]

This was the situation in New Hampshire: Goldwater characterized as an undesirable because of what he was saying; Rockefeller characterized as an undesirable because of what he had done of a moral nature; and the voters probably receptive to an image-candidate hero if they could but perceive one. And they did perceive an enhanced, idealized impressionistic image of Henry Cabot Lodge—over and over again—on their television sets.

Some 90,000 New Hampshire Republicans trudged through a blizzard on March 10 and cast their votes for a presidential candidate. Some 33,000 of them wrote in the name of Henry Cabot Lodge, the candidate who was not there. About 20,700 voted for Barry Goldwater; 19,500 for Nelson Rockefeller. Richard Nixon, also a write-in candidate, emerged with 15,600 votes. Of Ambassador Lodge, *Times* columnist Reston said:

JAMES RESTON: [He had] buried a couple of millionaires with a campaign that cost less than $25,000. The way in which the money was spent may indicate the coming political fashion. Paul Grindle, Robert Mullen and the other amateurs who dislodged Rockefeller and Goldwater operated on the assumption that too many TV shots of their candidate may soon become as boring as advertising jingles. They spent only $3000 on a single film clip [they did?!] of Lodge in action, fighting Communists in the U.N. and Nazis in Africa. . . . One television shot showed Ike beaming like a proud father on the handsome candidate and saying, "This is the man we want. . . ." Where this ancient film clip came from nobody knows exactly and the sound ended before Ike said what he wanted Lodge for, but the viewers got the idea that Lodge was Eisenhower's candidate for something and apparently the thing worked.[2]

For the record, the script of the "thing" that apparently worked is reproduced below as it was originally produced in 1960. You can use your imagination as to where it might have been edited to sound as if it specifically referred to the presidential primaries of 1964.

On reading this, you may think—and quite correctly—that there is no particular power in the narration. But again, at the risk of repeating *ad nauseam,* the rational import of the words that are said are probably the least important part of television propaganda. The effect comes from the dramatic whole: from the rapid sequence of still pictures, each a frozen moment in itself, slipping by so fast as to leave mere impressions of a greater-than-life character; from the musical scoring; from the zooming titles; and from the simulated conflict between Lodge and Vishinsky inside the United Nations.

MEET MR. LODGE

(Produced in October 1960. Length 4:16. Animation Camera Operator: Hugh Valentine. Narrator: Ray Morgan. Music and effects by Ross-Gaffney, Inc. Note that all visual material was still photographs treated under animation camera to simulate action and movement on the screen.)

FADE IN	*(Music:* OPENING THEME*)*
CONVENTION CROWD: ZOOM IN TO SIGN "LODGE FOR V.P."	*(Sound:* CROWD CHEERING*)*
ANOTHER CONVENTION PHOTO C.U. SIMILAR SIGN AND ZOOM BACK TO SHOW NIXON AND LODGE WAVING	
BASIC CAMPAIGN PHOTO OF NIXON AND LODGE WAVING MAIN TITLE ZOOMS IN TO FILL SCREEN: "MEET MR. LODGE"	
DISSOLVE TO:	
SEQUENCE OF STILL PICTURES SHOWING LODGE CAMPAIGNING ON THE ROAD	NARRATOR (VO): Since his nomination as the Republican Party's candidate for Vice-President, Henry Cabot Lodge has been traveling across America.
ZOOM IN TO MICROPHONE IN LODGE'S HAND	LODGE (ADD PUBLIC ADDRESS REVERB): My fellow Americans: this is a time of danger

SEQUENCE OF PHOTOS
SHOWING LODGE
SPEAKING TO CROWDS,
APPEARING ON TV PROGRAM,
TALKING INTO RADIO MIKE

and of challenge
for our country
and all that it stands for.

We are engaged
in a life and death struggle
with world communism
which is determined
to take over the world.

But no one is going to
take over our country
or take over the world.

We insist that the world
be free and at peace
so that we can get on
with the attack
against poverty and injustice,
hunger and disease.

The triumph of freedom
and the safety of humanity
depend on American leadership.

SEQUENCE OF PHOTOS
SHOWING LODGE WITH
VARIOUS ADMIRERS ON
THE CAMPAIGN TRAIL

(*Music:* REESTABLISH THEME)

NARRATOR:
Republicans, Democrats,
Independent voters
are responding warmly
to the kind of leadership
promised by Henry Cabot Lodge,
leadership based on
a great personal experience
with the cold war—
the vital issue
of this election year.

LODGE AND EISENHOWER
SITTING TOGETHER AND
TALKING

President Eisenhower
has spoken out
on the unique qualifications
of Ambassador Lodge

ZOOM IN TO EISENHOWER
TO VISUALLY SUPPORT THE
VOICE

DISSOLVE TO:

STATUE OF FIRST SENATOR
LODGE SHOWING YOUNG BOY
NEAR BY, PROBABLY OUR
H.C.L., SALUTING IT

PHOTOS OF LODGE AS A YOUNG
MAN: FIRST CAMPAIGN,
FIRST PUBLIC OFFICE

LODGE AS ARMY OFFICER:
STANDING ATOP TANK;
LOOKING AT MILITARY MAP

LODGE AND FAMILY
EXAMINING HIS ARMY
HELMET

LODGE OUTSIDE
THE SENATE

UNITED NATIONS BUILDINGS:
AERIAL VIEW,

to be our next Vice-President.

EISENHOWER:
I have known Cabot Lodge
for many years.
His career in the Senate
was in keeping
with the brilliant record
of his family.
Five of his ancestors
served in that body.
He began his own political career
in the Massachusetts legislature.
There Cabot Lodge
came quickly to understand
that good representative government requires a system under
which certain responsibilities
and powers
are allocated to each level:
local, state and national.

During World War Two,
I knew him as a soldier.
He was the only man
in the United States Senate
since the Civil War
to resign his seat
to fight in the armed forces.
He served
in the North African campaign
and continued to serve
with distinction
until the close of the war,
after which
the voters of Massachusetts
gratefully returned him
to the Senate.

In his most recent role,
as our representative
to the United Nations

ZOOM DOWN SLOWLY
TO GENERAL ASSEMBLY BLDG.

INSIDE GENERAL ASSEMBLY,
  CONTINUE SLOW ZOOM IN TO
  LODGE SPEAKING ON DAIS

the past seven years,
Ambassador Lodge
has demonstrated his
superb qualities of leadership.

SEQUENCE OF TITLES
  ZOOMS IN TO FILL SCREEN,
  EACH TITLE OVER A
  DIFFERENT PICTURE OF
  LODGE IN ACTION WITH
  GROUPS OF U.N. PEOPLE [3]

(*Music:* ASCENDING PASSAGES
LEADING TO RESTATEMENT
OF MAIN "BATTLE HYMN"
THEME [4])

"KOREA—1953"
"GUATEMALA—1954"
"FORMOSA—1955"
"HUNGARY—1956"
"SUEZ—1957"
"LEBANON—1958"
"TIBET—1959"
"CUBA—1960"

PHOTOS OF LODGE
  WITH U.N. DELEGATES:
  HE SEEMS TO BE THE
  MAN THEY ARE LOOKING
  TO FOR LEADERSHIP

EISENHOWER (VO; CONT'D):
He has stood firmly
on a platform of truth
to confound
the delegates of the Soviet Union
and its satellites
who have falsely represented
the peaceful intentions
of the United States.

LODGE:
  ADDRESSING SECURITY COUNCIL

LODGE (FROM U.N. TAPE):
The Soviet Union
has got designs
on the American hemisphere.

AMBASSADOR VISHINSKY

VISHINSKY (U.N. TAPE):
  (SAYING SOMETHING IN RUSSIAN
  THAT SOUNDS ANGRY)

REACTION SHOT:
    BRITISH AMBASSADOR,
    HEAD ON TABLE,
    AS IF DISCOURAGED
    BY RUSSIAN TALK

VISHINSKY CLOSE UP

LODGE LISTENING:
    DISGUSTED LOOK ON
    HIS FACE

STILL MORE VISHINSKY

LODGE ANSWERING BACK: LODGE (U.N. TAPE):
    HIS HAND IS RAISED   The United States
                                   has found within its embassies
THREE PHOTOS: in the Soviet Union
    LODGE WITH WOODEN "GREAT   and the satellite countries
    SEAL OF THE UNITED STATES"   well over one hundred
    WHICH, WHEN OPENED, SHOWS   clandestine listening devices.
    A HIDDEN MICROPHONE

                                   (Music: OMINOUS STING; RESUME
                                       THEME UNDER)

EISENHOWER AND LODGE WALKING   EISENHOWER:
    THRU WOODS: We salute him
    CLOSE UP ON EISENHOWER TO   for his enviable record
    REESTABLISH WHO IS TALKING   as a public servant
                                   because he has been
                                   a stout and skillful representative
BEST SHOT: of the United States
    LODGE AT UNITED NATIONS   and because his performance
                                   in the United Nations
AERIAL VIEW OF U.N. BUILDINGS   has brought growing respect
    AT NIGHT: ZOOM BACK SLOWLY   and admiration for that
    TO GIVE EFFECT OF DEPARTING   great national institution
                                   among our countrymen.

CLOSE UP: IKE TALKING, IN   It is
    PHOTO OF IKE AND LODGE TALK-   upon such a record
    ING. PULL BACK TO REESTABLISH that we acclaim Cabot Lodge
    VISUALLY THAT IKE IS TALK-   as our
    ING TO—AND ABOUT—   Vice-Presidential candidate.
    LODGE

(*Music:* THEME TO CONCLUSION)

LODGE AT DESK, SURROUNDED BY AIDES: HIGHLY DRAMATIC SCENE	NARRATOR: There is no substitute for the long experience in government and foreign affairs gained by Ambassador Lodge from his years in the Senate, the President's cabinet and in the United Nations.
BASIC CAMPAIGN PHOTO: NIXON AND LODGE WAVING	When you vote on November 8th, vote for
SUPERIMPOSE TITLES:	Vice-President Richard Nixon and
"VOTE NIXON-LODGE"	Ambassador Henry Cabot Lodge.
"THEY UNDERSTAND WHAT PEACE DEMANDS"	They understand what peace demands.

FADE OUT

NOTES

1. Theodore H. White, *The Making of the President 1964* (New York: Atheneum, 1965), p. 108.
2. James Reston, "The New Political Fashions of 1964," *The New York Times*, March 13, 1964, p. 32.
3. A visual background should never be changed while a title is superimposed over it. Such a background change makes the title seem to jump and is momentarily disconcerting to viewers.
4. An excellent background arrangement, including theme, variations, and related cues, of "Battle Hymn of the Republic" is available on disc or tape from Thomas J. Valentino, Inc., New York. But be very cautious in using "Battle Hymn" for political films. It has become cliché and may provoke derision more than the desired nuances of Americana from viewers.

CHAPTER

14

KEEP THE CANDIDATE
OFF THE SCREEN

To this date, I think there would have been a good chance to get the 1964 Republican presidential nomination for Henry Cabot Lodge if he had continued to win the primary elections as a candidate *in absentia* and come to the Republican convention in July as the conquering hero, home from the hot spot of the cold war by popular demand.

After Lodge had run away with the March 10 Republican primary in New Hampshire, I allowed myself the luxury of some daydreams. My phone would ring and it would be that elusive character from Boston on the other end, Paul Grindle: "All right, Gene. That image film did it in New Hampshire. It was all we had. The candidate wasn't even there. Now can you do the same thing in Oregon and some other primaries? Can you stop Nelson Rockefeller and Barry Goldwater with the image of Henry Cabot Lodge?" And I would pause for a long moment, as if giving deep consideration to all the ramifications of this proposition, and then answer coldly: "Maybe. If you keep Lodge out of the country, it would be worth a try. As long as television viewers only see him as we want them to see him, he might appear to be much more preferable to Rockefeller or Goldwater."

But I never saw Paul Grindle again. When the phone rang, it was Dennis Kane calling. (Dennis was the television director who specialized in political campaign programs.) Dennis told me that he was working for Nelson Rockefeller's organization and wanted to know what it would take to get me to make image materials for Governor Rockefeller and no more for Henry Cabot Lodge.

I paused for a long moment while my mind cleared from the sudden shattering of the Lodge/image dream, then answered Dennis with a remark that certainly made no sense to him.

GENE: That's the way the ball bounces.
DENNIS: Don't talk like a writer.

The Rockefeller organization is a private army: vast, intricately structured as to pecking order, and completely assured of its own potency. Except for failing to wrest the 1960 Republican presidential nomination away from Richard Nixon, the organization's most severe setback to date had been the New Hampshire primary. Yet, such is the power of unlimited money and many bright minds dwelling on a problem that within a few days after March 10, 1964, the organization had regrouped, analyzed its weaknesses, added a few hands, and begun to move into the next battle area, Oregon, with renewed vigor. More than a hundred staff members crowded the fourth and fifth floors of 521 Fifth Avenue, where the Rockefeller National Campaign Committee had its official headquarters. Baseball's illustrious Jackie Robinson was in charge of Special Committees, whatever they were. Over in a corner, experienced journalists Harry O'Donnell and Frank Leonard put out a pseudo-newspaper, the *Campaign Express,* whose headlines, post-New Hampshire, seemed like some very loud whistling in the dark: "RACE WIDE OPEN—G.O.P.

TAKES A NEW LOOK AT ROCKY"; "WOMEN SOUR ON LODGE AS CAMPAIGNER"; "ROCKY WORKER INJURED WHEN GOLDWATER GATE-CRASHERS TRY TO DISRUPT RECEPTION"; and "ROCKY ENJOYS POLITICAL TALK WITH IKE."

Charles F. Moore, a former vice-president of public relations for the Ford Motor Company and an old Dartmouth crony of the governor's, was acting as director of communications for the 1964 campaign. Charlie Moore's office was notable for the carpet on the floor: a deep blue with abstract splotches of gray, the gray being cigarette ash flung from Charlie's gesturing hand. "I want to know exactly what you are going to do on television before you do it, but if it doesn't work, don't use me for an excuse. The idea is to win in Oregon. W-i-n, win!"

Under Charlie Moore's division of the organization came Jerry Danzig's television department, which boasted of a pretty dark-haired secretary, Seena, whose personal décor made up for the lack of a rug on the floor. Under Jerry Danzig came Dennis Kane, whose job was to direct Rockefeller programs and commercials; Dick Swicker, whose job was to straighten out the bills and expense accounts; and the new writer, whose job was to make Oregon turn out differently from New Hampshire.

The organization had an intelligence unit, officially called the Research Department, located in a labyrinth of sterile steel-partitioned offices behind an unmarked door in one of the Rockefeller Center buildings along Sixth Avenue. The "researcher" trailing Senator Barry Goldwater was one Graham T. T. Molitor. Molitor's day-to-day reports of Goldwater's inaccuracies and changes in policy and style were carefully digested by Research Director Roswell (Rod) Perkins and then rewritten into advisory memoranda to the governor. At this point the secrecy stopped because the protocol of the organization demanded that everybody who was anybody get a copy lest their feelings be hurt by the thought that they were being excluded from something important.

Since the Research Department operated on the assumption that what Governor Rockefeller said on the campaign trail would help him do a Dale Carnegie, and since I was operating on the assumption that his words were evidently not winning friends and influencing Republicans to vote for him, Rod Perkins and the Research Department could not be numbered among my allies in the organization. Indeed, some of the impossible words coming out of the governor's mouth made me wonder if some of the intellectuals around him might not be political saboteurs.

GOVERNOR ROCKEFELLER (OPENING OF A TELEVISED SPEECH, APRIL 6, 1964): In the past few weeks, we have been witnessing the buildup of Operation Obfuscation—an all-out effort by the Democrats to cover up their dismal and tragic failures in world affairs.

"Operation Obfuscation"? I forcefully diverted all eyes from Seena to myself. "What ignorant egghead is putting words like 'obfuscation' in his mouth? What do you want people to think— we got another Adlai Stevenson here? You go down on Fifth Avenue, Jerry. Ask the first hundred people you meet what 'obfuscation' means. I'll bet they have you arrested for obscenity!"

Jerry Danzig never stopped smiling as he caught the verbal knife and threw it right back at me: "We know we must be doing something wrong. The question is, What are you going to do that's right?"

In mid-April, about a month after the New Hampshire primary, a survey of Oregon's registered Republicans showed that almost half—46 percent—wanted Henry Cabot Lodge to be their party's 1964 presidential candidate. Only 17 percent favored Richard Nixon at that date. Barry Goldwater was preferred by 14 percent. And, trailing the field, there was Nelson Aldrich Rockefeller with a potential 13 percent of the Republican vote.

Thus the challenge of Oregon: in one month, by the May 15 election, move the dust-eater to be the front runner.

Several assumptions seemed safe for plotting an image strategy. First, there was the organization. What would it do, what could it do in Oregon that was different from what it had done for the candidate in New Hampshire? No doubt it would move Governor Rockefeller around the state with as much splash and hoopla as possible and probably deluge television viewers with direct-to-camera "paid political" programs and commercials.

There was no reason to believe that this sort of campaigning would be any more effective in Oregon than it had been in New Hampshire, but an organization has to do what it knows how to do, ineffectual or not.

Second, I had to assume that the Rockefeller image on television would be as nonpersuasive in Oregon as it had been in New Hampshire because the moral-libertine characterization stemming from his divorce and remarriage was still too fresh. Since the usual sort of direct-to-camera television appearances did not promise to open minds that were closed to him, the alternative strategy would have to be *keep the candidate off the screen* (in the realistic, direct-to-camera sense) and greatly increase a controlled presentation of a fresh Rochefeller image via impressionistic television material. This fresh image should be so attractive and so strikingly presented as to leave an impression in Republican voters' minds stronger than the prevailing moral-libertine impression.

The question was what new characterization to use for Governor Rockefeller in Oregon. It must be genuine. It must be subject to presentation in a dramatic style.

I settled on using *ancestral motivation,* one of the personal characteristics common to successful politicians identified by Dr. Steven Ebbin in the late 1950s.[1] From interviews with a number of Connecticut politicians, Dr. Ebbin described certain elements of personality and campaign tactics that differed significantly between winning and losing candidates.

1. *Family tradition (Ancestral motivation).* Successful politicians credited their ancestors with having motivated them to politics.

2. *Party considerations.* Successful candidates minimize these while unsuccessful candidates focus on partisanship.

3. *Personalities vs. issues.* Unsuccessful candidates emphasize issues while the successful feel that personality was more important.

4. *Duty concept.* Unsuccessful candidates emphasize their duty to get things done in a way they think right. Successful candidates see it as a more generalized duty to their constituents.

The script of *Rockefeller's Way*, the basic short film used heavily in Oregon to obscure the immoral image with a striking characterization of the candidate as ancestrally motivated, is reproduced below. Again, as in the short Lodge film (which was, incidentally, exposed on Oregon television to the limits of Paul Grindle's budget), the impressionistic still-picture technique was used to prevent the audience from seeing too realistic a presentation of the candidate. Again, the persuasive power of the film seemed not so much to be in the words of narration as in the overall effect of the pictures flashing by and the music and the short dialogue of Rockefeller and his "Father" as characters in a dramatic story. The most moving moments, according to viewers, were when the talking stops and the emotion-generating magic of the music and pictures takes over.

The musical scoring for this film deserves special note because it represents the first time that I had carried the technique of a single musical theme to its utmost point, which was using it continuously—in many mood variations—from beginning to end, to help establish an unmistakable aesthetic entity for the piece. In *Rockefeller's Way*, wanting the music to generate the aura of Americana generated by "Battle Hymn of the Republic" and being afraid that "Battle Hymn" had become cliché from overuse, I took a slight sidestep and had "Battle Cry of Freedom" ("We will rally 'round the flag, boys, and rally once again") arranged for six male voices, cornet (not trumpet, which has too modern a sound), string bass, and snare drum. The voices never sing the words, but hum and go "lu, lu, lu" to the melody, thus stopping short of revealing what the song actually is and stopping short of introducing any words that must be listened to.

The cornet allows for a counterpoint melody to be heard across the melodious humming of the male voices. In my opinion, the highest point of the film—the point that is most stirring—is a sequence halfway through when the still pictures are showing Governor Rockefeller—with his new wife, Happy—campaigning in Oregon and paying attention to little children. This is not the conventional political baby kissing with Nelson Rockefeller, but a genuine love for children that keeps showing itself in his private and professional life. His feeling for the youngsters shows in his face. He picks a little blonde girl up and hugs her. The camera holds on that one still shot for five or six seconds. The cornet, in counterpoint to "Battle Cry," has been playing the nursery tune "This old man, he played one/He played knick-knack on my drum/With a knick-knack paddy-whack give the dog a bone/This old man came rolling home."

This is how professional techniques make a candidate seem to be a more attractive image candidate—a character that viewers like—on television.

ROCKEFELLER'S WAY

(Written and produced in April, 1964. Length: 4:16. Camera: Hugh Valentine. Narrator: Brett Morrison. Father's voice: Karl Weber. Music: arranged by Jerry Bilik; edited by Ross-Gaffney, Inc.)

FADE IN

PHOTO OF MARCHING BAND: ZOOM IN TO SIMULATE MARCHING MOVEMENT	(*Music:* FULL BAND, "BATTLE CRY" THEME, AVAILABLE FROM THOS. J. VALENTINO INC. UNDER TITLE "FREEDOM ARISE" MUSICAL BACKGROUND)
N.A.R. IN OPEN CAR,[2] PARADE	
N.A.R. AUTOGRAPHING BASS DRUM	
N.A.R. AND HAPPY, NEAR BUS, WAVING TO CROWD	
HUGE CROWD: N.A.R. IN CENTER	

MAIN TITLE ZOOMS FORWARD
TO FILL SCREEN

"ROCKEFELLER'S WAY"

DISSOLVE TO:

(*Music:* SINGLE CORNET PICKS UP
"BATTLE CRY" THEME)

PLAQUE AT ROCKEFELLER CENTER,
SLOW ZOOM IN SO THAT
VIEWERS CAN READ
INSCRIPTION

NARRATOR (VO):
On a granite slab,
John D., Junior,
had his personal credo
engraved for the world to see.
He was Nelson's father.

C.U. WORDS ON PLAQUE

FATHER (SLIGHT ECHO EFFECT):
I believe
in the supreme worth
of the individual
and in his right
to life, liberty
and the pursuit of happiness.

SLOW PAN UPWARD
FROM PLAQUE TO
TOWER OF
30 ROCKEFELLER PLAZA

(*Music:* CORNET ENDS IN STING
BY MALE VOICES)

DISSOLVE TO:

(*Music:* MALE VOICES BEGIN
HUMMING "BATTLE CRY"
THEME B.G.)

BARE GIRDERS OF SAME
BUILDING, UNDER CON-
STRUCTION IN THE 1930's

NARRATOR:
In the depths of the Depression
young Nelson Rockefeller
stood here,

CONSTRUCTION WORKERS

WORKERS ON GIRDERS

fighting to keep
Rockefeller Center alive

YOUNG N.A.R.
WITH WORKERS
AT DEDICATION
CEREMONY

DISSOLVE TO:

and its workers on the job.
Defying bad economic news,
he began a program
of employee benefits
which won him the respect
of organized labor
that has lasted to this day.

AERIAL VIEW:
SOUTH AMERICAN CITY

SHANTIES

HUNGRY PEASANTS

HOUSES BEING BUILT,
N.A.R. WITH LABORERS

Then a business trip
to South America
opened the challenge
of a whole continent
where most people
knew nothing but poverty.
Rockefeller worked in Venezuela
to bring decent living conditions,
small private businesses,
and democratic institutions.

N.A.R. WITH F.D.R.

N.A.R. TALKING TO
GENERALS

When World War Two exploded
President Roosevelt
put him in charge
of our effort to get
first Nazis, then Communists,
out of Latin America.

N.A.R. WITH
STETTINIUS

ESTADOS UNIDOS MEETING

UNITED NATIONS
OPENING CEREMONY

Later,
as Assistant Secretary of State,
Rockefeller carried the fight
behind the scenes
of the United Nations opening,
getting a provision
in the U.N. Charter
that was the seed
of today's N.A.T.O. alliance.

N.A.R. WITH TRUMAN
AND GLOBE OF WORLD:
ZOOM BACK

For Harry Truman,
Rockefeller developed Point IV,
our foreign aid program.

N.A.R. BEING SWORN IN
BY EISENHOWER

For President Eisenhower,
he cut down waste
and duplication in government.

IKE SHAKING HANDS WITH N.A.R.	First as organizer and then as Undersecretary of a new Department of Health, Education and Welfare, Nelson Rockefeller fought to expand Social Security for millions of Americans.
N.A.R. WITH BIG ORGANIZATION CHART	
N.A.R. WITH ELDERLY LADY	
GENEVA BLDG., EXT.	Then, back on the international scene as Eisenhower's Director of Cold War Strategy, he came up with the "open skies" inspection proposal at Geneva which caught the Russians with their propaganda pants down.
GENEVA: N.A.R. WITH GROUP AROUND CONFERENCE TABLE	
BULGANIN	
N.A.R.: SATISFIED	
BULGANIN AND MOLOTOV LOOK AT EACH OTHER, PERPLEXED	This was Rockefeller's Way.
N.A.R. SATISFIED WITH HIMSELF: CLOSE SHOT DISSOLVE TO:	(*Music:* START "LU, LU, LU" SINGING OF THEME IN CLEAR)
N.A.R. WITH IMPORTANT PEOPLE: WITH DEGAULLE WITH MAKARIOS WITH MARTIN LUTHER KING	
DISSOLVE TO:	(*Music:* UNDER FOR BACKGROUND)
PHOTO OF 1958 N.Y. STATE REPUBLICAN CONVENTION	NARRATOR: New York in 1958 was another fight against odds: to win the governorship when the majority of voters were Democrats, and to do something about growing unemployment,
CLOSE UP: CONVENTION SIGN "AVE ROCKEFELLER, VALE HARRIMAN"	

1958
ELECTION NIGHT
VICTORY SCENE

industries leaving the state
and social problems
left unsolved.

N.A.R. AND AIDE WALKING
DOWN LONG HALL IN STATE
CAPITOL
VERY SLOW ZOOM IN TOWARD
N.A.R. TO SUSTAIN CAMERA
MOVEMENT AS TITLES ZOOM
FORWARD, ONE BY ONE:

But Nelson Rockefeller
is nothing if not a fighter
and his way in New York
is a matter of record.

(*Music:* THEME UP FULL)

"MORE JOBS"

"BETTER HOUSING"

"BUDGET BALANCED"

"EXPANDED COLLEGES"

"AID FOR THE AGING"

DISSOLVE TO:

(*Music:* THEME PLUS CORNET
COUNTERPOINT)

ROCKY-FOR-PRESIDENT BUS,
PAN SIDEWAYS TO SIMULATE
MOVEMENT OF BUS

CROWD UNDER MOVIE MARQUEE
WELCOMING N.A.R.

NARRATOR:
Now, in 1964,
Governor Nelson A. Rockefeller
campaigns again.

N.A.R. ON STREET,
CAMPAIGNING

WITH HAPPY AT TRAIN,
WAVING TO CROWD

WITH HAPPY AND BROWNIE GIRL
SCOUTS

(*Music:* CORNET COUNTERPOINT
TO "BATTLE CRY" THEME
BECOMES "THIS OLD MAN"
NURSERY TUNE)

WITH GROUP OF CHILDREN
ON LOCAL TV PROGRAM

BLONDE GIRL WITH HANDBAG

N.A.R. HUGGING CHILD

DISSOLVE TO:

(*Music:* CORNET FINISHES KIDDY
TUNE AND DROPS OUT;
VOICES GO BACK TO HUMMING)

N.A.R. SPEAKING,
 STATION KMJ

N.A.R. SPEAKING
 AT LECTERN

N.A.R. SPEAKING,
 PROFILE AT MEETING

N.A.R. SPEAKING
 TO BIG CROWD,
 SLOW ZOOM IN
 TO FACES IN CROWD
 LISTENING

ROCKEFELLER (ADD SLIGHT
 ECHO):
I entered the race
for the presidency
because I believe deeply
in certain basic principles
on which this country
was founded
and which have been responsible
for its rise to greatness
and because I want
to further these principles
and serve the American people.

COLLEGE GRADUATES
 LISTENING

STUDENTS STANDING UP,
 QUESTIONING

THREE GIRLS IN AUDIENCE

OLD MAN, HANDS ON HIPS,
 DOUBTING

NARRATOR:
Now
people are asking
what makes Rocky run
untiring in his fight
to help people get along.
The answer may be
that the faith of a father
is often engraved
on the heart of a son.

N.A.R. TRYING TO EXPLAIN
 SOMETHING TO MAN IN
 WESTERN HAT

N.A.R. ALONE
 IN FRONT OF
 BIG N.Y. STATE MAP:
 ZOOM IN SLOWLY

DISSOLVE TO:

FATHER (SLIGHT ECHO):
I believe
in the supreme worth
of the individual
and in his right
to life, liberty
and the pursuit of happiness.

PHOTO OF N.A.R.
  ALONE IN SPOTLIGHT
  ON DARK STAGE
START CLOSE UP
  AND PULL BACK SLOWLY
  TO END ON LONGEST
  POSSIBLE LONG SHOT

(*Music:* "BATTLE CRY" THEME
WITH CORNET COUNTERPOINT
BUILDS TO CONCLUSION)

NARRATOR:
Experience, strength, dedication:
these are the makings
of a president
who can face up
to the problems of modern times
for us.

TITLES SUPER OVER PHOTO
OF N.A.R. IN SPOTLIGHT:

"VOTE FOR GOVERNOR
NELSON A. ROCKEFELLER"

In the Republican Primary,
vote for Nelson Rockefeller.
He can keep
the promise of the future.

"HE CAN KEEP THE
PROMISE OF THE FUTURE"

(*Music:* ENDS)

FADE OUT

No matter how "good" this short film, *Rockefeller's Way,* seemed to make test audiences feel about the candidate, it could lose its persuasive power through overexposure in Oregon. After seeing it more than a few times, viewers might become too aware of its contrivances. Charlie Moore and I agreed that playing it once a day on every one of Oregon's television stations for the last two weeks preceding the May 15 Primary was enough, if not too much. But at least one other good piece of persuasive material seemed imperative because of the great change in attitudes that had to be effected in such a short time.

I put another five-minute film program into production, another attempt to characterize for viewers an attractive image of Nelson Rockfeller without letting the candidate himself appear on the home screen for fear of the moral-libertine image that such appearances would rouse.

The germ of the idea for this second film arose accidentally. One of the first things Jerry Danzig wanted me to do was to watch the candidate in action in a television studio. He hauled me out to Portland and sat me in a client's booth, where I could watch Governor Rockefeller below me in the studio and at the same time on a television monitor. That particular program was a two-hour telethon. Dave Garroway had flown in from New York to be the host. The governor answered questions that were phoned in, as well as some that were asked by members of a select studio audience.

The governor answered the questions with his usual sincerity and competence, a persuasive performance *if* viewers' minds were not already closed to anything he might have to say.

But only once in the two hours did that program rise out of its pedestrian rut and seem to be an emotionally moving experience. This was for a minute or so when a Negro minister in the studio audience stood up to ask a question and prefaced his question with a not-too-articulate but highly expressive favorable opinion of the Rockefeller family's efforts on behalf of civil rights over the years. Suddenly here was a "rich" character: genuine, believable, persuasive.

A few days later, Dennis Kane filmed this same minister in his church, framing up the camera so closely that the top of the man's head and neck were cut off by the top and bottom lines of "TV safety."[3] Dennis was lighting and shooting for character, not words: the tight profile of the dark face in left foreground in clear relief against the white front of the church altar with its simple black cross in right background. No attempt was made to put words into the minister's mouth. The only technique used was overshooting: letting the man talk until he forgot the camera rolling within a few feet of his face and the words began to flow naturally, from the heart.

REVEREND JACKSON: You can see his record in New York—and you can find out he's been a man that's fearless. He's patient. He's kind. He's loving—and he loves people from the lowest to the highest. He's able—and all in between. And he's able to—that's the reason why we need a man of that caliber for our President.[4]

Again, do not look at the words and think that they are incoherent or unimpressive. As voiced by the Reverend Jackson in front of the altar of his church, they were terribly coherent and very impressive. Most human beings somehow manage to express themselves very adequately without proper grammatical construction or a strictly logical flow of ideas expressed in a series of discrete sentences. The convincing is the total product of their tone of voice, their gestures, their facial expressions, and their character, as well as what they have to say.

Working as a visual artist, director Dennis Kane went on to make five other character vignettes for me. There was a carpenter seen through a ladder in his shop, busy planing a board as he spoke of Rockefeller's concern for the "little people." There was Ed Cone, the mayor of Eugene, speaking from his lumber mill about the governor's skills in public administration while great stacks of logs dumped into the water by the mill. (I could just picture Dennis signaling: "Cue the logs!") Mrs. Clara Halbertson Koeber was not just an old lady talking about the candidate, but a gentle elderly widow sitting on the front porch of her home, fondling one of her pet kittens as she recalled Governor Rockefeller's long experience in public office.

MRS. KOEBER: All we have to do is look into his background and see what he's done throughout the years. He has always—and never fallen down on the job. He's always concerned about peoples and their welfare: the Rockefeller Foundation, there's so many things too numerous to mention.

Dennis filmed Don Du Shane, dean of students, on the University of Oregon campus as students strolled by in the background. ("Cue the students!")

DON DU SHANE: The reason he goes out on the campaign trail, early morning until late at night, the reason he takes embarrassing questions, the reason he takes tough ones, the reason he works himself is that something about the United States of America and something in his character makes it impossible for him to just sit back and watch things take their own easy way.

I don't know what it is that makes a man give up a comfortable life and sacrifice it for the sake of his country and the people in the country, but whatever it is, Governor Rockefeller has it.

Du Shane's statement was, of course, placed last in this film, *The People Speak*, because it so clearly underscored the ancestral motivation aspect of the candidate's character that was being delineated by *Rockefeller's Way*.

Note that the main element of contrivance—other than the theatrical contrivances to make the presentation more effective—in these two five-minute film programs was a matter of *selection*. Nothing false about the candidate was being said. Governor Rockefeller is in fact tremendously dedicated, as are most of his brothers, to working social improvement in the world around him. He does in fact labor like a Trojan, from dawn to midnight, always on the move, always lugging a few battered attaché cases or bulging red manila envelopes with papers needing his personal attention. To those who know him well, it is fairly obvious that he cannot help himself. Since his earliest years, he must have been subject to some sort of indoctrination from the original John D. or from John D., Jr. (Nelson's father), that he has to justify the very privileged position to which he had been born or else consider himself a failure.

For an image specialist, given the challenges of the Oregon situation, it was a matter of selection—selecting this genuine ancestral motivation to emphasize so impressively via "paid political" television materials that the less attractive moral-libertine characterization of the governor's image seemed insignificant by comparison. This sort of selection is not falsehood. Thus, the propaganda materials stemming from it are true—as far as they go. Unquestionably, both aspects of character—ancestral motivation and moral libertine—were valid considerations for Oregon's Republican voters. Do they want a President who, in his personal life, has violated the prevailing mores of the country? Could Nelson Rockefeller as President assume stances on American morality, on divorce legislation, on the crucial problem of birth control? (He continues to father many more children than the average citizen can afford.) On the other hand, what more could voters want in high public office than a man who is selflessly dedicated to social improvement? Nelson Rockefeller is highly experienced, highly resourceful, and completely above suspicion that he looks for personal profit in his public practices.

The two films, *Rockefeller's Way* and *The People Speak,* each playing once a day on every one of Oregon's television stations for the two solid weeks before the primary may have helped keep Rockefeller's selfless dedication uppermost in Republican minds as they went to the polls on May 15, 1964.

On seeing the final cut of *The People Speak,* some of the smaller bureaucratic minds in the organization were disturbed by one statement by a housewife and wanted it edited out of the film. Dennis Kane had filmed Mrs. Ruth Lyon pushing a cart in a supermarket as she spoke to the camera about Governor Rockefeller. In editing, Jim Gaffney had divided Mrs. Lyon's footage into three parts so that she would appear recurrently in the film as a unifying character. The first time she was on the screen, her dialogue made the point that Governor Rockefeller was the only candidate strong enough to unite the entire Republican party and that "we need to unite to win the election." The second time up, Mrs. Lyon mentioned that she had not given the divorce and remarriage much thought because she does not choose her political leaders on the basis of their personal life. The third film clip was taken from the end of Mrs. Lyon's "take," when she was evidently getting tired of the whole procedure of having a camera poked at her while she was trying to shop.

MRS. LYON: I think he's a strong man. I think he would make a good President.
     I'm not going to talk any longer. (LAUGHS) I need a Coca-Cola.
(EXITS, PUSHING HER SHOPPING CART)

"What do you want to give the Coca-Cola people a free plug for?" asked some small organization types. "It diverts viewers from thinking about the candidate." (At least they weren't worried that viewers might think Governor Rockefeller was getting a payoff from Coca-Cola for including the remark.)
I gave them the standard two-minute version of the image-

candidate credo: "Look, our job is to create an attractive character or image of the candidate up there on the screen. Viewers are not going to remember any specific words that these people are saying about Rockefeller. All they will remember is an impression that the governor is a hero to a lot of people—to a carpenter, a lumberman, a minister, a widow, a college dean, and a couple of housewives. And the richer the characterizations of these people on the screen, the more impressive their opinions of Governor Rockefeller will be. Never mind Mrs. Lyon's exact words—never mind that she expresses the desire for a Coke—that's the kind of woman she is and the more she reveals of her true self, the more will be the ring of sincerity in everything she has to say about the candidate."

The Coca-Cola line stayed in *The People Speak* as it played over and over again on Oregon television stations. But I had the sad feeling that the organization types had let it go because they could not stand up to my own appearance, demeanor, and presentation in defending its inclusion. I don't think they understood a word of what I was talking about, because their own thinking had been for too long in terms of words and not in terms of images.

NOTES

1. Steven Ebbin, "Personality and Politics: An Analysis of the Basic Factors of Political Success" (unpublished doctoral dissertation, Syracuse University, 1960).
2. "N.A.R." is Nelson A. Rockefeller.
3. Because television tubes and screens are somewhat rounded, the full frame of motion picture film may not be seen by home viewers. Therefore, directors are guided in shooting and editing by a set of "TV safety" lines, which circumscribe a smaller frame area within which all action and titles can safely be presumed to be seen by viewers.
4. Reverend Edgar L. Jackson, All Nations Church of the Nazarene, Portland, Oregon. Dialogue for *The People Speak*, Rockefeller National Campaign Committee film produced in April, 1964.

15

THERE IS NOTHING LIKE A
VILLAIN TO MAKE A HERO

Toward the end of April, when prints of the two short image films were en route to television stations in Oregon, Charlie Moore flung cigarette ash around his carpeted office at 521 Fifth Avenue and agreed with me that the California primary election scheduled for Tuesday, June 2, was going to be a very different kettle of f-i-s-h. Republicans in California were going to have two choices on the ballot, and two choices only, since no write-ins were allowed. They could vote for a slate of delegates to the Republican national convention that was pledged to support the presidential candidacy of Nelson A. Rockefeller. Or they could choose the slate of delegates pledged to support Barry M. Goldwater.

And Barry Goldwater was approaching the California primary in a very privileged position. He was the avowed conservative candidate. Most of the Republican organizations, especially in

Southern California, had been taken over by conservative and ultraconservative factions. Therefore, the main thrust of the party machinery in getting out the vote on primary day would be in getting out the conservative Republicans. The less active and probably less conservative Republicans would tend to stay home on primary day, as less active members of a political party usually do.

GENE: I'll tell you, Charlie, I did a study of the 1961 mayoral campaigns in New York City for my Ph.D. thesis and the situation in the primary struggle between Mayor Wagner and Arthur Levitt for the Democratic nomination wasn't too dissimilar from this Rockefeller/Goldwater/California situation. The mayor himself wasn't any great shakes of a hero image, but Levitt came across on television as a first-class bastard and Wagner focused his attack on Carmine De Sapio, a first-class political boss who became the villain of the piece. In the dramatic contrast and conflict between Mayor Wagner on one hand and the Levitt–De Sapio forces of evil on the other, the mayor managed to stampede a few hundred thousand less active Democrats to the polls who normally might have stayed home on primary day and left the field clear for the active organization-minded Democrats to elect the organization's candidate, Levitt.

CHARLIE: So Nelson doesn't look that much better than Barry on television.

GENE: Just right: the governor and Barry will come off as equally attractive images until you throw an image *villain* into the campaign, a villainous force that is clearly allied with Goldwater and clearly opposed by Rockefeller. There is nothing like a first-class villain to make a first-class hero in image-candidate terms.

CHARLIE: So who's the villain? Ronald Reagan maybe?

GENE: *They* are the villains, a collective They, an anonymous hateful They, a vicious violent They—The Extremists—the ultraconservatives whose paranoiac fantasies about communist conspirators in every walk of American life have caused them to libel, slander, persecute, bomb, and God knows what else, to take control of the California Junior Republicans and the California Republican Assemblies and a good part of the regular state party mechanism in an attempt to gain the political power needed to stop the march of time and turn the country back to simpler days, to the innocence of earlier years, to fundamentalist religion, to red-white-and-blue-July-4th patriotism, to no-entangling-alliances and no United Nations, to no income tax and no psychiatry and no fluoridation. . . .

CHARLIE: Can a faceless enemy be an influence on voting?
GENE: You bet it can. Whitaker and Baxter have been using it for years.[1]
CHARLIE: So what do you want to do in California?
GENE: I want to make one half-hour program—nonfiction, stark, simple, dramatic—that characterizes the extremists as the villains against whom Nelson Rockefeller is crusading in California. I want you to buy two or three half-hour periods, day time and prime evening time, on every television station in the state during the two or three days just before June 2. I guarantee you that what I put up on the home screens will not only rouse a few hundred thousand less active Republicans to go out to the polls and vote for Nelson Rockefeller as the champion of extremists' victims, but that the national media will pick up the conflict and put our candidate back up on a white horse again, because the national press has long been a target of extremist attacks.
CHARLIE: So we'll give it a try. I'll see you in California.

The Agent from 521 Fifth slammed the door of his bungalow behind the Ambassador Hotel and considered the gnawing anxiety that usually preceded irrevocable deadlines. There were nineteen days, including Saturdays and Sundays, between his arrival in California and Wednesday, May 27, the last date on which *The Extremists* could go before videotape cameras and be ready for a heavy schedule of play dates on California stations between Thursday night, May 28, and Monday night, June 1, primary eve. Nineteen days to research, write, and produce a job like that, and the traffic was so heavy on Wilshire Boulevard at 5:30 on Tuesdays and Thursdays that getting to the Beverly Hills "Y" for badminton was out of the question. Fortunately, the Agent had a second-best socially approved escape from professional tensions, playing revival hymns on the organ. And, more fortunately, there was a showroom of the Allen Organ Company just across Wilshire from the Ambassador. The first time one of the Rockefeller organization types came across the Agent giving out with 'Let the Lower Lights Be Burning" in the Allen show window, he shuddered violently and expressed his relief that campaigns did not come more often.

Jerry Danzig sent his cute secretary, Seena, down from Oregon to organize the big front room of the bungalow into a working office and the dressing room between the bungalow's two front baths into a working bar. Wes Willoughby, who had an encyclopedic knowledge of extremist organizations and a vast sampling of their literature, joined the program unit, coming either from Senator Kuchel's staff or from Spencer-Roberts, the Los Angeles advertising agency that was handling Governor Rockefeller's California campaign. Immediately after the May 15 Oregon primary, Dennis Kane (director), Dick Swicker (unit manager), and Jerry Danzig (executive producer) moved into adjacent bungalows.

As our knowledge of and contacts with extremist groups grew, day by day, we began to realize that perhaps our image villains were real people. One afternoon, Seena came running in from one of her "pool breaks," dripping all over a first draft of the script.

SEENA: I just saw a Minute Man!
WES WILLOUGHBY: How did you know it was a Minute Man?
SEENA: He had a helmet on and he was carrying a lead pipe, like the bomb that blew up Reverend Simmons' house.
GENE: Maybe a plumber?
SEENA: Don't be a smart-nose. We could be killed!
WES (PICKING UP CUTTY SARK): I'll hit him with a bottle.
GENE: You're supposed to smash the bottle and hit him with the jagged glass.
WES: Could I drink what's in it first?

Four highballs later, there wasn't a Minute Man to be seen—only Charlie Moore, putting golf balls and dropping cigarette ash on the hotel green. He suggested that we try looking in Lexington or Concord.

In Beverly Hills, a psychiatrist talked to me before his first patient arrived. I took notes.

NOTES RE WHY EXTREMISTS IN CALIFORNIA: Calif. a state of newcomers, esp. So. Cal., made glamorous by dreamworld of Hollywood.
Newcomers mostly those who were not adjusted and getting along well in their home towns, but who were driven by their un-

realistic dreams and community pressures to seek a better life in an El Dorado: the malcontents, the dissidents, the unstable, the unemployed.

Being disoriented to established and stable institutions of society, they tend to drift into more extreme organizations whose view of the world is black-and-white simple, childlike.

The tendency of these groups to hate change in society is the collective tendency of the unstable members who, unsuccessful in growing up themselves, want to hold society to blame for their unhappiness and insecurity.

The head shrinker's conclusions appeared to be validated somewhat as I traveled around the state, talking to victims of extremist groups. In Visalia, a college teacher told me of the vituperation that had been heaped on him because he dared to oppose the local cell of the John Birch Society, which was trying to ban the *Dictionary of American Slang* from school libraries because it contained "dirty words." In northern California, another teacher told me how one of her students had secretly recorded what she said in class because extremist groups suspected her of being too liberal in her favorable opinions about the United Nations. A film actress showed me headlines reporting how a small office that she and some friends opened in North Hollywood for the American Association for the United Nations had been demolished by a lead-pipe bomb. Then there was the Reverend Simmons.

DAVE GARROWAY: The Reverend John Simmons, Lutheran, organized a chapter of the American Association for the United Nations in his North Hollywood church. He blocked right-wing efforts to get information about UNESCO barred from the schools. He resisted extremist attempts to dominate the local schoolboard. He started a mental health clinic in his parish.

The Reverend John Simmons.

(THE LIGHTS GO DOWN ON GARROWAY; LEAVING REVEREND SIM-MONS ALONE IN THE SOLITARY "WITNESS CHAIR" ON A SMALL DAIS CENTER STAGE.

BEHIND REVEREND SIMMONS, THE HUGE BLOWN-UP PHOTOS OF FIVE EXTREMIST LEADERS GLARE DOWN ON HIM FROM WHERE THEY HANG ON THE SURREALISTIC SCAFFOLDING.)

REVEREND SIMMONS: The hate mail—the anonymous phone calls—began to come in the mid-1950s. The hate mail was usually sent anonymously, often with a penned note. Others of it came from extremist front organizations.

Whatever they said was that if you were in favor of the United Nations, you were subversive. They called you a communist.

The phone calls—well, they came all hours of the day and night. When the phone calls would come, I would answer or worse still my younger children or my wife would answer and a voice on the other end would say "Your father is a Commie—and we're going to get him."

Or they would only breathe very heavily into the phone and hang it up, only to call back again.

Sometimes in sheer desperation, in order that my family might get some rest, at two or three o'clock in the morning, I would turn the phone off by taking it off the hook, something I didn't want to do because I felt a responsibility to my parishioners in case they needed me.

(LIGHTS GO UP AND FOCUS SHIFTS TO DAVE GARROWAY IN THE FOREGROUND)

GARROWAY: On the first of February, 1962, Reverend Simmons was invited to be in a panel discussion at Temple Sinai on Wilshire Boulevard in Los Angeles.

The subject was "Is the Radical Right a Threat to Democracy?"

(LIGHT FADES ON GARROWAY AND FOCUS RETURNS TO REVEREND SIMMONS IN THE WITNESS CHAIR)

REVEREND SIMMONS: We were halfway through the meeting when Reverend Brooks Walker, a fellow member of the panel, was suddenly called to the telephone. He was gone for a few minutes and then returned to the auditorium, white as a sheet, and shouted: "My home has just been bombed!"

I'd only one thought at the moment—my own home. I ran from the auditorium to a telephone. Our line was busy. When I finally got through, I found out that I was too late. My home had been bombed too.

A bomb had been placed underneath the front window. When it exploded, the lead casing had ripped the glass and ripped through the house, just missing my wife's head with a piece of lead pipe by a few inches.

These extremists had already bombed my home and I went home.

I still wonder to this day, what kind of people are these who, when a man—or a father—is away from his home, will bomb it, threatening the lives of his wife and children.

May the Lord forgive them.

After the Reverend Simmons left the witness chair, Carl B. Pearlston, Jr., made his way slowly toward it, using two aluminum forearm crutches. This was a case of my "falling into it" as far as dramatic effect of the program was concerned. Pearlston's crippled condition was a temporary part of his convalescence from a recent leg or hip operation, but it made him look as if he had suffered great physical violence at the hands of the extremists that he was about to describe.

Pearlston was a graduate engineer (United States Naval Academy) and a Republican. He had tried to conduct a public forum in the Torrance High School auditorium on local problems of human relations and equal opportunities for racial minority groups. All his speakers were established state or local officials, but . . .

CARL PEARLSTON: . . . but *They* had made up their minds not to allow any public discussion on that subject. They were 30 or 40 people out of an audience of 400. Some were dressed alike in loud Hawaiian sport shirts as if it was a uniform.

They started shouting: "Is this a communist organization? Are you people in the audience communists?" . . .

The evening ended in chaos, which is what They wanted. I brought charges against the ones who had rushed up on the stage. They were convicted of disturbing the peace. They were also identified in court as local leaders of the John Birch Society.

One postscript I'd like to add. They have control of the Torrance Republican club now. As a matter of fact, extremists have control of just about every Republican club and Young Republican club in the South Bay area. When you go to meetings, they put out the Birch Blue Book, pamphlets by Billy James Hargis and the Courtneys and items such as that for sale.

I've been asked by them to get out of the Republican party. They don't believe there is any room in the party for anyone who disagrees with them.

The third witness on the program was Mrs. Bernice Wilson,

a grandmotherly retired schoolteacher, a Phi Beta Kappa graduate of the University of California. For twenty-five years, Mrs. Wilson had been an active Republican, often doing volunteer jobs at election time. Then, when she was serving as president of the Oakland Republican Assembly, They came.

MRS. WILSON: . . . more than a hundred of them, most of whom were not members, some of whom didn't even live in Oakland, or not even in Alameda County. They almost broke down the doors of the hotel dining room that we had rented.

I held them off for five and a half hours. Sometimes I thought it was like facing a howling mob. They kept on being disorderly until after midnight until most of our regular members went home in disgust.

Then they moved to unseat me. I turned the gavel over to another officer, who didn't fight them. They voted themselves into control. They all voted regardless of their lack of membership in the Oakland Republican Assembly.

In later weeks they moved in much the same tactic, with many of the same people, to take over the Berkeley Republican Assembly and then the Eden Township Republican Assembly.

Perhaps I should have been a stronger chairman. But I did hold them off—for almost five and a half hours.

These were courageous people: the Reverend Simmons, Carl Pearlston, and Bernice Wilson. They had no doubts about how much fresh abuse would descend on them because of appearing on this program. But they were willing to take it because they believed that a man like Nelson Rockefeller could indeed champion them and everyone who had been so badly mistreated by extremist elements in the state. There was no reason to believe that their hopes would be betrayed. Before they went on camera, Wednesday, May 27, they watched Governor Rockefeller record his opening three minutes of The Extremists.

GOVERNOR ROCKEFELLER: Good evening.

I have spoken out many times about the continuing effort of right-wing extremists to turn the Republican party away from its traditional path of moderation.

Nowhere has that effort been more intense than in the State of California. And no date seems more important in the calendar of the extremists than next Tuesday, June 2, when they are making their bid for great influence, if not control, over the state Republican party.

I believe every Republican in California should clearly understand this aspect of what his or her vote can mean on primary day. To further this understanding, I ask you to watch this next half-hour, as my good friend Dave Garroway reviews who the extremists are, reading from their own literature as to what they stand for and hearing eye-witness testimony about extremist tactics at the community level when you try to oppose them.

When you line up the evidence like this, all at one time, in the cold light of day, the extremists emerge as an incredible fringe on the American political scene.

I would prefer not to give any more publicity to what they have to say about President Eisenhower, Vice-President Nixon, Ambassador Lodge, Chief Justice Warren, President Kennedy, and myself.

But in all conscience, I could not pass this way, as a candidate for the presidency of the United States, and leave this job undone— and leave these people undenounced to continue their undermining of the Republican party, of the people of California, indeed of the nation itself.

Dave Garroway did a beautiful job in the studio that day. Not many television performers have his unique talent for reaching out and involving viewers in whatever he is talking about—Arlene Francis, perhaps, and Jack Paar and Arthur Godfrey, but not many.

Garroway conveyed the incredible garish fantasies of the extremists. There was the map they were circulating that showed the United States divided into new regions, each policed by United Nations troops such as Russians and Mongolians. There was the newspaper headline (Los Angeles *Mirror*, December 13, 1961) telling how an anticommunist meeting at the Shrine Auditorium had cheered when a speaker called for the hanging of Chief Justice Earl Warren. There was the February, 1964, issue of the John Birch Society's *American Opinion* magazine, with its explanation that President Kennedy was really a communist agent who was assassinated by his Russian masters because he was failing to subvert America on schedule. (Garroway held this document up gingerly and advised viewers to "take a bath" right after they read it.)

The name of Senator Barry Goldwater was mentioned nowhere on the program, nor was the evidence of Birchers and other extremists among the Goldwater slate of delegates presented. After the emotionally moving survey of extremist literature and the personal testimony of the three eye-witnesses, Garroway wrapped up the half-hour by holding up a copy of the *Los Angeles Times* with the headline "HOW ULTRA-CONSERVATIVES COULD TAKE OVER THE STATE G.O.P."

GARROWAY: As you can read in the papers almost every day now, the extremists—or ultraconservatives as they are sometimes called—are in position to dominate the whole state Republican party now. If that happens, they will dedicate themselves to unreal legislation far out of the mainstream of American thought.

The hope is, as Governor Rockefeller said, that the vast majority of California Republicans will come out of their homes on primary day in overwhelming numbers and use their vote to reject extremism and to reaffirm the Republican party's dedication to realistic, reasonable, responsible government.

This is Dave Garroway. Courage.

The very last minute or so of the program was strictly a visual reprise of extremist materials that had figured in Garroway's narration: car bumpers saying "PAY YOUR INCOME TAXES— KHRUSHCHEV NEEDS THE MONEY" and "STAMP OUT COMMUNISM"; headlines such as "BOMB BLASTS HIT TWO MINISTERS"; and the huge photos of the extremist leaders hanging on the scaffold. A single snare drum, the only musical instrument used in the half-hour, tapped steadily. Then an animated "X" slashed across the screen. The "X" receded in size until it became the "x" in the maintitle: *The Extremists*. Fade out.

On the night of Wednesday, May 27, 1964, seven videotape dubs of the program were made in the KTLA editing room. *The Extremists* was to start playing on stations around the state on the next evening, bicycling and repeating on a heavy schedule until primary eve, four days later.

On Thursday morning, May 28, Charlie Moore and Jerry

Danzig arranged a catered-breakfast screening of *The Extremists*. I was not invited, nor did I try to get invited, figuring that this would be a moment of glory for Charlie and Jerry and my purposes would be better served by letting them bask in it alone. Some of the most prominent Republicans in California, such as Leonard Firestone and Senator Thomas Kuchel, attended that screening. So did Governor Rockefeller. So did the governor's most intimate aides and advisers, Dr. William Ronan and press secretary Robert McManus, both of whom were strangers to me at the time.

That afternoon, Charlie Moore, Jerry Danzig, and one or two others who had been at that breakfast screening told me everything that had happened. Everybody had been deeply moved by *The Extremists* and broke into spontaneous applause when it was over. Then the local Republicans and the inner circle proceeded to argue against showing the program for two different reasons: political expediency and intraorganization rivalry.

POLITICAL EXPEDIENCY

I had been halfway through preparation of *The Extremists* on May 15 when Oregon Republicans trooped to the polls and gave Rockefeller a total of 93,000 votes to 78,000 for Lodge, 50,000 for Goldwater and 48,000 for Nixon. Although poll takers in Oregon had spotted the Lodge lead crumbling, none had predicted a Rockefeller victory of this scope.

To California Republicans who preferred anyone to Senator Goldwater, the Oregon returns were a heartening sign that perhaps Nelson Rockefeller was still popular with voters and could indeed be relied upon to stop Goldwater from getting the 1964

	Preferring Goldwater	*Preferring Rockefeller*	*Undecided*
Before Oregon primary	48%	39%	13%
Five days after Oregon	36	47	17
Ten days after Oregon	39	48	13

presidential nomination. Rockefeller's stock zoomed in popularity with California Republicans after May 15, according to surveys by the Lou Harris organization.

Since all the public-opinion polls on Thursday morning, May 28, were showing that Governor Rockefeller would defeat Senator Goldwater in voting by Republicans on the following Tuesday, June 2, "why," went the argument of California Republicans at *The Extremists* breakfast screening, "why rock the boat and unduly enrage the party's conservative and ultraconservative members with whom the more moderate and liberal Republican leaders would have to go on living after 1964?"

As reported to me, Governor Rockefeller was reluctant to go along with this reasoning because the persecution of innocent people by the extremists had been so marked in California. But then his closest advisers urged him to scrap the program, and to their advice he had to yield lest by overruling them at that moment, he might endanger the badly needed stability and efficiency of the organization.

INTRAORGANIZATION RIVALRY

"What did Bill Ronan and Bob McManus line up against it for?" I asked of some of the disconsolate television division people who dragged themselves back to the Ambassador on that Thursday before the California primary.

"Don't be naïve," came the answer. "*The Extremists* came out of left field from our part of the organization. Ronan and McManus didn't know about it. They weren't consulted about it. You can bet it was dead with them from the moment people at the screening applauded. Do you think they are going to let that show become public and make the governor into a hero when they didn't have anything to do with it?"

Jerry Danzig tried to cheer me up with a contract renewal. I went across Wilshire Boulevard and bought that organ in the Allen show window. For two hours, I played every hymn I knew with all stops down.

What happened next in California was a striking example of image reversal. Nelson Rockefeller's image shattered. Barry Goldwater's image suddenly seemed more attractive than ever to registered Republicans.

Saturday, May 30, was the Day of Doom. Nelson Rockefeller, Jr., was born to Margaretta Fitler Murphy Rockefeller on that day.

I was filming Senator Kuchel that afternoon, in a high place: the helicopter pad atop a downtown Los Angeles hotel, as my half-hearted contribution to some sort of primary eve television program that Dennis Kane and Jerry Danzig were trying to put together. I was worried that Senator Kuchel would be blown off the edge. The senator was worried about Happy's baby: "This can do it. This can open up all the old wounds. This can remind voters of the question of morality in Nelson's divorce and remarriage!"

If there was ever a wrong day on which to contrast Rockefeller immorality against Goldwater righteousness, Saturday, May 30, was it. Memorial Day: just the perfect setting for Barry Goldwater. And sure enough, in honor of America's honorable dead—in honor of America's honor—there was the senator from Arizona inspiring crowds to cheer themselves hoarse at red-white-and-blue rallies that could not be denied or excused as fundamentalist exercises.

	California Republicans		
Date of Survey	Preferring Goldwater	Preferring Rockefeller	Undecided
Friday, May 29	40%	49%	11%
Sunday, May 31	40	42	18
Monday, June 1	44	44	12

Senator Barry Goldwater won the June 2 California primary by 1,089,133 votes to Rockefeller's 1,030,180, a plurality of about 60,000. As expected, a good number of the state's registered Republicans—850,000, or about 29 percent of the 2,895,448 total—stayed home and did not vote in the primary.

If, if *The Extremists* had been allowed to present its particular aspect of the campaign drama, sharpening the hero image of Nelson Rockefeller by presenting him as the sworn opponent of the powerful despicable They, perhaps a few hundred thousand of those less active, less aware Republicans might have been roused enough to vote in the primary. Perhaps the hero image as characterized by *The Extremists* might have survived in more Republican minds under the dual onslaught of the baby and Memorial Day, both of which appeared to cause a revision in public attitudes about the two candidates.

If, if Barry Goldwater had lost the California primary, that would have meant three losses in a row (New Hampshire, Oregon, California) when Republican voters did the choosing of presidential candidates. Three losses in a row might have been ample basis for a move at the Republican convention to keep the nomination from going to Goldwater.

The antagonism of pro-Goldwater delegates and other anti-Rockefeller sentiment at the convention probably would have prevented the governor from getting the nomination, but Richard Nixon or Henry Cabot Lodge might have been named, either of whom could have attracted more votes than the luckless Goldwater, whose issue positions (and manner of stating them) appeared to be frightening to a substantial part of the electorate. Against Nixon or Lodge, President Johnson might have been reelected by a much smaller margin and, post-'64, might not have been so confident that his actions were supported by a consensus of the people. In the absence of a Democratic landslide, Republican candidates for various levels of public office might have done much better and a more reasonable semblance of two-party balance might have been maintained across the country. In Illinois, Charles Percy probably would have been elected governor. New York State voters probably would have returned Republic Kenneth Keating to another term in the Senate. And Bobby Kennedy, whose defeat of Keating was helped considerably by the Johnson landslide, might still be on the political sidelines.

But *if* did not happen. *The Extremists* was never shown in public and probably never will be except in propaganda classes as a political curio a generation from now.

Ironically, just the day after canceling *The Extremists,* Governor Rockefeller had to admit in public that extremists among Senator Goldwater's supporters were responsible for cancellation of two Rockefeller speaking engagements and also for more than two hundred telephoned bomb threats against the Rockefeller campaign office in Los Angeles.[2]

And, less than two months later, Governor Rockefeller was booed and heckled before a nationwide audience of viewers watching television coverage of the Republican Convention when he tried to introduce a plank in the 1964 Republican platform that denounced extremists and declared them unwelcome in the party.

But it was too late. He was now an interloper at Barry Goldwater's convention and the extremists had a firm foothold in the machinery of the Republican party.

NOTES

1. The late Clem Whitaker and Leone Baxter, man and wife, were very effective political propagandists operating out of San Francisco. Stanley Kelley, Jr., in *Public Relations and Political Power* (Baltimore: Johns Hopkins University Press, 1956), describes some of the Whitaker-Baxter use of the "faceless enemy" in local and national campaigns designed to influence public opinion.
2. *The New York Times,* May 30, 1964, p. 6.

16

AN EXERCISE IN FUTILITY

That contract renewal had a hook in it, and I was reeled in by the organization about three weeks after the June 2 debacle. The first thing I knew, the whole itinerant television department—Jerry Danzig, Dennis Kane, Dick Swicker, Seena Schnall, and The Writer—were installed in a motel about ten miles north of Scranton, Pennsylvania, in between some man-made hills of waste matter from the coal mines and a high viaduct of the Pennsylvania Turnpike, on which big trucks, rushing through the nights, sounded something like cash-receipt cylinders going through the pneumatic tubes in old-time department stores. Nobody knew of a badminton court nearby and Dennis Kane installed his big judo-trained body on my bed to make sure that I didn't go looking for the nearest church organ. Nothing bothers Dennis Kane. He is a very relaxed expert. To him the whole world is a location, and once he has scanned his immediate surroundings with his mental viewfinder, he goes to sleep, waiting for the script that will bring it alive before his cameras. It was Thursday morning, June 25, 1964, and very hot in the coal country.

After June 2, the handwriting on the walls of the Cow Palace in San Francisco, where the Republican national convention was to convene in six weeks, said, "BARRY GOLDWATER ON THE FIRST BALLOT," in letters so big that former President Eisenhower, former Vice-President Richard Nixon, Michigan Governor George Romney, Pennsylvania Governor William Scranton, and probably every other prominent Republican in the country could read it and quake. Now none of the so-called "moderate" Republican leaders could excuse their own lack of participation in past primary campaigns because Nelson Rockefeller was putting up such a staunch fight against Goldwater.

On Saturday, June 6, in response to a telephone call from the former President, Governor Scranton motored down to Gettysburg and there, apparently, was led to believe that *he* was now Dwight D. Eisenhower's choice to be the 1964 Republican nominee.

At least this was the gist of headlines in the morning papers of Sunday, June 7, as Scranton arrived at a governor's conference in Cleveland with plans to announce his last-minute, last-ditch, Eisenhower-backed fight against Goldwater on a network television program, *Face the Nation*, that was originating from Cleveland.

Evidently, President Eisenhower saw the same headlines and was disturbed by them. He placed a call to Governor Scranton in Cleveland to make sure that Scranton did *not* think that Eisenhower was backing him over Goldwater or any other Republican hopeful.

On television, Governor Scranton was still shaken and flustered by this unexpected turn of events. He compromised his intentions by saying on the air that he did not plan to go out and try to defeat Senator Goldwater.[1]

In *The Making of the President 1964,* author Theodore H. White summed up Scranton's misadventures at the governor's conference in Cleveland.

THEODORE WHITE: [Scranton] had known immediately after his Sunday *Face the Nation* appearance how weak and vacillating a personality he had displayed. His aides, with a frankness permitted them because of their adoration, had told him after the broadcast that it had been a "complete and utter bomb." Scranton was almost a joke; one of his fellow governors had referred to him as "Gutless Bill." The press had called him "the toothless tiger." He had tried to organize, overnight, a campaign for Romney, but on Tuesday afternoon, Romney had quit. . . .

He was alone.[2]

On Thursday, June 11, from the governor's mansion at Indiantown Gap, Pennsylvania, William Scranton sought to redeem himself. He announced his intention to take the 1964 Republican presidential nomination away from Barry Goldwater. Scranton's hope and plan was to build such a ground swell of rank-and-file Republican sentiment in the remaining four weeks before the convention that the delegates would have to acknowledge it and deny Goldwater the nomination. While Eisenhower's endorsement was no longer a sure thing, William Scranton did know of one prominent and sure ally in his anti-Goldwater crusade: Nelson A. Rockefeller.

Money had materialized for the purchase of a prime-time half-hour on the CBS television network, 9:30 Sunday evening, June 28. The organization's television department had been hastily reassembled and shipped to Pennsylvania with instructions to make Governor Scranton look like a hero and help him persuade a couple of million viewers to write a flood of pro-Scranton (anti-Goldwater) letters and telegrams that would make an undeniable deluge on the convention floor.

As I said, it was Thursday, June 25, and very hot. Furthermore, all I knew about William Warren Scranton was what was said in one or two hastily prepared throwaways. There were something over eighty hours until air and no guests, no film clips, no stills of the candidate, no videotape inserts, no musical background cues—just a location, Marworth, the elegant family home, which seemed to be the only feasible stage set available on short notice for a presentation that would enhance the image of the candidate and make his plea to viewers more persuasive.

Dennis and I had worked out a production schedule to the minute. Sometime in the small hours of Saturday night, a huge Teletape mobile television unit would arrive at Marworth from another location. At dawn, with or without sleep, the Teletape technicians would start setting up: running camera, microphone, and lighting cables into the various rooms of the big house and onto terraces for outdoor scenes, all connecting to the elaborate control room and bank of videotape recorders in the truck. By noon, before noon if possible, Dennis was to start putting the show together, rehearsing and recording sequence by sequence, all to be spliced together into the finished half-hour by about seven o'clock, when a small helicopter would be waiting on the lawn to carry Dennis and the videotape above the Sunday traffic to the West 40th Street heliport in Manhattan. There a CBS car or messenger would be waiting to rush the tape to the network control room.

Everything had been worked out to the minute, except what was going to go on the screen.

I spent a few hours alone, wandering the grounds and the ground-floor rooms at Marworth trying to envision "scenes" in a half-hour story that would generate some audience emotion about Governor Scranton, scenes that would help characterize him as an exciting and powerful man, as presidential timbre, as the man who should be carrying the Republican banner against Lyndon Johnson in 1964.

But the character of Scranton as the powerful crusader refused to jell, something about the house—something I could not put my finger on right away—was striking a discordant note. In the gallerylike formal living room, portraits of seven generals hung on the walls, officers under whom Scranton men had served in every war that had been fought for America's freedom. But the biggest, and by far the most impressive portrait in the house, was that of a woman: a determined and perhaps dominating woman.

She was his mother, the late Marian Margery Warren Scranton. They called her "the Duchess." At age sixteen, as a teen-age suffragette, she had picketed the state legislature in Harrisburg, demanding votes for women. When that goal was won, she moved to take over the Lackawanna County Republican Committee. In 1928, she had become Pennsylvania's Republican national committeewoman and, in later years, vice-chairman of the Republican National Committee.

The Duchess had apparently nursed her only son, Bill, on politics. And, just as apparently, she had dominated him in his earliest formative years, dominated him as she dominated his father and the entire Scranton household. In what must have been an act of rare masculine assertion, the father had finally stood up to the Duchess and insisted that young Bill be sent away from Marworth, away from his mother and his sisters, away from a household full of strong females.

As this sort of information about the candidate came my way from eye-witnesses, a danger signal began to sound in the back of my mind. What had Governor Scranton been called publicly for his spineless behavior at that governor's conference in Cleveland? Wasn't it "Gutless Bill" and "the toothless tiger"? On television interviews during June, had I not seen the governor's wife, Mary, who had seemed to be a strong woman, very sure of herself?

If William Warren Scranton was at heart a man whose conditioned behavior pattern was adjusting to strong females rather than asserting his own dominance in the rough, raw admirable manner of television heroes, then television viewers would be sure to pick up this nuance of character and it might tend to vitiate the candidate's persuasive power.

Governor Scranton might say all the right words against Barry Goldwater, but they would not quite ring true. Viewers would perceive his bark as being without much bite. His battle song would seem to sound from the larynx rather than the diaphragm. His racing form would be that of a swimmer who is afraid of the water. His blows would come from his wrists, not from a gladiator's heart. And nothing short of an heroic performance on television would generate anything near the tidal wave of emotion among rank-and-file Republicans that this stop-Goldwater crusade was counting on.

The campaign situation into which Scranton had precipitated himself was most atypical in that the opposition candidate was not present and viewers would not be comparing. Scranton might be battling Goldwater, but Goldwater was not battling Scranton. Goldwater, having won the crucial California primary, was away from the public scene, relaxing until the convention. It was intermission time in the political drama. The curtain was down while the scenes were shifted to San Francisco. And then on came Bill Scranton with a one-man olio act to woo an audience that had gone out for a smoke. Probably the strongest of image candidates could not have aroused rank-and-file Republicans to a massive walkout on Goldwater at that moment. And certainly, in image-candidate terms, Bill Scranton was miscast as Prince Valiant. It was not a natural role for him. He was not going to be very convincing. He was not going to be very persuasive.

He was probably going to throw a million dollars or more down the drain between his declaration of candidacy on June 11 and the nomination of Barry Goldwater on July 15. And the CBS half-hour could be nothing other than an exercise in futility stemming from the ignorance of political leaders about what does and what does not arouse public sentiment.

I had committed the production of this half-hour program to the Marworth location before I had any insight into the true character of the candidate, who was supposed to be presented as a crusading hero. Now all I could do was make sure that he did not appear in his informal living room with that dominating portrait of the Duchess or in any scene with his wife. Whatever scenes I constructed would have to underscore his masculinity. By process of elimination, the program construction gave him two key scenes to play: (1) early in the half-hour, alone in his study, Henry V alone in his tent on the eve of Agincourt delivering a soliloquy on bravery and courage and the dimensions of the coming battle; and (2) a closing scene of General Lee with his valiant young men in gray, inspiring them to make their suicide charge up Cemetery Ridge. That would be the last scene in the program except the epilogue. It would be as masculine and dramatic as possible. (It also would take Dennis over two hours to stage and almost knock the whole show off the air due to the split-second schedule of delivering the tape to CBS-TV control in New York on time.)

Taylor Grant, a topnotch television newsman and personality working out of Philadelphia, came up to Marworth to be the storyteller: starting on the terrace for exterior views, wandering through the house, setting the mood and drama of the anti-Goldwater battle, introducing the various "scenes," integrating what bits of newsfilm, videotape, audiotape, and stills we had been able to round up on such short notice, and talking to one or two secondary "characters" whose appraisal of Governor Scranton might help characterize him for viewers.

The governor's number-one boy in 1964 was a wholly male-animal whirlwind by the name of Bill Keisling. Keisling was then about twenty-eight, completely without polish but with a raw angry energy that—when coming from Scranton's mouth in the form of campaign oratory—imparted to the governor an aura of virile determination. Keisling had come from a newspaper background to be Scranton's top public relations man and speechwriter during the 1962 gubernatorial campaign.

As happens with most aides and advisers, Bill Keisling chafed angrily at the whole concept of image candidates and at my approach to this CBS-TV half-hour as a theatrical piece, as a political "drama" rather than just a speech. When Keisling's copy for Scranton in the study scene arrived at the motel where I was integrating elements of script for the teleprompter, his resentment of the image concept was obvious.

EXCERPTS, KEISLING COPY FOR SCRANTON STUDY SCENE: And some television experts have been around to see me too. They don't think much of the American people either. They say that you are lazy and indifferent. They say that if I talk to you about the serious business of this nation for more than two minutes, you will go to sleep or turn the channel.
If that's true, I cannot succeed.

This passage was struck from the final script. It was too angry, too raw for the governor to say. It was also not true. Viewer response to candidate images seen on television is not a matter of laziness or indifference. It is mainly a matter of viewers' conditioned responses to the appearance, demeanor, and presentation of "political characters," causing personal impressions of candidates, impressions that are—by and large—formed independently of just what the candidates happen to be saying at the time.

When this angry copy came down to the motel from Bill Keisling, I remember commenting to Jerry Danzig or Dennis Kane: "Scranton had better watch out for that boy. Keisling's very good, but he is still too rough for big-time politics."

Prophetic words. A few weeks later, during the San Francisco Republican convention, a letter allegedly written from Scranton to Goldwater was reprinted as front-page news. It said, in part:

SCRANTON (KEISLING): "Your organization . . . feel[s] they have bought, beaten and compromised enough delegate support to make . . . [Goldwater's nomination] a foregone conclusion. With open contempt for the dignity, integrity and common sense of the convention, your managers say in effect that the delegates are little more than a flock of chickens whose necks will be wrung at will."

From the rawness of those words, there was little doubt in my mind that Keisling had written the letter and now either was dominating Bill Scranton more than ever or was running wild, out of control. Follow-up stories from San Francisco confirmed my supposition. Governor Scranton had never seen the letter. Keisling had sent it off to Barry Goldwater after signing Scranton's name.

From the terrace at Marworth, about seven o'clock on the

evening of Sunday, June 28, 1964, distant shadows could be seen filling the Lackawanna Valley and creeping up the slopes of the Abingtons, whose peaks were still golden-green from the late-setting sun.

On the manicured lawn in front of the big house, a helicopter waited, its rotor turning idly. Teletape technicians, groggy from lack of sleep, were taking it a bit easier now, enjoying the governor's hospitality with cans of cold beer nearby while breaking down the cameras and lights.

At the cramped videotape console in the truck, Dennis Kane and his tape editor made their splices, laboriously joining together the best parts of the best takes of each scene. Each splice could take ten minutes, and the clock was ticking—150, 140, 130 minutes left to air. At eight o'clock, CBS-TV master control in New York had to be alerted that the program was a few minutes short: they should have public service stand-by announcements ready to fill the time period. Another emergency call to the West 40th Street Heliport: we were past its closing hour and it had to be kept open and illuminated.

Shortly after eight o'clock, Dennis jumped down from the control truck with one edited roll of videotape under his arm. (There had been no time to edit a safety roll.) We congratulated each other for having thought of everything that could have gone wrong and for managing to adhere to such an impossible schedule. Dennis squeezed himself and the videotape into the helicopter. Its rotors accelerated. The little craft shuddered violently, wrenched itself free of the greensward, and disappeared rapidly over the distant hills.

But we had not quite thought of everything. The helicopter pilot was a local boy who had never flown as far as New York before: he didn't know the route. Dennis managed to guide him to Manhattan by following highways from the air. The videotape just barely managed to get to CBS-TV master control on time.

What effect did the telecast have? Western Union did a land-office business for about twenty-four hours. By Monday morning, some 15,000 telegrams had come into Scranton headquarters.

But their political worth was probably less than the excess baggage charges for hauling them out to the San Francisco convention. One swallow does not a summer make, nor one exercise in image techniques a hero—especially when the exercise is so hastily prepared and the candidate so devoid of hero characteristics.

Scranton ended up campaigning for the election of Republican presidential nominee Goldwater.

NOTES

1. *Face the Nation*, WABC-TV, New York (and stations affiliated with the ABC-TV network), June 7, 1964, 12:30–1 P.M., E.D.T.
2. Theodore H. White, *The Making of the President 1964* (New York: Atheneum, 1965), p. 154.

PART FIVE

Summing Up

17

A CONCEPT OF IMAGE
CANDIDATES

What is unique about the personal image of a political candidate that television conveys to its viewers? An important clue to the answer of this question is found in the recent findings that *all* viewers tend to see the same personal image of televised candidates although the influence of that image on viewers may vary.

According to now-classic studies of American voting behavior, this should not happen. Voters are supposed to formulate varying mental images of the candidates according to their (the voters') *political predispositions.* To define that term, voters' political predispositions are tendencies, growing out of their habitual preference for the candidates of one party and their habitual rejection of opposition party candidates, to seek out and favorably interpret information leading to impressions of favored candidates and to avoid, misinterpret, distort, or forget information and impressions of opposition candidates. Wilbur Schramm has summed up the conventional wisdom about political predispositions with respect to television.

WILBUR SCHRAMM: Man is far from a *tabula rasa*, or clean slate, for mass communication to write on. . . . He has built up a sense of values which lead him to react positively or negatively to much of what the candidate will say. . . . The voter will have a strong sense of belongingness. . . . Perhaps he will have a sense of how the people in his "set" or his union or his luncheon club evaluate the candidate. In other words, before he even sits down to the television set, he is prepared to react in a preset way to whatever comes out of it.[1]

But, such scholarly opinion notwithstanding, this sort of selective distortion of candidate images as seen by television viewers failed to happen in a number of recent elections. A study by the Cunningham and Walsh advertising agency during the 1958 gubernatorial campaigns in New York concluded that voters, regardless of political affiliation, tend to see similar television images of the candidates. Respondents characterized the Republican challenger, Nelson A. Rockefeller, as dynamic and personable. The universal opinion of incumbent Governor W. Averell Harriman added up to a "strained and stiff" image.[2]

In 1960, Joseph and Marian McGrath studied members of Young Republican and Young Democratic clubs as a sample of politically predisposed television viewers, assuming that "if any group is liable to distort the images of a favored candidate, one would expect a highly partisan group to do so."[3] Yet after these two groups had witnessed the televised "great debates" between the Republican and Democratic presidential candidates, they characterized the two candidates in similar terms: "Kennedy was seen by both parties as more ambitious, aggressive, striving, active, dynamic, rebellious, etc. Nixon, in contrast, was seen by members of both parties as less ambitious, more easy-going, contented, passive, relaxed, conforming, etc."[4]

This unexpected phenomenon may be explained without denying established findings about the distorting influence of a voter's political predispositions by accepting the concept that all voters, as television viewers, have some other mental predisposition that influences them to react in a preset way to whatever comes out of their television set and, further, that this other mental predisposition is so firmly fixed as to overwhelm and obliterate a partisan distortion of candidate images due to political predispositions.

This other and stronger mental influence on viewer perception of candidate images might be called *media predispositions.*

HARVEY WHEELER: Television . . . has created its own symbolic language: what one's face looks like, how one's face corresponds to television's laboriously created stereotypes for good guys and bad guys becomes crucial. . . .

The moment the television viewer takes his place before his set, he brings with him a series of invisible visual values which have a strong political significance regardless of the viewer's conscious desire.[5]

Furthermore, television's stereotype dramatic characters, with their "invisible visual values" that condition viewers on a year-around, year-after-year basis, embody personifications of universally admired (or detested) characters in the popular American culture, the culture shared by all voters regardless of their political affinities.

PSYCHIATRIST'S OPINION RE NONPARTISAN AFFINITY FOR A FATHER-IMAGE CANDIDATE: [An] authority vacuum in the home and transfer of the directive roles from the father to the mother are reflected in the increasing interest in many levels of our government for a more authoritarian and paternalistic government, one featuring a maximum of security and a minimum of hazard. This may result in a tendency on the part of many people to secure such a state by vote.[6]

SOCIOLOGIST'S OPINION RE NONPARTISAN AFFINITY FOR A SINCERE-IMAGE CANDIDATE: Sincerity means performance in a style which is not aggressive or cynical, which may even be defenseless, as the question-answering or press conference technique of some politicians appears to be. The performer puts himself at the mercy of both his audience and his emotions. . . . It would not be fair to be too critical of the person who has left himself wide open and extended the glad hand of friendliness.

Forced to choose between skill and sincerity, many in the audience prefer the latter. They are tolerant of bumbles and obvious ineptness if the leader tries hard.[7]

All television viewers, to a greater extent than they might suppose, would seem to have mental picture galleries in their heads, the walls of which are hung with portraits of heroes, lovers, villains, stooges, fathers, statesmen, politicians, comedians, and the other stereotype characters in television's commedia dell'arte. With little conscious effort—or perhaps in spite of conscious effort—viewers probably match the images in their mental picture galleries against the images of candidates seen on television and derive an impression of the candidates' characters accordingly.

THE THEATRICALITY OF CAMPAIGN COVERAGE ON TELEVISION

Not only may the great preponderance of theatrical entertainment on television condition viewers to perceive political campaign coverage as a theatrical experience, but certain production techniques commonly used in television news programs may serve to heighten an illusion that the campaign is a "political drama" and the candidates are players therein who should be judged as dramatic characters.

The Reaction Shot

Kurt and Gladys Lang were early observers of television's tendency to dramatize news coverage into a theatrical experience. The Langs' study revolved about one news event: a "farewell" visit made by General Douglas MacArthur to Chicago in 1951, shortly after he had made his colorful "Old Soldiers Never Die" speech on returning to the United States from Korea. The Langs were interested in finding out if, and how, the reaction of eyewitnesses who saw the parade and public ceremonies honoring the general differed from the reaction of viewers who had seen these events on television.

Television, the Langs concluded, had magnified instances of

public enthusiasm over MacArthur to the proportions of an "impersonal absolute force" that had an "overwhelming" effect upon home viewers: "Selectivity of the camera and the commentary gave the event a personal dimension non-existent for particular participants in the crowds." [8] Whereas General MacArthur was in fact a controversial militarist who had to be removed from his Korean command by President Truman for fear that he would, on his own, take overt military action against Red China, from this television coverage the general appeared to be a conquering hero idolized by the American public.

Although the Langs did not use the technical term *reaction shots,* their findings indicated that selected scenes of parade watchers applauding and cheering the passing general intercut and hence juxtaposed with close-ups of the general was the prime technique that made a theatrical experience out of the television coverage and a face-value hero character out of General MacArthur.

As discussed in Chapter 3 with reference to the Nixon *Ambassador of Friendship* film, reaction shots are so typically a technique of film and television drama that their use in news coverage may (1) increase the emotional intensity of the coverage to the point of obscuring rational consideration of the subject matter, and (2) increase the illusion that the coverage is drama and not reality.

On September 26, 1960, Ted Rogers—as Richard Nixon's television adviser—fought out and lost a dispute with CBS television director Don Hewitt over the use of reaction shots on the first of the "great debate" programs. Possibly because he knew that his candidate looked awful in comparison with the healthier, handsome John F. Kennedy, Rogers demanded that reaction shots of one candidate listening to the other be barred. Rogers feared that reaction shots would dramatize the image contrast between the two presidential candidates and take the focus off the substance of their dialogue.

But director Hewitt ruled that to eliminate the reaction shot was "cheating the audience" and that it was wholly natural for the viewer watching the discussion to want to see the reaction of the other participants from time to time.[9] In what sense would the elimination of reaction shots have "cheated the audience"? Certainly the average person sitting in an auditorium where a platform debate between presidential candidates was in progress would hardly be close enough to observe the effect of one candidate's words on the other as revealed by the nuances of the listening candidate's facial expressions. Rather, the expectation of reaction shots—and the sense of being "cheated" when they are not used—is probably something cultivated in television viewers by continued exposure to reaction-shot drama and news coverage.

The Rigid Time-Period Factor

Television's slavish devotion to the stopwatch may also serve to reduce the substance of political statements to incidental dialogue between dramatic characters in conflict. Newscasts typically edit a candidate's SOF remarks to the most pithy and provocative sentences and, without elaboration or evaluation of the condensed statement, juxtapose it with a contrary statement by the opposition. Time considerations and the desire for a fast "pace" can reduce face-to-face confrontations between candidates on news-feature programs to a travesty of political debate. For example, on Saturday evening, October 29, 1966, Station WABC-TV in New York City gave an hour of air time and facilities to put on a face-to-face confrontation between the four most prominent gubernatorial candidates: Governor Nelson A. Rockefeller, Republican; Frank D. O'Connor, Democrat; Franklin D. Roosevelt, Jr., Liberal; and Paul L. Adams, Conservative. The format of the program was rigid: each candidate was asked two questions on campaign issues by the program moderator. Each candidate had 90 seconds to answer. Each of the three other candidates had 60 seconds to rebut the answer. Between the rebuttals, the candidate giving the original answer had 30 seconds for re-rebuttal. The potential governors of a state in which 18 million people lived were given the following air time for discussion of important public questions: 90 seconds, 60 seconds, 30 seconds. What sort of comprehension of alternative proposals could viewers gain from such a flash exposure? Most probably only an impression, an impression based not on substance of argument but on style.

Editorial Abstention by Television Journalists

Even when candidates are given more time to answer and rebut answers of questions about campaign issues, viewers may be forced to judge style rather than substance of the arguments because candidates are often in serious disagreement as to the basic facts and such disagreements are rarely (if ever) set straight by the professional television journalists conducting the program. This failure should not be dismissed with the comment that the professional journalists might not be prepared to inform the viewer where the truth lies. Technically it is quite feasible (and hardly more expensive) to record candidate confrontations on videotape and delay broadcast twenty-four or forty-eight hours until the facts cited by the candidates can be authenticated and appraised by inserted remarks by the program moderator.

But however feasible in a technical sense, any appraisal of political candidates or their remarks by television newsmen would constitute a cardinal sin against the medium's most holy commandment: *Thou shalt not offend.*

JACK GOULD (TELEVISION CRITIC): You don't slap a customer in the face. . . . All the major advertising agencies have testified at F.C.C. hearings that this is the basic policy of television: you do not offend.[9]

A station that offered information, no matter how valid, that sharply contradicted a political candidate would run the risk of offending that candidate's supporters. That station might become "controversial" and scare away the advertising agencies, whose dollars are the lifeblood of television.

A few more courageous (and affluent) television stations have begun to endorse favored candidates in separately programmed and clearly identified editorial announcements by a spokesman for station management who is *not* a regular newscaster. (For example, WCBS-TV endorsed Republican John Lindsay for mayor of New York in 1965.) In accord with the FCC's "fairness doctrine," these stations are obligated to seek out rebuttal from (spokesmen for) other candidates, a step beyond the usual equal-time stricture.[10]

But editorials aside—and they are aside from newscasts and news-features programs—television's professionals follow a strict policy of letting political candidates stand at face value. This editorial abstention from campaign coverage may encourage viewers to appraise candidates on face value, which is what most viewers appear to do.

FACE VALUE

According to the Cunningham and Walsh study of the 1958 gubernatorial campaigns, although television viewers generally agreed that they were more favorably impressed by Nelson A. Rockefeller than by incumbent Governor W. Averell Harriman, few viewers could identify anything that either candidate had said on television. Commonly, the viewers remarked that the candidates were "just talking politics."

Elihu Katz and Jacob J. Feldman did a study of studies, reviewing thirty-one separate research projects concerned with the 1960 Nixon-Kennedy television debates. Katz and Feldman concluded that viewers had not learned enough from what was said by the candidates to cause any change of opinion on campaign issues but that the viewers had "learned something about the candidates themselves. They discovered how well each candidate could perform in a debate and they formed images of each candidate's character and abilities." [11]

Such scholarly findings indicate what may be one of the most important—and least acknowledged—aspects of candidate appearances on television: *the rational import of what they say may be a minimal part of the sentiment that they arouse in viewers.*

(Obvious exceptions to this generalized finding, such as obscenity or other utterances that are blatantly offensive to public sensitivities, are conceivable but improbable.)

A classic example of face value overwhelming rational import was provided by viewer response to a televised confrontation between Edward (Ted) Moore Kennedy, younger brother of the President, and Edward J. McCormack, Jr., attorney general of Massachusetts, in 1962. Young Kennedy had been nominated for the Senate seat vacated by his brother at a state convention of Massachusetts Democrats. McCormack, as a Democrat who was older and more experienced in public office, challenged Kennedy's nomination in a primary contest that led both men to face each other in front of television cameras and a large in-person audience.

EDWARD McCORMACK: You never worked for a living. You never held elective office. You are not running on qualifications. You are running on a slogan—"He can do more for Massachusetts." That is the most insulting slogan I have ever seen.

["Insulting" because the slogan implied that Ted Kennedy could get special favors for Massachusetts, such as federal contracts, because his older brother, John, was the President.]

If his name was Edward Moore, his candidacy would be a joke. Nobody is laughing. Your name is Edward Moore Kennedy.[12]

Ted Kennedy politely declined to answer any of the points raised by McCormack in the dialogue cited above because the candidates really should be discussing issues rather than "personalities." At this answer, the studio audience broke into great applause for Kennedy. "By the end of the day," reported *The New York Times*, "resentment over Mr. McCormack's tactics appeared to be mounting, particularly among women. Many called newspaper offices to register protests."[13]

The meaning and relevancy of McCormack's remarks had been obscured by face-value image considerations. Whether or not young Kennedy had ever worked for a living, an experience that might have helped him understand problems of the average citizen, and whether or not he had ever held elective office, an experience that might have prepared him for the high responsibilities of a United States senator, he was a handsome young replica of his brother. Whether or not Edward McCormack was a thoroughly seasoned public servant, his demeanor, the hard tone of his voice, and the aggressive intent of his remarks characterized him as the unpleasant and undesirable image candidate. Kennedy went on to win the nomination and election despite "a monumental lack of relevant experience. . . . A dazzling smile, a tireless handshake and a great deal of native political acumen pretty much completed his arsenal of qualifications." [14]

Recent findings by social scientists Nathan Maccoby and Leon Festinger illuminate this phenomenon of face value prevailing over rational import from a completely different angle. Viewers, under controlled conditions in the Festinger-Maccoby experiments, were found to learn persuasive television messages better when hearing the audio and watching unrelated video than when they watched the speaker giving them the message directly, that is, audio and video together. The distraction of watching something unrelated to the audio message was apparently less than the distraction of watching the speaker. [15]

IMAGES INTO IMAGE CANDIDATES

The image characterizations of candidates conveyed to viewers by television *can* vary significantly from images of the same candidates conveyed to listeners by radio and to readers by the print media.

The potential contrast between television and newspaper images of candidates is fairly obvious, as was illustrated by the various literary-fiction techniques of newspapers cited in Chapter 9. A newspaper, if it chooses, can put selective emphasis on coverage that reflects favorably on the favored candidate and describes the opposition candidate as an ineffective failure or worse. But newspapers can only describe, they can only write, a continuing and possibly biased political novel to stimulate the imagination, the mind's eye of the reader. The newspaper-stimulated image of a candidate can be largely fiction and differ sharply from the television image, or the newspaper-stimulated image can be largely the truth and differ sharply from the television image. It is the literary-fiction image that appears to be obliterated in voters' minds by the televised image when both media are fully covering the candidates. There are several reasons for this. Television most closely simulates intimate personal persuasion between candidate and voter, and personal persuasion has been found to be the most effective influence on voting.[16] Further, television images are universally perceived, whereas newspaper images, especially the more highly fictitious images conveyed by the more intensely partisan papers, achieve a limited exposure. (Refer to the inverse correlation between newspaper partisanship and circulation discussed in Chapter 9.) When the newspaper-stimulated image of a candidate differs sharply enough from the television image and is largely the truth and is generally reported by all the printed media, it may well prevail in the minds of television viewers. The 1964 Republican presidential primary in New Hampshire (Chapter 3) provided an apparent example of this situation. Newspapers had provided all the intimate details of Nelson Rockefeller's divorce from a wife of thirty years and of his subsequent remarriage to a much younger woman who had to give up legal custody of her four children to gain her own marital freedom. Before Nelson Rockefeller appeared on New Hampshire television screens, viewers held a striking characterization of him that was too recent to be readily obliterated by Governor Rockefeller's personable television image. In a similar manner, the printed media were generally describing Barry Goldwater's impulsive and rash pronouncements on important public questions, a personal characteristic that apart from the substance of his statements may have created a striking image of Goldwater as a "dangerous" candidate, an image that served to obscure Goldwater's most attractive appearance and demeanor on New Hampshire television.

The potential contrast between a newspaper image and a

television image of the same candidate may be commonly recognized, but not the potential contrast between a radio image and a television image of the same candidate.

DR. ITHIEL DE SOLA POOL: Television humanized Eisenhower by revealing him to be somewhat more sensitive and withdrawn than the iron soldier the public had previously imagined. TV did not improve the image of Stevenson, though it certainly helped him become known. Radio was the medium that conveyed an overwhelmingly favorable image of Stevenson.[17]

In 1960, political reporter Earl Mazo observed a sharp contrast between radio and television images of a candidate. The night of the first Nixon-Kennedy debate, Mazo had been covering the Southern Governors' Conference in Hot Springs, Arkansas. Because the Hot Springs station was not directly on the network cable, the assembled governors heard the first debate on radio an hour or so before they saw it on television.

EARL MAZO: Before the encounter on radio was half finished, every Kennedy partisan in the room was disparaging the idea of a fine, upstanding young man like Senator Kennedy having to clash verbally with a crusty old professional debater like Vice President Nixon. But the attitude changed immediately when the magic lantern of television came on.[18]

On radio, Mazo observed, Nixon's deep resonant voice conveyed more conviction, command, and determination to the listening governors than Kennedy's high-pitched voice, with its Boston-Harvard accent. On television, Kennedy looked sharper of the two, more in control, more firm, more the image of a President who could stand up to Khrushchev.

In summary, television apparently does more than just present political candidates. Television transfigures candidates into personal images or characterizations that can be quite unique to the medium. Thus, it is necessary to have a term to describe this unique image, a term such as *image candidate*.

In summary, an image candidate is a leading character in the political drama presented by television before an election. His characterization tends to be universally perceived, regardless of viewers' political predispositions, due to viewers' media predispositions to see the candidates in terms of television's stereotyped desirable and undesirable characters, stereotypes that may in themselves be projections of characters valued or detested in the United States culture at large.

Such television production techniques and policies relevant to campaign coverage as the use of reaction shots and editorial abstention by the medium's journalists may work to enhance the viewer's illusion that he is watching a theatrical drama rather than political reality and that the image candidates are to be judged as characters in that drama. Most image techniques employed by political propagandists to enhance the appeal of their client-candidates seek to exploit television's inherent theatricality and viewers' tendencies to see the candidates as dramatic characters. By controlling the presentation or theatrical setting of candidates on paid political programs and commercials, propagandists can encourage viewers to perceive a favorable characterization of the client-candidate.

A candidate's appearance and demeanor appear to provide viewers with the most substantial clues to his character. The rational import of what the candidate says on television, as long as it is not blatantly offensive to the great central cluster of the electorate, appears to have very little influence on viewers' perception of image.

NOTES

1. Wilbur Schramm, *Responsibility in Mass Communication* (New York: Harper & Row, 1957), pp. 52–53.
2. *Television and the Political Candidate* (New York: Cunningham and Walsh, 1959), pp. 19–22.
3. Joseph E. and Marian F. McGrath, "Effects of Partisanship on Perceptions of Political Figures," *Public Opinion Quarterly*, XXVI, No. 2 (Summer, 1962), p. 246.
4. *Ibid.*, p. 243.
5. Harvey Wheeler in Earl Mazo, Malcolm Moos, Hallock Hoffman,

and Harvey Wheeler, *The Great Debates* (Santa Barbara: Center for the Study of Democratic Institutions, 1962), pp. 14–15.

6. C. W. Wahl, M.D., "The Relation Between Primary and Secondary Influences," in Eugene Burdick and Arthur Brodbeck (eds.), *American Voting Behavior* (New York: Free Press, 1959), pp. 275–276.

7. David Reisman, Nathan Glazer, and Reuel Denney, *The Lonely Crowd* (Garden City, N.Y.: Anchor Books, 1953), pp. 225–226.

8. Kurt and Gladys Lang, "The Unique Perspective of Television and Its Effect," in Wilbur Schramm (ed.), *Mass Communication* (Urbana: University of Illinois Press, 1960), p. 554.

9. Jack Gould, *Television* (Santa Barbara: Center for the Study of Democratic Institutions, 1961), p. 4.

10. Station obligation to actively seek rebuttals to station editorials on public questions, the so-called fairness doctrine, was set down by the Federal Communications Commission, *In the Matter of Editorializing by Broadcast Licensees*, pamphlet, 13 FCC 1246, June 1, 1949.

11. Elihu Katz and Jacob J. Feldman, "The Debates in the Light of Research: A Survey of Surveys," in Sidney Kraus (ed.), *The Great Debates* (Bloomington: Indiana University Press, 1962), p. 203.

12. *The New York Times,* August 28, 1962, p. 16.

13. *The New York Times,* August 29, 1962, p. 15.

14. Editorial, "A New Senator Kennedy," *The New York Times,* November 7, 1962.

15. Leon Festinger and Nathan Maccoby, "On Resistance to Persuasive Communications," *Journal of Abnormal and Social Psychology,* 68, No. 4 (1964), 359–366.

16. Joseph T. Klapper, *The Effects of Mass Communication* (New York: Free Press, 1960), pp. 129–130.

17. Ithiel De Sola Pool, "TV: A New Dimension in Politics," in Eugene Burdick and Arthur Brodbeck (eds.), *American Voting Behavior* (New York: Free Press, 1959), p. 243.

18. Earl Mazo in Earl Mazo, Malcolm Moos, Hallock Hoffman, and Harvey Wheeler, *The Great Debates* (Santa Barbara, Calif.: Center for Study of Democratic Institutions, 1962), p. 6.

18

APPLYING THE CONCEPT TO
SOME RECENT ELECTIONS

☆————————————————————————————☆

Today some small states and some fairly large cities located near dense population centers where television stations are clustered still may not have ample television service of their own. And innumerable political contests in smaller communities across the land will continue to function as if television did not exist. Even candidates for high-level office, if that office happens to be below the top-of-the-ticket spot on the ballot, may find themselves slighted by television, which tends to concentrate on the top race.

With those exceptions, however, the most prominent candidates for the most important public offices in the United States today can expect a good amount of television news coverage and should expect to make liberal paid-political use of the medium. These candidates are going to be image candidates whether they like it or not. And as image candidates, their ability to exploit—or to protect themselves from—the unique influence of television will depend on their knowledge of and their manipulation of the three major variables:

1. *Political Party Registration.* Except in the case of primary elections, when those voting tend to be the more active members of the same party, registration figures provide a rough indication of how many voters would vote for each party's candidate, other influences on the voter being equal or nil. If there is a sizable independent bloc of voters, it may be prudent to check out whether they are truly independent or whether they habitually lean toward a local party that has discouraged registration for some reason.

2. *Campaign Issues.* Are there fresh, genuine, and clear differences between the major candidates on important public questions? Are newspapers—other than overtly and habitually biased papers—generally carrying news that is both (1) threatening to large blocs of voters and (2) identified with one of the major candidates?

3. *Candidate Images.* How do the separate characterizations of the major candidates, as seen on television, compare and contrast with stereotype characters of television drama? Can a contrast be achieved by juxtaposing one candidate with a personified evil such as a political boss (who looks like a political boss)? Do any of the major candidates enjoy or suffer a pre-campaign reputation so striking as to prevail in viewers' minds and not be obliterated by that candidate's appearance, demeanor, or presentation? Does one candidate, usually the incumbent, have a clearly superior ability to make news that has a striking visual aspect or that can be portrayed in television newscasts and paid-politicals in terms of persons affected by the news?

Lest the influence of television be overestimated, it is prudent to remember that the most common effect of image candidates on viewers is *crystallization* rather than *conversion.* For example,

Kurt and Gladys Lang speak in terms of crystallization as the factor helping Senator Kennedy more than Vice-President Nixon when the two men were seen face to face in the 1960 television debates: "The largest gain for Kennedy came from crystallizers and illustrates his success in rallying behind himself a larger number of uncommitted than Nixon." [1]

By this statement they mean that the superior image of Kennedy should be thought of as rousing more voters *who were already inclined toward a Democratic candidate* to go out and vote for—or better yet, work for—Kennedy as compared to the influence of the weaker Nixon image on voters *who were already inclined toward Nixon.* Crystallization is the sort of conservative terminology preferred by social scientists to explain the influence of television in a manner compatible with the common finding that most voters end up voting for the candidate of the party to which they (the voters) are habitually inclined.

But, lest the influence of television be underestimated, one should remember that examples of massive conversion largely due to a sharp contrast in competing image candidates are becoming more common. The election of Eisenhower in 1952 and 1956 involved the conversion of many Democrats for whom the sentiment generated by the soldier-hero-father image of Eisenhower was stronger than their habitual sentiments toward a Democratic presidential candidate and their sentiments, if any, toward the personal image of Stevenson. (The landslide election of President Johnson over Senator Goldwater in 1964 was in part due to the conversion of many Republicans, but that conversion was obviously due more to clear issue differences between the two candidates than to image considerations.)

Of course, as noted in Chapter 1, the increasing incidence of conversion by image candidates may be as much due to weakening alignments of voters with political parties as to the unique and pervasive ability of television to convey image differences.

Consideration of a few more recent elections—in terms of image candidates—may help clarify the probable role of television in American politics of tomorrow.

NEW YORK CITY'S
MAYORAL ELECTION OF 1965

Images, all images: John Lindsay, Republican; Abraham Beame, Democrat; William Buckley, Conservative; Frank O'Connor, Democrat. Lindsay, Beame, and Buckley were candidates for mayor on the November ballot. Frank O'Connor was a would-be mayoral candidate, the district attorney in Queens who was persuaded by Democratic organization bigwigs to drop his own mayoral ambitions and take second position (candidate for City Council president) on Abe Beame's "team" before the primary elections. It was a fatal error for the bigwigs stemming from the conventional conceit that any candidate of a party that outnumbers its opposition by 3 to 1 cannot lose. It was a fatal error in the age of television. Little Abe Beame was a short, undramatic graduate of City College who had left teaching to become a career civil servant and slowly climbed the ladder of municipal government to become city controller during Mayor Wagner's last term (1961–65). Like it or not, little men with Brooklyn accents are simply not found in the television viewer's mental picture gallery of heroes. And this particular little man had no class, no style, no inspiration, no special inner fire (that is, "demeanor" in image candidate terms) that might compensate for his shortcomings of appearance.

Frank O'Connor was not only more attractive as an image candidate, but in television materials prepared for his campaign as City Council president on the Democratic ticket, O'Connor displayed a keen awareness of television's unique ability to exploit image rather than substance. One of his assistants talked, perhaps too freely, to someone who was preparing an article about O'Connor:

THE NEW YORK TIMES MAGAZINE: O'Connor's masterwork was presented to the TV public toward the end of the campaign. A five-minute tape . . . the show was easily the most effective piece of political advertising in the entire election.
The camera panned in on the candidate standing in his den

"where my family and I sit around and talk and read and listen to music." And there on the wall was a picture of John F. Kennedy shaking hands with O'Connor at a windswept airport. . . .

The Camera rolled to the patio where Mary O'Connor, a pretty matronly woman, awaited her husband. Off to the right, one of the twins was shooting baskets.

After introducing his family, O'Connor said: "I am grateful that I have a good home to come to at the end of a hard day, and I often thank God for my blessings. . . .

Few people in all the world could execute such a performance. There is Bing Crosby. There is, perhaps, Spencer Tracy. And there is Frank O'Connor.[2]

Congressman John Vliet Lindsay, forty-three, Republican and Liberal party candidate for mayor, had everything the American hero on television is presumed to have: blond hair, a face handsome in the tightest close-ups, a well-modulated voice controlled with an actor's discipline, tallness of stature, vigor of youth, the self-confidence of a winner, and the sweet smell of success.

William F. Buckley, Jr., mayoral nominee of the Conservative party, performed on television, mixing penetrating gibes with serious political comment and characterizing himself as a sort of young Jack E. Leonard with a cause. (Leonard is a night-club comedian whose forte is insulting members of his audience.) Buckley wittily described his opposition, Lindsay and Beame, as being so close together that he couldn't jam a piece of Scotch Tape between them. When asked by reporters what he would do if he won the election, Buckley quipped that he would demand a recount. Except for news conferences in his midtown office, Buckley's public campaign appearances were almost wholly limited to television. He often appeared with Lindsay and Beame on television's regularly scheduled news-feature programs, which were (by virtue of their regular scheduling) exempt from having to give equal time to three minor mayoral candidates who were also in the race.

In the typical manner of a candidate relying on his attractive television image, John Lindsay became as nonpartisan as possible. He cut himself off from the national Republican party and, in public at least, held Republican Governor Nelson Rockefeller (and Rockefeller's millions) at arm's length. Lindsay secured the nomination of the Liberal party and became the candidate of a paper party—"Independent Citizens for Lindsay"—as well, in order to further diffuse his Republican identity.

There were no clear issue differences between Lindsay and Beame. Even though Beame was not the incumbent mayor, Lindsay pegged his oratory on the traditional out-candidate's theme of *time for a change*. He also followed the by-now-familiar image tactic of associating the opposition candidate with some alleged evil force that could be personified: he attacked three "villainous" Democratic organization overlords (Charles Buckley, Bronx; Stanley Steingut, Brooklyn; Adam Clayton Powell, Harlem) to whom little Abe Beame was allegedly in thrall. This tactic seems to be a natural for television because it is expressed in terms of *compassion* rather than direct verbal attack at the person of the opposition candidate; that is, Lindsay could effectively deprecate Beame by expressing his regret that Beame was a creature of the bosses. Compassion is a familiar attribute of the television hero.

As Election Day approached, the crucial question seemed to be whether or not the contrast between Lindsay and Beame as image candidates would be great enough to convert large numbers of Democrats into voting for Lindsay. A second question concerned the influence of William Buckley's brilliant television image. Buckley was the nominee of the Conservative party. The Conservative party is usually considered an offshoot, to the political right, of the Republican party. Would Buckley pull votes away from Lindsay?

Table 11 shows what happened. The figures suggest variations in expected voting—that is, variations in voting that might have flowed from the influence of habitual party loyalties alone—due to the influence of candidate images.

Even though Democratic registration had outnumbered the combined Republican and Liberal registration by better than 2 to 1, John Lindsay—as the Republican-Liberal candidate—was able to convert enough Democrats to be elected mayor. But he could only gain a winning plurality for himself. His teammates, Timothy Costello and Milton Mollen, were much weaker image candidates. The greatest number of votes polled by any candidate went to Frank O'Connor, who, in second place on the Democratic ticket, had the influences of an attractive image and superior party registration going for him.

The influence of television image is particularly clear in the case of William Buckley. On television his performance was brilliant, witty, fascinating. That he also happened to be propounding a clear conservative doctrine that sharply contrasted with the positions of Lindsay and Beame on many issues was apparently not comprehended by over 100,000 New York City voters who were dazzled by his image. Such a conclusion seems reasonable in view of the fact that Buckley ran 100,000 votes ahead of his own ticket. If those 100,000 voters had understood what Buckley was saying on television, their votes would have represented endorsement of the singular conservative doctrine and therefore they should have voted straight Conservative. It also seems reasonable to conclude that since those 100,000 votes were politically naïve and were wooed by the attractiveness of the Buckley image, without Buckley in the race those votes would have gone to John Lindsay because little Abe Beame had a far less attractive image.

The ticket splitting was so common in this election that— because ticket splitting is a more complicated process than straight voting—71,000 New Yorkers (2.7 percent of those voting) ended up without any choice for mayor. In New York's 1961 mayoral election, by contrast, when the most attractive image candidate (Mayor Wagner) was on the big party ticket (Democratic), ticket splitting was far less: only 1.7 percent of the voters ended up without a lever pulled down for a mayoral choice (see above, Table 10).

Again, in 1965, the three most minor mayoral candidates could not in total attract 1 percent of the vote although once again—because of Section 315, the equal-time law—we can pre-

TABLE 11

NEW YORK CITY MAYORAL ELECTION RETURNS, 1965

Mayoral Candidates (and Party)	Vote* (in thousands)	Percentage of Vote	Other Candidates on Regular Party Tickets	Their Vote (in thousands)
ERIC HASS (Socialist Labor)	2	0.1		
CLIFTON DE BERRY (Socialist Worker)	4	0.2		
VITO BATTISTA (United Taxpayers)	11	0.4		
Subtotal: Three Minor Candidates	17	0.7		
WILLIAM F. BUCKLEY, JR. (Conservative)	339	13.0	ROSEMARY G. MOFFETT (City Council president)	208
			HUGH MARKEY (city controller)	257
ABRAHAM D. BEAME (Democrat)	1031	39.4	FRANK D. O'CONNOR (City Council president)	1366
			MARIO A. PROCCACINO (city controller)	1195

JOHN V. LINDSAY (Republican, Liberal)	1156	44.2	
TIMOTHY W. COSTELLO (City Council president)			939
MILTON MOLLEN (city controller)			1004
Votes with No Choice for Mayor	71	2.7	
Totals	2614	100.0%	

* Vote as reported by the New York City Board of Elections, rounded to the nearest thousand.

sume that they were given much more than 1 percent of the television campaign coverage.

With enough money and control of Abe Beame, a political propagandist familiar with the image candidate concept of television's influence on voting might have changed the outcome of this 1965 election.

First, the propagandist would have had to get the real Abe Beame out of the way for the duration of the campaign. Ideally, something should have happened to Beame that would have aroused voter compassion for him, anything that would have prevented viewers from repeatedly seeing the image contrast between Beame and Lindsay on television.

Second, all Beame's television appearances should have been exclusively on his own "paid-political" programs and commercials, during which (figuratively) he would be taller because he was standing on an unseen soap box and his image character would be more intense—more attractively intense—by virtue of nonrealistic (theatrical or impressionistic) presentation. The purpose of such treatment would not have been to make the Beame image more attractive than the Lindsay image. That would have been impossible. But the *contrast* between the two images might have been somewhat softened, somewhat blurred for Democratic viewers so they would not feel so impelled by their *media predispositions* to vote for Lindsay as the obvious hero image of the political drama being watched on television. Since there were so many more Democrats than Republicans and Liberals combined, the goal of an image specialist working for Beame should have been to help Democrats follow their own political predispositions to vote for Democratic candidates. The political predispositions of Democrats might have been made temporarily more intense than usual by a propaganda campaign directed at reviewing the struggles and glories of the Democratic party. The name of every revered Democrat and the bodies of every living Democratic celebrity should have been dragged into the persuasion, not to say one word on behalf of Little Abe—of whom the less said or shown the better—but to arouse latent sentiments of registered Democrats about their party identification. Television could have been used, but would hardly have been necessary, in such a Democratic-awareness campaign. Direct mail would suffice, because Democrats tend to read broadsides put out by their own party headquarters. Planted coverage and paid advertising in the *New York Post* might have helped, because its readership is largely Democratic.

The key word in appraising or trying to manipulate the influence of image candidates is probably "contrast." If there is a great contrast in party registration figures, it will probably take a great contrast in candidate images or campaign issues to overcome it. The goal of the image specialist is not only to make his candidate appear as much in the idiom of the television hero as possible, but to prepare materials that will amplify any contrast that helps his client and that will minimize any contrast that might influence voters to prefer the opposition.

NEW YORK STATE
GUBERNATORIAL CAMPAIGNS OF 1966

Frank O'Connor finally got his chance to run for a top-of-the-ticket office as Democratic candidate for governor in 1966. But again, as had happened the year before to his mayoral ambitions, it was prominent members of his own party who foredoomed his gubernatorial aspirations, namely, Franklin Delano Roosevelt, Jr., and Senator Robert F. Kennedy.

Roosevelt wanted the Democratic nomination for himself and, failing to get it, became the Liberal party's candidate for governor. Judging from political party enrollment figures in the state, a separation of the Liberal vote from its usual alignment with the Democratic ticket would still allow Democratic candidates to enjoy their party's 800,000 registered-voter superiority over the Republican registration. (The actual 1966 enrollment figures were: Republican, 2,794,320; Democrats, 3,616,775; Liberals, 87,596; and Conservatives, 54,027. Independent voters were estimated at 1 million.) But Roosevelt was a Democrat, not a

Liberal, and furthermore he was *Junior*, so the big question mark was how many Democrats would vote for *Junior* instead of O'Connor as a gesture of reverence to the late President.

By what he failed to do, Senator Robert F. Kennedy hamstrung O'Connor's chances to be elected governor. The senator failed to make with the Kennedy millions when money of that dimension was essential to pay the production costs for a catalog of television image materials and for air time enough to saturate statewide audiences with exposure to those materials. That O'Connor had an attractive television image and that he knew how to exploit it had been made clear a year earlier during the city campaign. But when it came to financing O'Connor's statewide television or holding tight to the purse strings, Senator Kennedy would have had everything to gain by holding tight. As long as he remained the most prominent Democrat in New York politics, he could exert a strong influence over the state's huge delegation to the Democratic national convention in 1972 or whatever year he chose to make his own move for the presidential nomination.

Meanwhile, the current occupant of New York's Executive Chamber in Albany, Governor Nelson A. Rockefeller, had plenty of money to make masterful use of television image materials. From their bitter experiences in the 1964 presidential primaries, the Rockefeller organization had learned well that television communicates images rather than ideas, that talk is the smallest part of image, and that a candidate speaking directly to camera can do himself more harm than good if his unadorned bare face immediately stimulates viewers to think of his shortcomings.

And many New Yorkers might have been aware of Nelson Rockefeller's shortcomings in 1964: his divorce and remarriage; his sales tax after promising no additional taxes; and the passage of his Medicaid plan, which was promising to be frightfully expensive. According to his own polls, taken in 1965, the governor's popularity was at or near its lowest ebb.

In view of these probable public antagonisms, Rockefeller's use of television was precisely correct. His one-minute "paid-politicals" began appearing in the summertime, some three or four months before Election Day. The governor himself rarely appeared on these film spots, and when he did, it was in a completely theatrical setting that established a mood and led viewers to perceive him in the character of a wise and compassionate public leader.

One of these commercials consisted of a traveling shot of a white line that marks the center of a road. A quiet announcer's voice gave the impressive facts of the Rockefeller road-building program. Another commerical showed nothing but a hand laying out small objects on a table: first a spoon and hypodermic needle, implements used by narcotic addicts; then brass knuckles, a knife, and a gun, implements used by addicts to get the wherewithal for narcotics. Then the hand picked up the objects one by one, as the quiet announcer's voice described the governor's program for the care and cure of addicts.

A third showed negative footage of a child at play, the reversed light values of the negative sensitively conveying the shadowy sorrow of a retarded child. In the last few seconds of the minute, the governor appeared to speak a few words about his program to expand and modernize state schools. The preceding negative footage had set a context of compassion for his appearance. No viewer could think of him in context of the divorce or the sales tax at that moment. A fourth showed the governor enacting the role of a governor. He spoke for the entire minute, but he was not exactly speaking directly to camera. His setting was a podium, and he was saying important words to an unseen audience. Few viewers would notice the theatrical lighting, the studio camera angles, and the lack of background noise as clues that the film was a simulation designed to convey the image of a leader rather than some footage clipped from an actual appearance.

These were consummate image techniques, the product of Jack Tinker and Partners, an affiliate agency of the McCann-Erickson/Interpublic complex. But in dissecting them for purposes of this discussion, I do not mean to infer that there was anything untrue about *what* they were saying. The contrivance was in selection—selecting things that reflected well upon the Governor—and in presentation—communicating them in television's singular language of theatrical images so as to arouse conditioned (unthinking) responses in viewers. The achievements of the Rockefeller administration during his first two terms (1959-1966) were remarkable. His use of image commercials to rouse viewer sentiments about those achievements and about himself in such a manner as to obliterate rational consideration of criticisms and costs was probably—to him—a questionable means to justify his ends, that is, further achievements. His inadequate use of image techniques in 1964 had allowed Barry Goldwater to gain the presidential nomination and to give the Republican party its greatest setback since the 1930s.

Toward the end of the 1966 campaigns, when he could not avoid appearing unadorned in two televised confrontations with O'Connor, Roosevelt, and Adams (Conservative party candidate), Governor Rockefeller had only to relax and be his personable self. The rigid time strictures of the programs eliminated any meaningful discussion of campaign issues. Indeed, as every good image candidate should know, the more compressed the attacks by challenging candidates, the more they tend to impart a characterization of aggressiveness to the challenger.

Governor Rockefeller was elected to a third term on November 8, 1966, by 2,713,261 votes, a margin of more than 400,000 over the 2,290,407 votes received by Democratic candidate O'Connor. Franklin Delano Roosevelt, Jr., the Democratic "spoiler," ended up with some 520,000 votes on the Liberal ticket.

When asked to account for his loss, O'Connor mentioned Roosevelt's defection, Rockefeller's expenditures (probably over $4 million), and a rising trend toward conservatism. His thinking seems hazy on this last point, since the large vote gained by the Conservative gubernatorial candidate in 1966 probably took more away from Rockefeller than from O'Connor.

Governor Rockefeller, when asked to account for his reelection, put his finger right on the crucial point: "He [O'Connor] never

convinced the people he was a viable alternative."³ As a person-
ification of political reality, no matter what his shortcomings,
Nelson Rockefeller had gotten across to millions of viewer-voters
as the preferable image candidate.

CALIFORNIA, 1966:
MAN VERSUS IMAGE

The title of an editorial in *The New York Times* on October
6, 1966, was "Man Vs. Image."

THE NEW YORK TIMES: Of all the governorships to be decided this
November, California's state election provides the sharpest test of
political behavior in the age of television.

There have throughout history been leaders who gained power
through personal charm or skillful deception rather than qualities
of character and mind. More recently, modern communications have
made it useful for a political candidate to be photogenic or have a
pleasing radio voice. But the advent of television has carried these
tendencies much further.

With its neatly segmented half-hour programs, its well-crafted
dramas with their simplified issues, clearly discernible heroes and
villains, and fully resolved denouements, and its "sincere" well-
rehearsed announcers and masters of ceremonies, television has
created a new way of looking at reality for millions of viewers.

The newest word of political jargon—"image"—is drawn from the
television world. Its widespread use denotes the fact that for many
viewers—who are also voters—how a man looks and projects himself
is more persuasive than the facts about his experience, competence
or depth of understanding. The image now rivals the substance as
the ultimate political reality.

Ronald Reagan, the Republican candidate for Governor of California, personifies this intrusion of television and show business
values into serious politics. After innumerable appearances in
movies, as host of "Death Valley Days" and other television programs, and as paid lecturer on the luncheon club circuit, Mr. Reagan is now playing the role of a gubernatorial candidate. He is tall,
lean and bronzed by the sun; he smiles handsomely and speaks
well. His standard speech is a skillful script combining moral platitudes, pseudo-indignation, homey examples, and harmless jokes. He
knows very little about drawing up a state budget or administering
a vast complex of state agencies and institutions; he has few if

any specific programs on the hard public problems that vex the lives of real governors. But if the opinion polls are correct, a majority of California citizens are now inclined to vote him the man in the white hat with the fastest draw and send him to Sacramento to round up all the bad guys.

Governor Pat Brown, the Democratic incumbent, is not an exciting leader but he does have the experience, he has programs, and he has proved that he can administer the affairs of a great and growing state honestly, intelligently and compassionately. He has made mistakes and has few simple answers, because in real life hard problems rarely yield to simple one-shot answers.

Governor Brown belongs at the State Capitol in Sacramento, dealing with the stubborn public problems he knows so well; Mr. Reagan belongs in the studios in Hollywood, gracing the movie and television screens he knows so well. On November 8, Californians will, we trust, understand where reality ends and fantasy begins.[4]

On November 8, 1966, over 6 million of California's 8,340,868 registered voters came to the polls. Over 2,540,000 cast their ballots for the two-term incumbent Governor Edmund "Pat" Brown, Democrat. About 3,480,000 voted for screen actor Ronald Reagan, Republican. The winning margin for Reagan was over 900,000. His winning tally was 58 percent of total votes cast. Newspapers called his victory a "landslide" and immediately began talking about him as a potential Republican nominee for the presidency in 1968.

Even though Edmund Brown had been a good governor; even though he had first been elected in 1958 by a margin of 1,000,000 over his Republican opponent, former Senator William Knowland; even though he had been reelected in 1962 by a margin of 300,000 over former Vice-President Richard Nixon, the Republican party's 1960 standard-bearer; and even though registered Democrats outnumber registered Republicans by a margin of 3 to 2 in California the governor's loss to Ronald Reagan in 1966 —to a man who had never before in his life held public office and whose political alignments over the years had ranged from liberal Democratic to Goldwater conservatism—the governor's loss to Reagan was not remarkable according to the concept of image candidates' influence on voting, but rather inevitable.

Reagan was the image, himself one of the familiars in viewers' mental picture galleries of heroes. All he had to do in campaigning was to resemble himself and do nothing to break his image. Viewer conditioning would do the rest. To fail to vote for Ronald Reagan would be to abandon the hope that real life can be the pleasant, exciting but harmless, adventure that it appears to be on television.

Political analysts tried to look for political causes and political trends in the Reagan victory, hardly aware that Reagan was "soft-selling" all the key issues (as *Newsweek* put it) so that nothing he said would rouse any sentiments contrary to those roused by his general appearance, demeanor, style of presentation, and reputation.

Governor Brown himself ascribed his loss to a combination of "white backlash," a defection of Democrats who had become affluent and Republican-oriented during his eight years, and the primary wounds inflicted by Los Angeles Mayor Samuel Yorty, a fellow Democrat. A characteristic trait of politicians who lose badly because of sharp image contrasts seems to be the inability to admit that the key reason for their loss really had little to do with politics in the traditional sense but with the pervasiveness and peculiar influence of a new mass medium.

With enough money and control over Governor Brown, an image specialist might have reversed the outcome. As in the New York City 1965 mayoral contest, the image specialist's goal would have been to minimize the image contrast between Brown and Reagan so that fewer Democrats would be converted by their media predispositions to deny the habitual voting tendencies caused by their political predispositions.

Control over Governor Brown would have been necessary to prevent him from going on television and "speaking to the people," thereby contributing to their perception of the sharp contrast between his and Reagan's image. Control would have been necessary to stop the governor from leveling any sort of personal attack against Reagan on a medium that converts verbal attack into a characterization of aggressiveness. Brown should have ignored Reagan rather than repeatedly accuse him of inexperience or associations with right-wing extremism or making movies with monkeys (*Bedtime for Bonzo*). Brown's television exposure should have been limited to the kind of theatrical-impressionistic "paid-politicals" that the Jack Tinker agency was preparing for Nelson Rockefeller in New York. Most of Brown's television money should have been spent for the Tinker-type impressionistic treatments of his achievements in office, which were real and something to be proud of. Other (nontelevision) propaganda should have been directed at Democrats only to make them temporarily more aware of their Democratic identification. In image-candidate terms, Brown's strong cards were the 3-to-2 Democratic registration and his record in office. His weakest card was his image comparison with the pure image of Ronald Reagan.

He played his weakest card. And he lost.

Eight months after the election, in midsummer of 1967, prominent California Democrats were still revealing their inability to comprehend the magical spell that their new governor was apparently weaving over the state. "He's the Batman of politics," said one. "He has a remarkable immunity to the slings and arrows that ordinarily afflict people in public office."

"Every time he comes on the box, it's a plus, even if the circumstances are unfavorable," said another prominent California Democrat. And, during his first year in office, many circumstances were unfavorable to Reagan: proposals on which he had to backpedal; actions that offended legislators, state employees, and other special interests. Yet his popularity, measured by public opinion polls, continued to climb. "He defies political gravity," remarked Assembly Speaker Jesse Unruh, one of the most professional politicians in the state.[5]

The incredulity of political activists notwithstanding, Ronald Reagan could be elected President of the United States. He is the purest image candidate on the American scene and we still have no idea how far a man can go in politics today by exploiting the conditioned image responses of television viewers.

CONNECTICUT REELECTS
GOVERNOR DEMPSEY

When there is a contrast in only one of the three main influences on voting, the election returns can be expected to reflect that contrast.

In 1966, the only contrasting influence acting on Connecticut voters was their habitual party loyalties. Enrolled Democrats (458,730) outnumbered Republicans (381,003) by a ratio of 55 to 45. While there were also many independent voters in the state (about 484,000), there was no reason to believe that they would not follow the party preference patterns of their neighbors and give 55 percent of their votes to the Democratic candidate and 45 percent to the Republican. This would not be a safe assumption if there was a sharp image or issue contrast in the campaigns, but there was neither.

Perhaps Democratic incumbent Governor John N. Dempsey had a somewhat more attractive image. He was a genial native of County Tipperary, Ireland. He had the prestige of high office. His opponent, E. Clayton Gengras, was an unknown Hartford insurance man when he received the Republican nomination for governor.

Perhaps Gengras had a somewhat stronger influence on voters as far as campaign issues were concerned. Although he had nothing startling to say, his target—Governor Dempsey—had been in office six years, time enough to allow the usual time-for-a-change sentiment to be exploited. Gengras used the "crisis" approach, calling for new state action on highway safety, water pollution, juvenile delinquency, civil rights, and so on. Governor Dempsey reassured everybody that all was right as right can be, claiming that his administration had already given Connecticut "a government with a heart." He promised, in future years, to make "our beloved state an even finer state in which to live."

Assuming that the contrary influences of the somewhat superior Dempsey image and Gengras issue positions balanced each other out, one could predict that the remaining influence contrast, party loyalty, would prevail and that Governor Dempsey would win with 55 percent of the vote. Further, by some simple arithmetic it was possible to estimate his winning margin well in advance of Election Day. There were 1,324,359 voters registered in the state. About two-thirds to three-fourths of them could be expected to come to the polls on November 8 for a total vote of about 1,000,000. Dempsey's 55 percent would be 550,000. Gengras' 45 percent would be 450,000. Dempsey's winning margin would be 100,000.

The actual vote turned out to be: total 1,006,540; Gengras, 444,081, or 44.1 percent of the total; Dempsey, 562,459, or 55.9 percent, a winning margin of 118,378.

An important question here is why state Republican leaders, including candidate Gengras, did not see an inevitable loss of this dimension ahead of them. (Toward the end, in the most inner circles, they acknowledged to themselves that Gengras would lose but by perhaps 10,000 or 12,000 votes.)

The image-candidate concept is inexact, but inexorable. The state Republican leaders must have known, in advance of the nominating convention, that 55 percent of the voters would be more prone to vote for the Democratic incumbent in the absence of a strong countervailing issue influence or image influence. They should have known that they would have little chance of raising sharp issue contrasts, because Governor Dempsey had run a trim, progressive, scandal-free administration. (The Republicans did manage to muck-rake up the fact that Attilo R. Frassinelli, Democratic candidate for lieutenant governor, owed the town of Stafford $16,727 in personal property taxes and interest.)

Before the convention, it should have been obvious to Republican activists that their only chance to win was to put forward an extremely attractive image candidate. But they nominated the unknown Gengras, whose very name might stimulate immediate connotations of gangrene or poison gas. Republican strategists launched their candidate on a three-month marathon rat race, rushing him from shopping centers to railroad stations to shake hands with startled housewives and commuters, hardly an image-creating tactic.

The Connecticut Republicans lost miserably, but in the essence of their tactical errors may lie the saving grace for American politics in the age of television.

In the opening chapters it was pointed out that beyond the pervasive growth of television itself, the apparent increase of image-candidate influence may also be due to a declining intensity of voters' habitual tendencies to vote for the candidates of one political party. Since intensity of party loyalty and degree of party activity are obvious correlates, however, it seems very probable that considerations of image have the least influence on such party leaders as delegates to a nominating convention. Party leaders, as members of the community at large, doubtlessly have the same media predispositions as their neighbors that lead to similar characterizations of candidates based on television and cultural stereotypes, but the intensity of party leaders' political predispositions probably negates the possibility that attractive opposition images will influence their preference for the candidate of their own party.

Further, making a judgment from experience, I would say that because party leaders and delegates are so concerned with party activity and political considerations, they find it difficult to conceive that the greatest part of the electorate might be relatively unconcerned with political considerations and might be prone to image influence. Talk of image-candidate influence may be a foreign language to political activists. They deny it. They cannot comprehend it. The concept runs contrary to what they regard as important: the political positions and party identity of the candidate they choose.

Thus, nomination by convention rather than open primary may be a saving grace for politics, since it offers relatively more assurance that the nominee will have positions of substance and that there will be a greater degree of meaningful political debate in the course of the campaigns.

NOTES

1. Kurt and Gladys Lang, "Reactions of Viewers," in Sidney Kraus (ed.), *The Great Debates* (Bloomington: Indiana University Press, 1962), p. 315.
2. Sidney E. Zion, "Frank O'Connor Takes the High Road," *The New York Times Magazine,* January 16, 1966, pp. 74–75.
3. *The New York Times,* November 11, 1966, p. 29.
4. © 1966 by The New York Times Company. Reprinted by permission.
5. Gladwin Hill, "Reagan Assessed as Being 'the Batman of Politics,' " *The New York Times,* July 23, 1967, p. 47.

CHAPTER

19

1968

☆——☆

Here is a prediction of candidate behavior, the use of television, and the outcome of the 1968 national election based on image-candidate considerations. To keep the discussion short, for it is only incidental to the larger concern of this book, grant that President Lyndon Johnson is in good health and receives the Democratic party's presidential nomination to run for another term.

PARTY LOYALITY: INSIGNIFICANT NUMERICAL SUPERIORITY OF DEMOCRATS

At mid-1967, a national breakdown of voters' party preferences was about 44 percent Democrat, 36 percent Republican, 20 percent independent, and the remainder undecided or claiming allegiance to smaller parties. There was evidence of a slight uptrend in voters claiming preference for Republicans, particularly since the Republican "comeback" elections of 1966. This uptrend promised to narrow the apparent Democratic-Republican preference gap by November, 1968. However, it should be noted that we are talking about a *presidential* election and that party loyalty becomes a less significant influence on voters as the issues and personalities involved in a given election become more remote from the voters' immediate sphere of existence. A habitual Republican may vote almost automatically for the Republican nominee for dog catcher in his home town, but perhaps less automatically for the Republican gubernatorial or presidential nominee.

CAMPAIGN ISSUES: REPUBLICAN CANDIDATE CAN SELL "HOPE"

Whether or not open hostilities have ended, the Vietnamese war will be exploited by delicate, subtle, but highly impressionistic Republican paid-political programs and commercials. Their predominant tone will be *lament,* not attack. They will lament the shortcomings of Lyndon Johnson's character, his lack of intellectual stature, his lack of a sense of history, which would have given him the wisdom to cope with the troubles in Southeast Asia short of committing half a million American boys to mortal danger. After all, Congress never declared war on North Vietnam. They will imply it was Lyndon Johnson's insufferable ego that caused him to escalate congressional consent for a police action into tragic confrontation of East and West.

Republican campaign propaganda will try to characterize the President as a man who cannot bring the war to an end, essentially amplifying the posture first voiced by Vermont's George D. Aiken, senior Republican in the Senate.

SENATOR AIKEN (PARAPHRASED FROM *The Wall Street Journal*): The Johnson Administration, however well-intentioned its motives and reasonable its policies, is a prisoner of the past, unable to take a fresh look and fresh initiatives, irrevocably alienated from the foe.

The Johnson Administration is so deeply committed that it can no longer see the national interest except in terms of its own survival as the Government in power.

Only a Republican Administration, unfettered by the past, can end the war.

Such a position neither condemns nor supports President Johnson's specific efforts in Vietnam. It cannot be declared unpatriotic by the "hawks." It cannot be declared warlike by the "doves." It is a position that sells hope.

CANDIDATE IMAGE: CONTRAST STRONGLY FAVORS SEVERAL REPUBLICANS

Because of the President's image deficiencies, nothing he has to say on television will generate much hope—not that he is unaware of his inability to communicate the substance of his positions via television. The September 23, 1966, issue of *Time* magazine quotes him as saying: "Every time I appear on television, I lose money."

In the Johnson years, typical viewer reaction (*What the eye rejects, the mind dismisses*) has added up to a feeling of disbelief so common that it has earned a special name: the credibility gap. This feeling may have nothing to do with President Johnson's competence in office, but everything to do with his staying in office. He has tried contact lenses, face make-up, electronic prompting devices, everything short of plastic surgery to improve his television image. But his appearance, demeanor, and style of presentation are simply contrary to the ideal characterization of a President that exists in the minds of television viewers.

During the 1968 campaigns, the President will not appear on any television discussion programs such as *Meet the Press*. He will not allow viewers to compare him. with the Republican candidate in a televised face-to-face confrontation, with possible exception if Richard Nixon is the Republican nominee. (This would require a fast waiver of Section 315, as in 1960.) The

President will not appear speaking direct-to-camera on any of his own paid-politicals, but will make heavy use of impressionistic minute-length commercials that seek to generate sympathetic audience sentiment about the Johnson administration's less controversial achievements. The only television coverage he will allow is newscast and news-feature coverage of him making public appearances, being mobbed by admiring crowds, making grand entrances into arenas full of party faithful, and speaking to huge audiences.

In decreasing order of effectiveness, these five Republican presidential candidates could best use television to establish the essential image contrast with President Johnson: Rockefeller, Romney, Percy, Reagan, Nixon. Each has image attributes and image shortcomings, with the shortcomings especially significant in the case of Nixon.

Governor Reagan, while visually the image incarnate, still is known primarily as an actor, a commonly known reputation that might act to mitigate the response of viewers nationally based on media predispositions. After all, being governor of California is one thing, and being President of the United States—with final say over the use of nuclear weapons—is quite another.

Actually, shortcomings of the Republican candidate's image are the only thing that could possibly prevent the election of a Republican in 1968. The existence of the credibility gap should be ample proof that television viewers are repelled by the Johnson image as negative poles of a magnet are repelled by each other. All the Republicans have to do is put forward a candidate who can be perceived as a positive pole, a more attractive alternative.

Still, this may not happen. It is possible that former Vice-President Nixon will be the choice of the Republican activists who do the nominating. His views, currently conservative, and his unstinting campaign activities for Republican candidates over the years will have endeared him to many convention delegates. It will matter little to the delegates that he is not an attractive image candidate. The flaws in his character are too well known.

He is not handsome in the television idiom. He will insist on sitting on the front edge of a desk and "getting his views across to the people," little realizing that his excellent voice is primarily effective on radio rather than television.

As this book goes to press, the big conservative Republican money that backed Goldwater in 1964 and Reagan in 1966 is flowing in to back Nixon in the few open Republican primaries that he chooses to enter. This money can pay for huge doses of television image material prepared apart from Nixon's own efforts on television. In contrast, Governor Romney's primary campaigns may be less well financed and less able to make full use of image materials. The big money usually flowing to liberal-moderate candidates from the so-called Republican Eastern establishment may be only a trickle until Governor Rockefeller solves his own deep-down indecision about his own presidential prospects. If Nixon wins one or two open primaries, he has a good chance of being nominated.

In summary, according to the image-candidate concept, Richard Nixon would have the least chance of defeating President Johnson in 1968; Governor Reagan would have a slightly better chance; Governor Romney, Governor Rockefeller, or Senator Percy could readily be elected to the White House if they used television correctly and, during the campaigns, did nothing or said nothing that could be construed to offend or frighten large segments of the electorate.

YEARS TO COME

It will not come as an omnipotent Big Brother or even as an amoral television personality such as *Lonesome Rhodes*.[1] American politics in the age of television will not decline with a bang, but a whimper, a subtle increase of incompetence in high places at crucial moments, a subtle corrosion of our government's traditional dedication to being representative of and responsive to a consensus of informed public opinion. But not everyone takes such a dim view.

ARTHUR SCHLESINGER, JR: If voters had to depend on television alone
for the information on which they base political judgements, the
results would undoubtedly be poor for American democracy. Yet
so long as television is considered a supplement to newspapers,
magazines, political meetings and solitary midnight brooding by
individual citizens, and not a substitute for them, it has in certain
respects enriched our politics. . . . Its power to convey the quality
of political leadership is vast.[2]

Such reassurance, in light of the evidence and experience reported in this book, is not reassuring. The quality of political leadership is not at all what television conveys, most of the time. It did convey the admirable qualities of Schlesinger's friend John Kennedy, but only because in President Kennedy great intellectual stature and executive capability were combined in an extremely attractive image candidate. How much more common are homely men of stature and capability. Television will not convey their qualities of public leadership, but their characterization or image based on politically insignificant factors of appearance, demeanor, and presentation. Who can be so sure today that tomorrow's homely Jeffersons and Lincolns and Roosevelts and the substance of tomorrow's debates on public policies will not be obscured at the polls by tomorrow's Ronald Reagans?

"So long as television is considered a supplement to newspapers, magazines, political meetings and solitary midnight brooding by individual citizens, and not a substitute for them . . ." How long is that going to be? Television may be considered a supplemental medium of political information for the majority of Americans voting today because the majority of today's voters were out of their childhood and perhaps considerably literate before television did grow to be pervasive in this country. But what of the generation now maturing to voting age, the *now* generation that is *turned on* and *happening*, the young Americans to whom television may have been an electronic baby-sitter from the earliest moment of their preliterate consciousness? It is generally agreed by those who probe the mysteries of the mind that very first impressions register deeply and possibly—as the superego or conscience—silently govern much behavior in adult life. Adults voting now may be responsive to a conditioning by television much more superficial than the conditioning being impressed upon our babies with the power of a primal mythology.

The printed media of our press, reinforced by our schools (which teach the habit of *reading* when information of substance is needed), will remain the public's first (or last?) line of defense against extreme exploitation of television images for political purposes. The publishers of our newspapers, magazines, paperbacks, and hard-cover books are not unaware that they may have additional responsibilities in the age of television.

NEWSPAPER PUBLISHER JOHN HAY WHITNEY (FRONT PAGE *Herald Tribune,* OCTOBER 30, 1961): News is not simply what happens. It is what newsmen find out and what we read with understanding. The world has never been so well reported nor, at the same time, seemed so confusing. Big stories that used to be the bread and butter of journalism now get reported almost at once to millions by radio and television. Eighty-five per cent of the readers of morning newspapers have already heard the headline news before they sit down to read.

Yet they do sit down to read. The reason of course is that they feel deeply the need to know more. . . . A newspaper must, I think, dig harder than ever before beneath the surface of events . . . and sharpen its analysis of causes and implications.

Our schools perhaps could do more by teaching about television: its image language and its persuasive techniques that function largely independent of the apparent content of programming. Marshall McLuhan has given us the catch phrase "the medium is the message." The teaching profession could try to explain and help the young develop some resistance to television's message.

But the great contribution toward the preservation of the rational element in American voting behavior should come from the medium of mass communication that has perpetrated the era of image candidates upon us. In years to come there are three major changes or additions that television station owners and journalists should make—must make—in their coverage of political campaigns.

1. *More Editorial Endorsements of Candidates by Stations.* Editorial endorsement is especially needed when the weight of substance is on the side of the less attractive or less affluent candidate who cannot adequately impress viewers with the merit of his proposals on public problems or the potential quality of his political leadership.

The Federal Communications Commission allows, even encourages, editorializing by stations as long as they seek out and air rebuttal editorials by the opposition.

This requirement, however fair, may become prohibitive when there are too many candidates for the same office entitled to rebuttal. But journalistic timidity rather than too many rebuttals does appear to be the main reason why most stations today abdicate their opportunities to advise and prod viewers to think about nonimage considerations before an election.

2. *More Prime-Time, Specially Scheduled, Preelection Face-to-Face Confrontations Between the Two or Three Major Candidates.* More "great debates" in the interests of more rational voting behavior? After nineteen chapters of evidence and experience proving the subrational influence of image candidates?

Just so. Not because more face-to-face confrontations would do other than favor the more attractive image candidate, but because the impression left by these confrontations would be more natural and less contrived than other forms of television presentation now leaving dominant impressions upon the electorate.

More prime-time "great debates," with the relatively huge audiences that would be attracted by this purest form of staged political conflict, should neutralize or at least lessen the impact of the image specialist's work. Daily newscasts—easily, if occasionally, manipulated—would no longer be the most prominent form of campaign coverage by the station. Paid-politicals, programs and commercials, would no longer be home free with their contrived illusions. And consequently, great wealth to pay for paid-politicals would not be so necessary a requirement for reaching voters via television.

3. *More Prime-Time, Specially Scheduled, Preelection Programs Clarifying the Rational Substance of Difference Between the Major Candidates on the Major Campaign Issues and on Non-image Qualifications for Office.* Where more prime-time debates would play into the hands of the more attractive image candidate, the station should then put on an equivalent number of prime-time programs that take the images apart, appraise them for

shadow and substance, and work to build viewer comprehension of rational differences between the public policies advocated by the major candidates.

Programs produced in this format should, but do not necessarily have to, use the documentary technique of conveying the essence of issue differences in terms of human images who might be affected by the proposals.

Another comprehension format could be the relatively inexpensive appraisal of candidate remarks (played back on video tape) by one or more experienced journalists or nonpartisan experts.

There are three reasons why these three forms of campaign coverage have not been taken up by the television industry. First, station owners and journalists may not have been aware of the singular subrational image influence that their medium tends to exert upon voting. Second, it is a safer, more conservative business policy not to put on any material that might offend the supporters of any candidate.

The third negative is the one that the television industry cannot do anything about. Section 315 of the Communications Act of 1934 requires that all stations, on penalty of losing their license, offer equal time to all qualified candidates for the same office if they have offered time (i.e., an on-the-air exposure) to one candidate for that office. Since 1959, that restriction has not applied to newscasts, regularly scheduled news-type interviews, and certain other bonafide news programming, but it does apply to specially scheduled prime-time preelection debate and documentary formats; and because confusion, not comprehension, results from programming too many political alternatives in a given period of time, stations will tend to avoid putting on such programs where they cannot control how many candidates appear.

The Congress of the United States has been rigid about not changing Section 315 unless circumstances forced them or made it convenient for them to do so, as is described below. If you look closely, however, there is a pattern in the history of their actions and failures to act on Section 315, a pattern that does not do them honor: *self-interest taking precedence over the public interest.* Until this pattern is brought out into the open, there may be no chance of getting Congress to enact the changes in Section 315 now essential to enable television's responsible journalists to begin to counteract their medium's inherent tendency to emphasize image.

You have to appreciate the fact that the American press was born free and that this freedom was a phenomenon in human history. Since the advent of modern mass communications with Gutenberg's movable type in the fifteenth century, the more courageous scientists and philosophers had been fighting the age-old concept that church and state authorities had an exclusive prerogative to decide what was right and true in human affairs and, consequently, to decide what common man should read.

John Milton, in his *Areopagitica* (1644), a treatise against Puritan censorship, argued that common man can distinguish between right and wrong and that, to exercise his reasoning ability, man should have unlimited access to the ideas and thoughts of other men. From Milton, such libertarian concepts as the "open marketplace of ideas" and the "self-righting process" (whereby truth survives) evolved.

The colonial press in America had a rough time with authoritarian controls. In 1718, Cotton Mather's henchmen put James Franklin in jail as a measure to stop publication of Franklin's *New England Courier*, which had become a voice of dissent in the Massachusetts colony. In the 1730s, John Peter Zenger was put on trial for libel because his *New York Weekly Journal* had allegedly poked fun at Governor William Cosby.

The "spirits" of '76 that infused the American Revolution were brewed by publishers of pamphlets and newspapers. In the new United States, the press was envisioned as a necessary and vital voice of the common man. Thomas Jefferson held that the opinion of the people should be the basis of the new government. The First Amendment of our Constitution guaranteed that Congress would make no law "abridging the freedom of speech or of the press." The libertarian assumption was that if the press was guaranteed freedom, it would proceed in no other way than to publish diverse opinion, for the simple reason that if there was a substantial unpublished dissent, its adherents could always go out and start up a newspaper of their own.

About 130 years later, our technology produced a new medium of mass communication that used a finite band of the energy spectrum in which there were just so many wavelengths available and no more. From all accounts, the early days of radio resembled an electronic Spanish Main sailed by enterprising buccaneers, a latter-day gold rush with broadcast pioneers trampling each other for the listener's attention and the advertiser's dollar. Between 1920 and 1925, more than 500 stations went on the air.

WALTER EMERY: Some stations stepped up their power, jumped frequencies and changed hours of operation at will in a frenzied effort to enlarge their coverage areas. . . . Some broadcasters attempted to interfere and drown out the signals of lower-powered stations.[3]

Broadcasters and public alike demanded federal action to relieve this chaos of the air waves. In the Radio Act of 1927, Congress made it law that (1) the broadcast spectrum was public, not private, property; (2) a federal agency would be set up to license stations for exclusive use of available frequencies; (3) these licenses would be issued and renewed periodically only if the public interest was served thereby; and (4) nothing in the Radio Act would be construed to give the government power of censorship over broadcast communications.

Two words frequently heard in debate preceding passage of the 1927 Radio Act were "monopoly" and "propaganda." These were frightening words in those days, "monopoly" bringing to mind recently curbed abuses of the public by industrial combines and "propaganda" evoking fresh memories of World War I atrocity stories that had been bragged about by "propaganda experts" after the war. Congressional fear of "monopoly" and "propaganda" showed in H.R. 9971, the emerging Radio Act, when it came to the Senate floor for action. It contained a provision that radio stations be considered "common carriers in interstate commerce" available for use by the public at large with respect to any discussion of public issues. Senator Clarence Dill noted that this "common carrier" provision was causing "more objection to the bill than probably all the other provisions combined." [4] He introduced a successful amendment that required equal treatment of political candidates only. The Dill amendment became Section 18 of the Radio Act and, later, Section 315 of the Communications Act of 1934.

SECTION 315 (PRIOR TO 1959): If any licensee shall permit any person who is a legally qualified candidate for public office to use a broadcasting station, he shall afford equal opportunities to all other such candidates for the office in the use of such broadcasting station, and the licensing authority shall make rules and regulations to carry this provision into effect: *Provided,* that such licensee shall have no power of censorship over the material broadcast under the provisions of this paragraph. No obligation is hereby imposed upon any licensee to allow use of its station by any such candidate.

By this legislation, which was eventually tested and supported in the courts, Congress was saying that in order to preserve the libertarian principle underlying the First Amendment's guarantee of a free press—that is, the principle of common man having access to all opinion about public controversy—some regulation of broadcast journalism was necessary even though that regulation (of telling stations that they had to give equal time to competing candidates) was in itself a violation of the First Amendment.

Over the years, however, it appeared that the net effect of Section 315 was not to foster political broadcasting but to inhibit it. Fearful of numerous equal-time claims from minor candidates who might be politically insignificant and/or public nuisances, stations held back broadcast coverage of major-party candidates. The major-party candidates did not complain too much because they usually had money to buy "paid-political" time, which minor-party candidates—when offered their "equal opportunities to use station facilities"—could not afford. In addition, stations were covering major candidates' activities and statements on newscasts as if newscasts were not subject to Section 315.

Early in 1959, this loophole was abruptly closed. The Federal Communications Commission ruled that Lar Daly, a minor candidate for mayor of Chicago, should receive television time equal to some news film that stations had shown of the incumbent Democratic mayor and the Republican mayoral candidate. Apparently, the FCC had come to realize that any appearance of a candidate on television can influence voters, whether or not political oratory is involved. (This is the essence of the image-candidate concept.)

FCC CONFIRMING OPINION RE LAR DALY: The candidate has several roles in which he may appear on television. The most obvious appearance is as a candidate for office. Of no less importance is the candidate's appearance as a public servant, as an incumbent office holder, or as a private citizen in a non-political role.

. . . While not always indispensable for political success, for some purposes television may enjoy a unique superiority in selling a candidate to the public in that it may create an impression of immediacy and intimate presence. It shows the candidate in action and it affords a potential for reaching a vast audience.[5]

If the Lar Daly decision was enforced, it was apparent—not only to broadcasters—that Section 315 would be in clear violation of the First Amendment's provision that Congress could not make a law that abridged freedom of the press.

EDITORIAL IN THE *Washington Post,* JUNE 18, 1959: . . . the President of the United States, if he happens to be a candidate for reelection, could not be shown on television attending a summit conference or laying a cornerstone without giving equal time to all other candidates for the presidency.

Whatever congressional fears of broadcast "propaganda"— and there was ample evidence of such fears—in the summer of 1959, Congress amended Section 315 to exclude from equal-time claims appearances of candidates on "bona-fide" newscasts, news-interview programs, documentaries (only when the appearance of the candidate was incidental to the subject matter), and on-the-spot coverage of such political events as party conventions.

An impression that Congress was getting more liberal about

political broadcast regulation in enacting the 1959 amendment was heightened by further legislation affecting Section 315 in 1960. Adlai Stevenson, former governor of Illinois and two-time Democratic presidential candidate, proposed a "great debate" for the presidency: "Only television can establish such a forum. I propose that it provide a quadrennial clearing of the air by use of the air." [6] Governor Stevenson's proposal was promptly put before Congress in bills that had two rigidly prescriptive elements: (1) a definition of "substantial presidential candidates as those of parties whose presidential candidates had polled at least 4 percent of the popular vote in the preceding national election; and (2) a stipulation that every radio and television station, during each of the eight weeks preceding Election Day, would have to give one hour of free prime time to each "substantial" presidential candidate.

The outcry against these rigid prescriptions was loud and long. Minority-party spokesmen objected to the 4 percent "substantial candidate" requirement as effectively barring them from the free time. Historians pointed out that the 4 percent requirement would have excluded such illustrious presidential candidates as John C. Fremont in 1856, Theodore Roosevelt in 1912, Robert La Follette in 1924, and Strom Thurmond and Henry Wallace in 1948. Constitutional objections to the free-time prescription for "substantial candidates" were raised; this formula would constitute dictation by government as to what should go into a particular program, thus taking private property (station facilities) for public use without just compensation.

CBS president Frank Stanton, who had originally suggested the presidential debate idea some years earlier, proposed that in 1960 the broadcast industry be allowed to voluntarily make time available to presidential candidates without being subject to the usual equal-time claims.

Cautiously, ever so cautiously,[7] Congress went along with Dr. Stanton's idea and enacted Senate Joint Resolution 207, which suspended Section 315 with respect to nominees for President and Vice-President only and until Election Day, 1960, only.

In 1960, besides Republican Richard Nixon and Democrat

John Kennedy, there were fourteen minor presidential candidates on one or more state ballots who might have claimed equal-time had there not been Senate Joint Resolution 207.[8] Without fear of their claims, the networks proceeded to put on the Nixon-Kennedy "great debate" series and all sorts of other informative programs about the national elections that are generally overlooked when recalling political broadcasting in 1960.

SPOKESMAN FOR THE NATIONAL BROADCASTING COMPANY: . . . apart from "The Great Debates," we were able to present the personalities and issues of the campaign more extensively and in more varied ways than ever before. For example, we developed an 8-week series of full-hour evening programs called "The Campaign and the Candidates," which presented a detailed background on the campaign issues and nominees, to give the public a full insight on what sort of men they were and what they stood for; four hour-long programs in this series were devoted to interviews in depth with the four major candidates.

In addition to our regular news programs, we also covered the campaign in such programs as "Meet the Press," "The Dave Garroway Today Show" and Chet Huntley Reporting." In all, from August 24, when the suspension of equal time became effective, until election day, we offered 24 hours and 15 minutes of campaign coverage, not counting our regular newscasts.[9]

CBS went so far as to present an hour documentary about minor parties in American political history, a program that included SOF statements by three 1960 minor presidential candidates whom the network regarded as "responsible" rather than "frivolous." [10]

Encouraged by the wide acclaim for television coverage of the 1960 campaigns, broadcasters rushed back to Congress in 1961 with various proposals to further liberalize Section 315. They pleaded for more latitude in producing documentary and debate programs that did not have to include insignificant minor candidates.

STATION NEWS DIRECTOR: Because it is not possible to present extensive coverage of political activities within the framework of newscasts and news interviews . . . many news directors, myself included, assume additional programming responsibilities in the production of documentary, special events and face-to-face programs. It is in this area of programming that Section 315 has proved completely unworkable.[11]

But such argument in 1961, then again in 1962, and then again in 1963, ran into a stone wall. Some members of Congress showed a deep apprehension that maybe broadcasters had too much latitude already.

OPINION OF FOUR CONGRESSMEN: Our friends in the broadcasting industry having been given a glimpse of power in the political arena, are now hungrily pursuing its ultimate: the right to hound people out of office who do not please them, the right to openly groom a successor for an official in disfavor, the right to control completely what an official or candidate may say to his audience in his own behalf, the right to use the airways to argue for its own political point of view, its own candidates, and with impunity.[12]

This sort of apprehension seems to be more intense in Democrats than in Republicans.

SENATOR CLAIR ENGLE (D., CALIF.): I would be very reluctant to see this broadcasting industry get in the same position as we are with the press, where we don't get any help at all. . . . We Democrats resent that and we are not going to permit this licensed medium on the airwaves to ever get into the kind of position we have with the American press where the Democrats always get the worst of it.[13]

In 1963, as in 1961 and 1962, with but one exception all proposals affecting Section 315 died in committee. The exception was House Joint Resolution 247, which, on September 7, 1963, was reported favorably by the Senate Commerce Committee, parent body of the Senate Subcommittee on Communications. H.J. Res 247 was virtually a duplicate of the 1960 action that had temporarily suspended Section 315 until the coming Election Day with respect to presidential and vice-presidential candidates only.

In three years, a mountain of controversy had brought forth a mouse. And the mouse turned out to be short-lived.

Because the 1960 temporary suspension of 315 had facilitated the Nixon-Kennedy debates, three years later H.J. Res. 247 became popularly known as the "great debates" proposal for 1964.

It passed the Senate on October 2, 1963, with two minor amendments and was returned to the House for consensus on these amendments. There seemed to be no obstacle in the path of the legislation. President Kennedy was on record as willing to debate his Republican opponent in 1964, a sporting gesture, because Kennedy was commonly supposed to have won the 1960 election because of his televised debates with Nixon.

On November 22, 1963, President Kennedy was assassinated.

On February 13, 1964, the House of Representatives indicated its disagreement with the Senate's two modifications of H.J. Res. 247 and asked for a conference. On May 7, Senate and House conferees met, resolved their differences, and agreed to file a conference report. On August 18, this report came to the Senate floor for acceptance.

In some manner, by that date President Lyndon Johnson, Democrat, had indicated to the Senate majority leadership, Democratic, that he did not want to engage in televised debate with his Republican opponent, Senator Barry Goldwater. This instruction from the White House put some Senate Democrats on the spot, namely, those who had been majority members of the Subcommittee on Communications that had reported favorably on H.J. Res. 247 almost a year earlier. Communications Subcommittee chairman John Pastore (D., R.I.) seemed to indicate the political pressures that had been brought to bear on him as, on the night of August 18 on the floor of the Senate, he damned the H.J. Res. 247 Conference Report with faint praise, referring only to the "great debates" that would be allowed by H.J. Res. 247 and omitting all mention of the rich and varied campaign coverage that had been facilitated by the temporary suspension of Section 315 in 1960.

The political machinations did not escape Senate Republicans.

SENATOR NORRIS COTTON (R., N.H.): We should be fully aware in the Senate Chamber tonight that . . . the Conference Report is going to be put to death by the majority party. . . .

I say this with all the sincerity at my command: the question is not whether the President wants to debate or whether Senator

Goldwater wants to debate. . . . The question is merely one of saving this bill which was carefully and properly drawn, which affords an opportunity for joint appearances or separate appearances and gives the people of the country an opportunity to see and hear the candidates.

I believe that those who feel compelled to kill the bill tonight . . . are doing so with regret and sorrow. . . . Politics are being talked, but the question is one of future policy.[14]

On the night of August 18, 1964, forty-four senators, all Democrats, voted to table the Conference Report and thus remove H.J. Res. 247 from further consideration. Forty-one senators, including every Republican present and those Democrats who were compromised by their membership on the Communications Subcommittee, which had favorably reported H.J. Res. 247 in the first place, voted to accept the report.

Called to account for his vote against H.J. Res. 247 on that night, one Democratic senator spoke of "principals" rather than "principles."

SENATOR ABRAHAM RIBICOFF (D., CONN.): I thought the Kennedy-Nixon debates in 1960 were worthwhile and would hope such debates might be revived in the future. Such a decision, however, would seem to be one in which the judgement of the principals should have great weight.

Senator Goldwater has previously stated that he did not believe it would be wise for a President of the United States to engage in such debates, and President Johnson has not indicated any wish to do so.[15]

So the flash of an assassin's rifle ended up illuminating a primal element of self-interest in congressional rigidity about Section 315. Suddenly every past action—or refusal to act—on the equal-time law could be seen as part of a pattern. In 1927, the proposal that stations be required to present all sides of controversy on public issues was dropped and replaced by a requirement that protected candidates only from "monopoly" and "propaganda." In the early 1950s, although scholarly studies and expert testimony indicated that Section 315 was inhibiting campaign coverage and largely excluding minority candidates from the air, Congress did not act. The major parties had money to buy air time for their candidates, and, besides, the major candidates were being covered on news programs, which were functioning at that time as if Section 315 did not apply. In 1959, Congress acted to amend Section 315, but just enough to ensure return to the unofficial situation of earlier years. In 1960, the temporary suspension of 315 served the public interest by allowing expanded broadcast coverage of the national campaigns, but it also specifically served the presidential candidate of the majority party in Congress, Senator Kennedy, who—less known nationally than Vice-President Nixon—had much more to gain from the prominence of the televised joint appearances than Nixon did. In 1961, 1962, and 1963, disregarding widespread acclaim for television coverage of the 1960 campaigns, Congress refused to further liberalize Section 315, even on a temporary experimental basis, because whatever the public interest in being better informed about political choices, members of Congress were all deeply concerned about their own interests as incumbent candidates soon to run for re-election. If—due to station fear of equal-time claims from minor candidates—Section 315 was *preventing* stations from putting on more special prime-time programs in which viewers could compare and contrast the major candidates, this could only serve the more prominent incumbents. In 1964 the public interest clearly would have been served by a repeat performance of 1960's rich and varied campaign coverage by the broadcast media. But in 1964 the self-interest of the majority party in Congress required that its presidential candidate, now an incumbent with more to lose than to gain by televised confrontation with his personally attractive opponent, be protected!

This is the sorry history of political broadcast regulation in the United States. For technical reasons, Congress got a finger-hold on a medium of the American press and ended up manipulating coverage of political campaigns so that congressional interests were protected first and the public interest second.

But history is proving Jefferson and his libertarian brethren to be correct: freedom of the press cannot be comprised with impunity. The equal-time statute is proving to be a meaningless protection against the deliberate manipulation of candidate images by biased newscasters in that the statute does not and cannot reasonably be applied to newscasts. It has no effect on equalizing the influence of paid-political image propaganda because all candidates for a given office will *never* (well, *hardly ever*) have equal financial resources. Under Section 315, a station selling air time to a wealthy candidate is obligated only to offer equal time at equal prices to other candidates for that office. If the other candidates cannot afford to make equal purchases of air time, the station has discharged its obligations under 315 and the wealthy one's paid-politicals are home free. Indeed, congressional rigidity on Section 315 can now be labeled as the factor most responsible for *fostering the influence of image propaganda on biased newscasts and paid-politicals* because 315 as it now stands inhibits stations from putting on specially scheduled prime-time *noncontrived* debate and documentary programs whose influence might counter the contrived image propaganda.

Congress is not unaware that great wealth is a prerequisite for the effective use of television today; but, blinded by their self-rooted fear of free television journalism as a factor that might equalize disparities of wealth between candidates, they have actually begun to consider financing high-level campaigns with government monies as a means of equalizing the advantages of wealth. A federal law was passed in October, 1966, that would have generated as much as $30 million to reimburse the Republican and Democratic national committees for expenses incurred during the 1968 presidential campaigns. An apprehensive Senate made this law inoperative in May, 1967, but their apprehension had nothing to do with the singular subrational influence of image candidates. Immediately President Johnson sent his own proposals for a campaign financing law up to Capitol Hill. The pressure will be on to enact it or something similar.

SENATOR RUSSELL LONG: Governor Rockefeller reported expenditures of $5.2 million [in the New York gubernatorial campaign of 1966]. On the other hand, his unsuccessful opponent Frank D. O'Connor,

the Democratic nominee, reported expenditures of only $576,000. . . .
Mr. O'Connor was obviously faced with a insurmountable obstacle. One-half million dollars will not buy as much prime TV time as $5 million.[16]

Pray that our senators and representative, all honorable men, soon hear and speak about and open their eyes to the reality of image candidates, which poses a far greater threat to democracy than the "evil" of unregulated television journalism. A federal law to finance paid-politicals would be the pin on the hand grenade, the flood gate on the dikes. State legislatures and city councils would seize the precedent to appropriate public monies for the expenses of statewide and local campaigns and we would be subjected to a deluge of image propaganda hitherto unimaginable in a nontotalitarian country.

The alternative is a rededication of American faith in a free and responsible press, by further relaxation of Section 315, even though that faith will surely be sullied on occasion by biased newscasters and station owners. (But only *occasionally*. Antitrust laws prevent large combines of broadcast stations.)

A modest amendment to Section 315 might do the trick of allowing great improvements in the quality (and influence) of television campaign coverage, for example, a public comprehension amendment that permits special preelection programs presenting *at least two* candidates for the same office to be exempt from equal-time claims by all the candidates for that office:

Appearance of a candidate on any program originated and produced by a television station licensee which presents the views of two or more candidates (for that office) for the purpose of clarifying and comparing the political alternatives represented by those candidates shall not be deemed a use of station facilities by the appearing candidates and therefore not subject to claims for equal use of station facilities by other candidates for that office.

This amendment would enable—not require—television journalists to schedule more prime-time face-to-face confrontations between the two or three major candidates for our highest public offices as a means of counteracting the influence of contrived image materials (which is in turn largely dependent on wealth of the candidates). This amendment would enable—not require—television journalists to put on more prime-time preelection programs designed to encourage public comprehension of nonimage differences between the qualifications and public policies of the major candidates.

There probably would not be a wholesale rush by television stations to put on these two types of preelection programs. Television has become habituated to journalistic timidity that does not offend. But we must believe that some of the medium's more responsible and more mature journalists will rise to the challenge, once given more freedom from the strictures of 315, and put on the sort of programs that set good examples for the industry's laggards.

A public comprehension amendment to Section 315 would raise some fine problems of its own. It clearly sets television apart from radio, yet the two media have always been considered similar because of the similarities in their transmission over the public air waves. This amendment demands that differences of effect between television and radio be the prime consideration.

Unquestionably, with television journalists given freedom to determine who are the politically significant candidates and how many of them can be presented sequentially without causing more confusion than comprehension, some minor candidates—serious and frivolous alike—are going to be excluded from television except for token exposure given to them in the interests of acquainting the public with political diversity.

But the minor candidates would still have their equal-use claims on radio stations under Section 315, and it is quite possible (and should be demonstrable) that radio is a more suitable medium for the exposition of political viewpoints that are relatively singular in substance, relatively divergent from the so-called political mainstream.

Sometimes, in the name of a greater freedom, it becomes necessary to transgress on a smaller freedom. The greater freedom in this case is the voters' freedom from undue subrational influence of television's image candidates. As it is sometimes necessary to fight fire with fire, it is now time to set television journalism free—or at least *freer*—of political broadcast regulations. The alternatives are unspeakable.

The fate of American politics in the age of television now rests with the Congress of the United States.

NOTES

1. Big Brother is the image demagogue always "watching you" via two-way television in George Orwell's *1984*. Larry "Lonesome" Rhodes is a guitar-strumming hobo who develops political ambitions after becoming a top television personality in Budd Schulberg's screenplay *A Face in the Crowd*.
2. Arthur Schlesinger, Jr., "How Drastically Has Television Changed Our Politics?" *TV Guide*, October 12, 1966, p. 10.
3. Walter B. Emery, *Broadcasting and Government* (Lansing: Michigan State University Press, 1961), p. 13.
4. Senator Clarence Dill, *Congressional Record*, Sixty-ninth Congress, 2nd Session, 1926, p. 12358.
5. Clause 23, Lar Daly decision, FCC #59–565–74196, June 15, 1959.
6. "Adlai Stevenson's Plan for a Great Debate," *This Week* (New York *Herald Tribune*), March 6, 1960, p. 15.
7. The FCC was told to report to Congress on the effects of S.J. Res. 207 on broadcast coverage of the 1960 elections. The Senate authorized a "watchdog" subcommittee to spend $35,000 on a similar study.
8. This number included minor presidential candidates of parties such as the Tax Cut party, Prohibition party, Vegetarian party, and American Beat Consensus, as well as the more substantial States Rights and Socialist parties.
9. Testimony of Robert Kintner, president of NBC, Senate Subcommittee on Communications, January 31, 1961, *Hearings*, p. 66.
10. Testimony of Frank Stanton, January 31, 1961, in *ibid.*, p. 36.
11. Robert J. Shafer, director of news, Station WRC-TV, Philadelphia, letter to Senator Harrison Williams, Jr., July 6, 1962, inserted in transcript of Senate Communications Subcommittee *Hearings* (Political Broadcasting), July 10–12, 1962, p. 88.
12. Representatives John Bennett, John Bell Williams, J. Arthur Younger, and Samuel L. Devine, minority views on H.J. Res. 247, Eighty-eighth Congress, 1st Session, 1963.
13. Senator Clair Engle, Senate Subcommittee on Communications, July 11, 1962, *Hearings*, p. 71.
14. Senator Norris Cotton, *Congressional Record*, Eighty-eighth Congress, 2nd Session, August 18, 1964, pp. 19411–19413.
15. Senator Ribicoff, letter to author, August 29, 1964.
16. Senator Russell Long (D., La.), *Congressional Record*, Ninetieth Congress, 1st Session, April 13, 1967, p. S5077.

INDEX

☆————————————————————————☆